# —HOOKED ON ICE FISHING II—
# PANFISH

## SECRETS TO CATCHING WINTER FISH, FOR BEGINNERS TO EXPERTS

### TOM GRUENWALD

Published by

 **krause
publications**

700 E. State Street • Iola, WI 54990-0001
Telephone: 715/445-2214

www.krause.com

Please call or write for our free catalog of outdoor publications.
Our toll-free number to place an order or obtain a free catalog is 800-258-0929
or please use our regular business telephone 715-445-2214
for editorial comment and further information.

Library of Congress Catalog Number: 95-77307
ISBN: 0-87341-489-6

Printed in the United States of America

# Dedication

*T*o...

God for creating all the wonders of winter, ice, and the wonderful, fascinating
world within and beneath;

My savior Jesus Christ, it is you who guides me through each day and your love
that lights the way.

My wife, Lisa, for your enduring love, patience and understanding;

My children, Alyssa Jo and Brianna Kay, it is you who make a fascinating new
adventure of each day and provide a glimpse of heaven here on Earth.

My parents and grandparents, your inspiration and encouragement remain in
my thoughts and prayers each day;

My colleagues and good friends, Paul, Joanna, Ken, Becky, Nate and Diane
Grahl, without your help and encouragement, this book would not be
possible.

My good friend Terry Jann, whether you know it or not you've become a trea-
sured part of our family;

My good ice fishing friends Jim Lindsey, Larry Smith, Tim Duffy, Steve Heem,
Wil Wegman and ice anglers throughout the world...let's enjoy and preserve
our cherished pastime for many generations to come.

# Contents

# Preface

# *Panfish, Favorite of the Masses*

*A*nother pre-dawn winter morn atop the ice.

Still. Dark. Frigid. Only the iridescent glow of my sonar screen dimly lights the ice in a cold, indigo blue.

I sit perched on the frosty tailgate of my truck, jigging, the unforgiving, silent cold stinging my numb, red fingertips exposed to sub-zero cold. Shivers resonate through my body as I inhale the dry, icy air, yet I welcome the tranquility of the frigid silence—a silence graced only by the soft whisper of gentle, chilling winds sifting peacefully through soft shoreline pines; a peaceful silence broken only by the occasional eerie sound of cracking ice as the pack expands, resounding its haunting, heart-stopping echoes through the depths below.

Above, a peaceful snow swirls gracefully from the heavens, lightly seasoning the cold, dark air. A few flakes scatter across the sleeve of my winter coat, presenting a fascinating array of designs available for close scrutiny; their white, lacy symmetry obvious against my dark coat in the stark, glowing shadows of lunar light. I inhale a deep, slicing breath of cold, laced with the distinctive aroma of smoke generated by a wood-burning stove cozily placed in the corner of some distant cabin.

For contrast, I take a sip of thick hot chocolate topped with whipped cream, savoring the sweet vapors rising from the liquid, bathing in the hot steam drifting past my icy nose and the richness of this hot potion as it washes over my throat.

Then, I suddenly rest my cup.

So far, the glow of my sonar has revealed little more than depth, bottom content and some light weeds growing along bottom. But as hoped, several fish suddenly have appeared—and two are heading straight for my lure. Careful to continue the same jigging motions used to attract them, I watch as they approach to inspect the bait.

After pausing briefly, one attacks. My eyes quickly shift from the electronics to my rod, where the sudden movement of my float and tightening of my line indicate a strike. In one smooth motion, I raise my right hand to set the hook—while at the same time reaching for the reel handle with my left. As the hook finds home and the rod doubles, I feel an adrenaline rush surge through my bloodstream. My heart skips a beat, my hands and knees tremble nervously, my mouth waters. For a moment, the world is small—just me, my ice rod and a fish.

Ecstasy.

Seconds later, a chunky yellow perch splashes from the hole and flips onto the ice, instantly coating itself with a blanket of fresh snow. As I lift the colorful, golden-green fish adorned with brilliant orange fins to my outstretched hand, I can't help but smile. In my mind, there is no greater thrill.

According to a recent study prepared by the U.S. Fish and Wildlife Service, I'm not alone. Panfish anglers were found second most numerous only to bass anglers, with more than 10 million Americans seeking these favorite of species—namely sunfish, perch and bluegills. Trout, also covered in this book, were third most popular, followed by crappie, also included here.

Additionally, it appears many of these anglers enjoy fishing multiple panfish species. For example, of the 8.3 million crappie anglers surveyed, slightly more than half also pursued other panfish. That's a lot of anglers, and compounded, a lot of fishing time and effort dedicated to panfish. So if you're an avid panfish angler, you're among a growing contingent—a contingent likely making up the majority of anglers, angling effort and days fishing, both summer and winter alike.

But before continuing, I should define the term "panfish." There is often a great deal of debate among ice anglers regarding exactly what a "panfish" is, so for our purpose, let's define the term. Traditionally, panfishes are most commonly considered members of the sunfish family, including sunfish, bluegills, crappies and rock bass. The yellow perch of the perch family and bullhead of the catfish family are sometimes included within these realms, although bullheads aren't as readily caught through the ice.

For the scope of this book we will define "panfish" as any respectable species commonly caught through the ice, that at maturity in an average environment will typically fit comfortably in an average-sized frying pan. Oh sure, a large cisco, perch or state-record crappie might undermine this classification, but notice I said "typically" and "at maturity in an average environment." In exceptional situations, some of the panfishes might not fit perfectly, but for our purposes, this definition will better distinguish the term "panfish" and help eliminate species such as walleyes, pike or lake trout from consideration. Yet for many, this definition will also include a few new species that may extend beyond the range of species commonly considered panfishes, including stocked trout, smelt, golden shiners, white perch, cisco, kokanee salmon—even arctic grayling.

Also keep in mind confusion of definition is often compounded by misnomers. A good number of panfish species go by regional names; I've heard bluegills called sunnies, 'gills and bream; cisco called tullibee and even inappropriately misnamed "whitefish" in some parts of the country. Kokanee salmon are often fondly called "kokes" by those familiar with them. There are also allied species such as white and yellow perch or black and white crappies, often referred to categorically as simply perch or crappies. However, confusion can be avoided by using proper common names, which we will refer to throughout this book.

Our secondary definition of "panfish" will help more clearly classify panfish. As defined here, panfish will constitute any species not only commonly caught through the ice and fitting in a pan, but also having a place within the middle reaches of the food chain in the environment they're found. This is important, because limiting our definition to species found in the midst of the food chain not only helps further define the term panfish, but also means these species are sought by larger, natural predators. This has considerable implications in our classification, because competition with, and fear of, larger predator gamefish species often influences typical winter panfish locations, habitats and habits.

In addition, nature has made panfish by our secondary definition highly opportunistic—meaning that with few exceptions, they're able to adapt and survive in a variety of environments, so they're readily available. And most panfish by our definition are also highly prolific—mostly for the sake of species survival. Yet at the same time, this also provides an often abundant resource for ice anglers.

With panfish now defined, you might ask why I'd write a book devoted strictly to icing them. A better directed question might be, why not?

By our definition, panfish are present virtually everywhere in millions of acres of river backwaters, ponds, lakes, flowages and reservoirs ranging in size from 1 acre to 100,000 acres or more. And being on the lower end of the food chain and prolific reproducers, they're usually quite abundant. In fact, panfish are so prolific in some waters their numbers exceed food supplies, making them stunted but very active and willing to strike—providing good fishing waters when action is desired over quality and size, such as outings with children or beginning anglers.

However, while desirable from an action standpoint, excessive quantities of panfish are not healthy for any environment. Overpopulated, stunted panfish populations knock lakes out of balance, offering tremendous numbers of smaller fish, but few if any larger ones, a condition that may be caused by a number of physical, biological and chemical limitations. Better balanced are lakes where populations of panfish are reduced due to natural environmental constraints. In such cases, forage is divided among a smaller number of individuals and they're likely to become larger, although less competitive and aggressive. These waters make better targets for experienced ice anglers looking for the challenge of finding and catching fewer—perhaps less eager to bite—but larger panfish.

So whether you're looking for action or a challenge, panfish are fun for ice anglers of all ages and skill levels. In fact, many of today's most accomplished ice anglers will admit mastering their angling prowess catching panfish, and even for the most seasoned veteran, trophy panfish still offer exciting challenges.

Sure, folks who seek panfish strictly for food or as a way to leisurely pass time may catch them on a variety of live bait and lures and almost any type of gear. But those who fish more for the challenge of maximum efficiency have learned to use specialized tackle and techniques to create their own consistency. These ice anglers appreciate that there are a few tricks for finding winter panfish, and once these fish are found, know that customized gear, lures and baits, and highly refined techniques, can dramatically improve their odds of icing them.

And often such action can be experienced throughout the winter in waters close to home, without a great deal of expensive equipment. Combine all this with high quality table fare and the fact these abundant, easily accessible, colorful, eager to strike, tasty fishes are loads of fun to pursue and catch, and you'll have rounded up all the reasons and more you'll need to muster up the initiative to chase this worthy prey—and much of the reason panfish are such popular quarry for winter anglers of all ages and skill levels.

However, as abundant and cooperative as panfish can be, whenever you're dealing with a variety of species like we're covering here and their diverse habitat preferences, inherent behavior and habits in a variety of environments, your odds of creating consistent catches can be greatly improved by closely examining each species and fishing situation on an individual basis.

In many respects, a white crappie is very similar to a black crappie, a sunfish to a bluegill, a rainbow trout to a brown trout, even a white perch to a white bass for that matter, so general patterns can be applied to catching them. Yet all are different species with varying traits, and each responds differently to an immense variety of sub-ice environments. If you learn to better understand each, you'll discover it's possible to develop systematic, strategic approaches to best meet the unique situations and conditions you're facing and create consistent methods for finding and catching your intended target species.

Introductory concepts for such systems were outlined in book one of the *Hooked on Ice Fishing* series. Within the pages of this book, we'll review these concepts, then build on them, picking up where the first book left off and begin covering methods for identifying more detailed winter panfish patterns, along with special and little known tips and subtleties that make ice fishing for panfish more comfortable and productive.

We'll delve into the methods for remaining safe and comfortable in the cold while pursuing winter panfish. We'll cover how to use systematic, mobile approaches to help with preparing, searching and locating winter panfish through research and the strategic use of lake maps, electronics, and highly refined, never before revealed approaches and techniques. We'll identify the preferred habitats, behavior, habits and movements of various panfish species throughout the winter, given various conditions. We'll demonstrate a versatile array of productive, fine-tuned presentations covering a variety of unique situations and conditions, then suggest the best equipment, baits, methods and techniques for catching panfish given each unique set of conditions— even recommend productive times to fish them.

The most popular panfish species are then covered thoroughly within individual chapters, where you will discover the habits of these species based on the research and experiences of the nation's leading fisheries biologists, winter guides and ice fishing experts. You'll also gain insight into the best angling techniques of ice pros and ice tackle designers from around the country—so you're sure to learn new tips that will help you catch respectable sized panfish with more consistency.

Seasoned ice angling veterans know good panfish catches aren't always easy, and that trophy panfish—plate-sized bluegills, slab crappies, jumbo perch and feisty white bass—can be every bit elusive as fussy trophy bass, finicky lake trout or light-striking walleye. But they've learned tricks to improve their odds. This is the exciting world of winter panfishing, one that we'll explore and reveal within the pages of this book, providing solid information you can use to catch panfish in a variety of waters across the ice fishing belt, throughout the winter.

So regardless of your reason for pursuing cold weather panfish, if you're a bona fide "hardwater" panfish enthusiast, this book was written for you.

# *Acknowledgments*

*T*hanks and praise to God and my savior, Jesus Christ, for the faith and visions you've provided; warm hugs to my wife, Lisa, daughters Alyssa Jo and Brianna Kay, for your encouragement to follow through on them. A most heartfelt thank you to my parents and grandparents for their endless love and support, all of you I love much. To Paul and Ken Grahl and HT Enterprises, my most sincere thanks for your help with photography and research, your contributions have been an invaluable part of making this book possible. A hearty handshake to Nate Grahl for his effort generating hardcopy illustrations from the mere sketches in my mind—your talent is sheer genius.

Very special thanks to Northern Outfitters, Fishing Hotspots, Vexilar, Lowrance, Zercom Marine, Humminbird, Jim Lindsey and HT Enterprises for their generous contributions of information and illustrations; and the many guides, tournament anglers, tackle manufacturers, engineers and sales representatives who took time from their busy schedules to share their knowledge, experience, insights, photos and illustrations. Your camaraderie is refreshing, and in many cases, the bond of friendship has become extraordinary. I can speak for ice anglers around the world when I say thank you for your commitment to excellence. Often it is your willingness to share information and product ideas that help make this sport we love that much more enjoyable and productive.

# Introduction

# *The Formula for Sweet Success*

$A$nytime someone ventures into trying something new, there's a certain element of excitement...and fear. Fear of the unknown, that is. For many, it's hard to ask questions for fear someone more familiar with the topic will fall into fits of laughter at the questioner's expense. Yet if you don't ask questions, you'll never move beyond the obvious.

Learning basics generally isn't too hard. It doesn't matter if you're trying to learn more about laying carpet, reupholstering furniture, fixing a leaky sink, driving a car, golfing or learning to ice fish. You must start somewhere, and usually, the basics can be gleaned by studying up on the topic. In today's information age of magazines, books, radio, television, videos, CD-ROMs, the internet and beyond, that's not difficult. The trick is getting hands-on experience, the practical edge that helps push you over that difficult initial "speed bump" of fear separating beginner from experienced participant.

When it comes to ice fishing, most educators do a tremendous job covering and demonstrating basic equipment, tackle and techniques, helping overcome that speed bump of fear. However, they often overlook the importance and particulars of putting that knowledge to work in the right location.

To me that's a problem. Beginning ice anglers are generally eager to learn, and often taught the basics of *how* to use equipment and tackle, but not enough about *where* it should be used to achieve the best results. So they leave their classes and seminars anxiously, and soon heading to a nearby lake, set up their equipment with high hopes—and all too often, come home disappointed.

Why? They're making the all-too-common beginner's mistakes: fishing in the wrong location, or perhaps the right location at the wrong time, possibly even using the wrong equipment for the situation.

Of course, not even the most educated "expert" can locate and catch panfish all the time. But a number of techniques and tools exist that can dramatically tip the odds in your favor. The key is learning to understand each panfish species and how they relate to their environment. By understanding each species and the special relationship to their environment, you can choose key locations, and the best seasonal and daily times to maximize your productivity.

While this process involves a number of factors and variables and can become quite advanced, we must start somewhere, and I've found the basic formula for success can be boiled down to 12 important variables I call the "Deadly Dozen." Each details important panfish-catching elements, and once you learn these factors and become adept at applying them to various situations and conditions, you'll begin catching winter panfish with more consistency. For many, a big part of the ice fishing thrill

becomes learning to identify key location patterns by applying these deadly dozen factors, then capitalizing on them.

For now, don't get hung up with the possible complexities of the formula, rather, look at this introduction for what it is: A listing of important variables and a brief review of each. We'll look at details later.

## Lake Type

### Variable Number One

*When choosing a place to fish, you must decide what species you wish to seek, identify the lake types most likely to support a healthy population of the species and size you want to catch, then begin searching for specific habitats in those bodies of water most likely to concentrate them.*

The first and most important variable revolves around learning to better understand individual panfish species and how they relate to their environment. Targeting a specific species, then understanding their preferred environment, or lake type, is the first key to success.

Stocked trout and ciscoes, for instance, thrive in large, deep, cold water lakes. Traveling to a small, shallow lake to fish stocked trout or cisco is not only likely to bring poor results, but probably none at all. That's not to say stocked trout or cisco won't be present in smaller, shallower lakes; sometimes they are. But they likely won't be present in

numbers conducive to consistent catches, because only marginal populations probably would be available.

Sunfish and bluegills, however, are likely to be abundant in smaller, shallow water environments—but virtually nonexistent in large, deep, cold water trout and cisco lakes. I'm not saying sunfish and bluegill won't be found in larger, deep lakes. They can be, but the population will likely be marginal. Thus, by understanding your target species and the environment they're most likely to thrive in, you can choose key waters to better focus your fishing efforts.

This can also be taken a step further. If you learn to understand each panfish species and their relation to a unique environment—whether preferred or marginal—you can create better strategies for identifying where to find the most productive fishing. For example, large, deep, coldwater lakes may not support an ideal environment for supporting bluegills, but one or two shallow, vegetated, muck-bottom bays might offer the best available conditions, helping you eliminate water and find the fish you're looking for. Furthermore, while such restricted environments would not be conducive to growing a large population of bluegills, those present may grow to trophy proportions. This is not a lake to take the kids, but is a good lake for the trophy hunter.

In short, panfish inhabit various winter environments, including rivers, river backwaters, ponds, natural lakes, flowages, reservoirs and Great Lakes bays. Each offers unique sets of conditions, and to be consistent anglers, we must recognize and learn how to best apply

the right techniques for finding and catching our target panfish within them.

## Population Cycles

### Variable Number Two

*Find the right lake type featuring a population cycle boost, and you'll be riding a wave of terrific ice fishing action.*

Next, it's important to understand population cycles. Say you wish to catch mid-size, "eater" crappies. You start by learning the preferred lake type from knowledgeable anglers or professional biologists. You research and find the proper lake types, preferably featuring areas meeting the preferred criteria for the size fish you're seeking at the time you're fishing. Then, you go there—but you don't catch the fish you desire.

The reasons for this could be many, but an important one to consider is a downward ebb in population cycle. Crappies, like most panfish species, experience ebbs and flows in population densities based on a number of environmental factors. In the case of crappies, population cycles are strongly based on successful spawns. A couple years of cold, low-water spring seasons resulting in poor spawns decrease the number of smaller fish, leading to a depletion in the population of new fish, leaving a gap in the number of larger crappie year classes available several years down the road.

In contrast, a couple of high-water, mild-spring seasons can result in good spawns, bolstering the population. So to be successful, you must not only choose the right lake during the best times, but you must also fish during an upward swing in the population for the species and size you're seeking.

## Habitat/Structure/Cover

### Variable Number Three

*Once you've chosen the proper lake type offering a solid population of the panfish you're seeking and undergoing an upward swing in cycle, you must select the highest percentage areas offering the best combination of habitat, structure and cover most likely to attract them, based on the conditions during the time you're fishing.*

Once on the ice, you'll want to further narrow down the amount of area to be covered—target locations I call them—where you're likely to find winter panfish, and this varies from one lake type to the next. In river backwaters or small, shallow ponds and natural lakes shaped like the proverbial bowl, panfish may simply relate to cover like vegetation, downed timber or stumps. If distinct drop-offs or deeper holes exist, they may hold on these edges, or simply cruise along them, essentially swimming around searching for forage.

In larger, deeper, more structurally diverse lakes, flowages and reservoirs where bottom features include distinct drop-offs, rises and falls at various depths, panfish may relate to any number of different areas, migrating between them as the winter season progresses, perhaps even moving periodically for various distances between them each day. By learning such things, then learning to predict when, where and how far these movements occur and how long they will last, you can better pinpoint locations panfish will hold, migration patterns between these locations, and where and when these movements are most likely to occur, thereby deciphering the best seasonal and daily times to fish.

Of course, many factors influence these key locations, unique movements and peak periods—many of which we'll examine in more detail throughout this book. For now, understand that each panfish species prefers specific habitats, structures and cover types within their unique environment.

Again, consider the contrast between cisco and sunfish. Massive schools of cisco often suspend high over deep water, away from structure and cover, where the only shelter from predators is their sheer number. Although sunfish may utilize such habitat, it's usually only when forced by environmental conditions, such as a severe cold front, little or no oxygen or forage availability in preferred vegetated areas, or simply because they've been chased out of preferred areas by predators or competing species. Sunfish would much rather hide on structures and flats offering good cover in the form of moderate to dense vegetation, wood or manmade cover.

## Depth

### Variable Number Four

*After finding the most ideal lake type for the species you're seeking undergoing a high swing in the population cycle—and searching for the most ideal combination of habitat, structure and cover where your target species is most likely to be found based on the time and conditions you're fishing—identify those areas nearest the deepest available water—and choose these areas wisely based on the depth of the lake.*

Another primary consideration when choosing a specific location for the time you're fishing is the depth the best habitats, structures and cover are found.

A sunken island located in 15 feet of water just outside a shallow bay might be good first ice structure on a shallow lake with a maximum depth of 40 feet, but midwinter, a sunken island in 30 feet of water might be better. Best of all might be a point running from a shallow feeding flat into 30 feet of water, because it offers more options for the fish throughout a longer time period. Given ideal weather conditions, panfish might slide up the point and scatter into the shallows. After the passing of a severe cold front, however, you'll likely find most fish on the deep end of the point. Again, be sure to evaluate the structure you intend to fish, based on the lake type, time you're fishing and the conditions.

And regardless of lake type, always start looking for panfish around the most suitable combination of habitat, structure and cover nearest the deepest available water, because deep water offers environmental stability. Consider a shoreline point extending from a shallow flat toward a deep hole. Early in the season and during twilight periods offering mild, overcast, stable weather conditions, you might find bluegills holding in vegetated bays or shallow, shoreline flats, but during mid-season or bright midday periods, they might relate to deeper weed lines, drop into deeper pockets or even the deeper hole.

Just keep in mind the terms "shallow" and "deep" are relative. Following a severe cold front, panfish might move into the deepest available water adjacent to where they're holding—which might be 10 feet down on a shal-

low lake, while on a nearby larger, deeper lake, the same fish might drop 20 or 30 feet down. And depth on a lake with a maximum depth of 10 feet versus one with a maximum depth of 40, 100, or 200 feet would certainly be rated differently, because panfish would have dramatically different sets of conditions and location options. For instance, ciscoes in a lake with a maximum depth of 40 feet might suspend in 20 feet of water, where on one with a maximum depth of 200, they might suspend in 30, 40, 50, 60 or even 100 feet.

Depth makes a difference in another respect as well. Deep lakes, having more volume, cool more slowly in fall and warm more slowly in spring than shallow lakes—meaning they freeze later in fall and thaw later in spring than shallow waters. This means if the same species existed in both lake types, the shallower one, which cools first, would freeze first and offer the best early season action. Late ice, however, the deeper lake—which warms more slowly—would likely offer safer ice fishing later into the spring.

The implications here can be tremendous. Knowledgeable anglers, knowing the first and late ice seasons offer terrific action but are also short-lived, are quick to fish smaller, shallow waters at first-ice, and by the time groups of anglers find the ice solid and start attacking these waters in droves, they've moved onto fishing larger,

deeper, less-pressured waters that have just iced over—in effect, allowing themselves to extend the short-lived first-ice bite by moving from lake type to lake type. Ditto late ice, when they fish smaller, shallower lakes first, then, after many ice anglers have put their ice drills away for the season, extend the famed late-ice season by fishing larger, deeper lakes, which are more resistant to thawing.

## How Far Winter Has Progressed

### Variable Number Five

*After carefully considering the species you're targeting, the lake type and environment in which they're found and their preferred habitat, structure, cover and depth, always remember panfish move under the ice seasonally, and that these movements will vary with the weather, how far winter has progressed, lake type and a variety of biological, physical and chemical parameters.*

Pinpointing winter panfish location can be further narrowed down by considering how far the winter has progressed.

Individual panfish species make under-ice movements, many of which involve depth changes. While these may be quite sudden, they're usually gradual, and can be predicted as changes in seasonal and daily conditions occur. Seasonally, bluegills typically will be found in shallow vegetation at first ice, then hold along or suspend over deeper weed lines, holes and structures during mid-winter before returning shallow as the melt-off approaches. Ciscoes may be scattered in shallow or mid-depth water during first ice and deep water in mid-winter, but by late season typically gather in large schools within mid-depth holes and pockets near shallower water.

Either species may move slightly deeper or shallower based on the lake type and current conditions on a daily basis, too. Panfish make general movements within areas

of seasonal constraints. For example, first ice bluegills may move from deep water pockets and holes onto shallow feeding flats, often following specific paths, called migration routes, at specific times. The length and duration of these movements will vary with the conditions.

Given ideal conditions and weather, panfish might move into the shallows and feed actively several days in a row. A great deal of activity on the ice, however, might cause them to not move as far into the shallows. Severe cold fronts offering bright, sunny skies might cause them to not move into the shallows at all.

Again, keep in mind depth is relative, so the distance, duration and depth of these movements will vary depending on your lake type, the deepest available and most easily accessible deep water, water characteristics, the local conditions and how far winter has progressed.

## Forage

### Variable Number Six

*Fish where the food is.*

Forage is a biological parameter that all by itself may heavily influence winter panfish location. You might find the right lake type undergoing an upswing in the population cycle and just the right combination of your target species preferred habitat, structure, cover, depth and other qualities for the time you're fishing—even identify primary migration routes amid them—but if there isn't an adequate amount of food present, panfish likely won't be there in number.

Furthermore, if large numbers of your target species attack an area of concentrated forage, fishing may be poor because the abundance of natural food creates a lack of interest in angler presentations. And by the time these fish finish foraging heavily upon existing food, scatter the forage and fishing starts to improve, another change in their feeding habits and further under-ice movements are likely to occur.

Thus, one of the main factors in locating panfish consistently is finding structures offering moderate amounts of forage. Excessive amounts of available forage usually result in well-fed fish and poor fishing action. Then again, areas supporting low forage densities won't attract fish. The trick is to find good "combination areas" harboring moderate quantities of forage—large enough to draw fish, but few enough to provide some competition among individuals.

Although you may discover overlaps in forage use among panfish, to reduce competition species typically seek different environmental niches—some may feed on shallow water plankton amid vegetation, while others graze on plankton suspended over deep water. Some will feed on shiners in weeds, others on shiners over hard bottom, mid-lake structures, or shad suspended high over deep water. Even among a single species, smaller panfish might feed on hard bottom, shallow water structures offering insects and crustaceans while larger individuals relate to deeper, soft-bottom structures offering plankton and worms.

Contact a local fisheries office to determine the preferred forage of the species and size you're targeting on your lake type, then ask about the habits of these forage bases and locations where you're likely to find moderate numbers of them—or perhaps more importantly, moderate, yet diverse numbers of several preferred varieties. By learning to understand the habits of your species favored forage bases and forage niches, you'll learn to better pattern the fish, too.

## Bottom Content

### Variable Number Seven

*Always remember your target lake's bottom content—along with other interrelated physical, chemical and biological variables—may affect parameters that dictate the preferred location and positioning of your target species.*

Bottom content is a good example of a physically influencing location parameter—one that may have a profound effect on numerous water characteristics.

Like many other variables in nature, bottom content directly and indirectly affects other important parameters. For example, muck bottoms supply a greater concentration of nutrients, which tend to sustain more plant and animal life. The result is lush vegetation and thick blooms of tiny plants called phytoplankton floating freely in the water, reducing water clarity, another physical parameter.

Lakes featuring less-fertile bottom contents such as sand or rock typically feature clearer water. This allows more sunlight penetration, in turn, causing light-sensitive species such as crappie to become less active during periods of bright light, or sends them scurrying into heavier cover or deeper water during bright, midday periods. Improved clarity also allows better and deeper vegetation growth, a physical parameter that increases photosynthesis and its important chemical by-product, oxygen.

In contrast, darker colored water results in reduced sunlight penetration in the depths, reducing vegetation growth, slowing photosynthesis and limiting oxygen production. This is important. Consider, for example, how various forage and panfish species have different levels of tolerance to oxygen concentration. Areas not supplying adequate oxygen will be vacated by both forage and fish. So even if you're fishing the right lake type featuring a good combination of habitat, structure, cover, perhaps even forage at the right depths and featuring varying bottom content, without adequate oxygen, it won't likely support panfish.

Darker water also means reduced sunlight penetration resulting in shallower weed lines, whereas clear water means deeper weed lines. Either way, the decreased or increased amount of cover will influence primary panfish depth patterns and migrations. Similarly, thick ice and heavy snow cover will diminish sunlight intensity as well, influencing a variety of physical, biological and chemical parameters, creating varying degrees of winter panfish activity, positioning and movement.

Different environments also often display vastly different varieties of bottom content. Although shallow, dark water lakes typically feature a large percentage of mud or muck bottoms and deep, clear lakes are more likely to be predominantly sand or rock bottomed, variations occur. And because certain types of prey prefer specific bottom types, bottom content can heavily influence under-ice location. A sand or rock bar on a largely muck bottom lake, for instance, might provide that little something different panfish relate to.

Why? Go back to variable number six, fishing where the food is. Because worms are likely found in muck bottoms, and insects in rocky bottoms, areas where the two meet offer a diversity of forage that attracts panfish.

## Interspecies Competition

### Variable Number Eight

*Consider interspecies relationships in the lake you're fishing; they often have a strong impact on panfish location.*

With this understanding, we can now delve another step deeper into the mysteries of winter fish location. Let's say you find the right lake type, identify the right combination of preferred habitat, structure, cover, depth, forage, bottom content and oxygen concentration in a particular area, and begin catching perch—then the action suddenly stops.

Why? It could be simply the perch are moving along a migration route, breakline of some kind, or perhaps a slight shift in location or activity level is occurring. Or it could be a predator or another competing panfish has moved in, and perch are responding by moving into heavy cover to hide until the danger passes. Either way, predator/prey relationships are important considerations when attempting any winter panfishing.

Remember, panfish are forage to many larger gamefish. Just as when a school of hungry panfish blasts into a concentration of plankton, ultimately causing them to scatter and hide—if a larger gamefish such as a pike moves in to feed on the perch, the situation will cause them to hide and scatter, too.

Similar phenomena occur when competing fish move in. You might be catching some smaller perch, then the action stops. It's possible a pike or walleye is close, but it could be a large school of bluegills or crappies outcompeting the perch for food. This doesn't happen often, because perch, bluegills and crappies typically prefer different ecological niches when found in the same environ-

ment. But at times, overlap for forage occurs and will affect your fishing.

## Intraspecies Competition

### Variable Number Nine

*Consider the population cycle, density and "balance" of your target species on the lake you're fishing, and how it may effect fish positioning, activity levels and movements.*

Just as another species may cause a change in your target fish's feeding mood, so may a larger member of the same species. Take bluegills for example. As you'll see later in this book, although the environmental needs of bluegills are similar no matter what their size, smaller bluegills have slightly different needs than larger ones, causing them to often hold in slightly or dramatically different areas—a key that can be used to increase your consistency with larger bluegills.

However, there are times panfish of different sizes utilize the same areas. When this happens, depending on the lake's balance, larger bluegills may chase the small ones away, slowing the feeding activity of the smaller fish—or, at times, the sheer number of smaller fish may simply reduce the ability of the larger fish to feed effectively. Either way, consider the influence of intraspecies competition.

## Time of Day

### Variable Number Ten

*Consider the species you're seeking and importance of the time of day when planning your winter angling strategies—and the importance and effect of interrelated variables such as bright, high skies, water clarity, ice thickness and snow cover on them.*

Time of day also has a pronounced effect on activity levels and movements. Some species are more adept at night feeding. Crappies, for instance, have large eyes and see better than most prey species during twilight and evening. Because this is a predatory advantage, you're more likely to find crappie actively feeding during these periods. Trying to find active crappies during midday, however, can be difficult—but locating midday schools of active, small-eyed perch that are less light-sensitive isn't unusual.

Time of day may also influence daytime movements. Bright conditions following passage of a cold front, for example, will send most panfish scurrying deeper or into heavier cover, especially in clear water. Even suspended fish may make vertical movements into greater depths. However, if thick ice and heavy snow coat even the clearest water environment, these movements may be altered. Given extremes, even light-sensitive species such as crappies may move shallow and feed at high noon, simply because diminished light penetration allows a change in behavior.

More importantly, to pattern these fish be sure to consider where such movements are likely to occur based on the prevailing conditions. Ask yourself where these fish might be moving to and from—not just during, but also before and after these changing light conditions, and try to determine how long or short these movements are in duration and distance.

## Weather

### Variable Number Eleven

*Either adapt your strategies to the prevailing weather conditions, or try to time your trips during sustained periods of mild, overcast, low pressure systems or extended periods of stable, favorable weather, preferably just before the arrival of a significant weather change.*

Because this variable is completely out of our control, it's the one that most commonly wrecks havoc with any winter fishing system. As with open water fishing, sudden changes in barometric pressure, wind, heavy snows and the passing of cold fronts and their associated bright skies may dramatically influence fish activity levels and movements beneath the ice. Even the experts can't explain exactly why, but here are some weather conditions that appear to affect ice fishing success:

- Periods of stable conditions are good for fishing.

- Panfish seem to bite better on partly cloudy days than bright, sunny days, because there is less light penetration into the water.

- South and west winds are good for fishing, but north and east winds are poor.

- Thin ice and little snow cover let light in, causing panfish to hide deeper in cover or at greater depths during bright conditions.

- Thick ice and heavy snow cover reduce the sun's brightness under water, allowing panfish to move shallower and feed, particularly early and late in the season. Mid-season, such conditions may reduce photosynthesis, slowing or stopping oxygen production, lessening the distance of movement or perhaps even causing panfish to move deeper or suspend.

- Panfish usually bite well during periods of light snow. Heavy snowstorms and blizzards may cause panfish to hide in cover or move deep. Fishing is often poor for a day or two after a big winter storm or passing of a severe cold front.

**Noted ice angler Dave Genz with an impressive Nebraska bluegill. (Courtesy Mark Strand Outdoors)**

- When you hear weathermen talk about warm and cold fronts, listen carefully. Warm fronts associated with low pressure systems usually bring active panfish up to feed. Cold fronts and bright, high pressure systems tend to send them deep, where they're not as active.

- Finally, listen when the weatherman discusses the barometer. Many experts find fishing best when the barometer is rising, others like fishing when pressure suddenly drops.

## Presentation

### Variable Number Twelve

*Always consider the species you're seeking, their location, depth, and activity level along with the local conditions when attempting to choose the proper presentation.*

The final variable in the formula for ice fishing success is presentation. Once you've targeted a species, determined their preferred lake type with an upswing in population cycle, found the best combination of habitat, cover, depth, forage, bottom content, water clarity and oxygen concentration for the time of winter you're fishing, and considered the influences of inter- and intraspecies competition, time of day, local conditions and weather, it's time to drill a few holes and start fishing. Now knowledge of how to set, rig and use equipment and tackle comes into play.

Panfish by our definition are small enough to fit in a pan, and with only a few exceptions, most feature small mouths. With such small mouths, it shouldn't be surprising to learn they eat primarily smaller forage items such as plankton, insect larvae and small minnows—and as anglers, we must try to match their natural feeding habits by using primarily smaller lures and baits. Often, this translates into the use of light, ultralight and micro-action jigging equipment, including wispy ice rods and spring bobbers, lightweight reels, thin diameter lines, minimal amounts of terminal tackle and tiny ultralight and micro spoons, jigs, hooks and baits. Specifically what equipment, lures and baits will perform best depends on the species you're targeting, their location, depth, local conditions and timing, and the fish's activity level—and careful consideration of the aforementioned deadly dozen factors.

At times, tip-ups may also play a role in successful presentation. However, since winter panfish often strike lightly, tip-up fishing for panfish requires special tip-ups and ultralight rigging methods for ultra-smooth trip settings. Special settings on ultra-smooth underwater and thermal tip-ups, use of lightly set wind tip-ups, ultralight "umbrella" style tip-ups and super-sensitive tip-downs with ultralight rigging are most commonly used. Again, which model and presentation strategies best fit the situation depends on the species you're targeting, their location, depth, and activity level. Of course, there are a lot of details to consider in presentation, but because these vary greatly with the species and conditions, we'll reserve further discussion for the coming species-specific chapters.

## The Deadly Dozen Variables Equal Success

Certainly nature isn't subject to any single set formula—there are many correlations, combinations and direct and indirect effects of the above "deadly dozen" factors and variables that all influence winter fish location—and we'll explore many of these areas in more and greater detail in future chapters. For now, it's only important to recognize these most important variables, and understand that considered together, they help create a general formula, or foundation, for success.

The true thrill of ice fishing is learning to identify these key location patterns, then capitalizing on them by determining the proper presentation based on the environment, daily conditions, fish's activity levels and moods. Compute these variables properly, and the results will equal more consistent, more enjoyable ice fishing—by the definition of many winter panfish anglers, sweet success.

# Chapter 1

# *Comfort in the Cold*

We can learn all we want about winter panfish location and presentation, but there's one thing required to accomplish any winter fishing approach: Time. And applied to ice fishing, that means time on the ice and time in the cold.

Before getting into specifics about locating and catching winter panfish, we must first tackle ice safety and staying warm in cold weather. No fish is worth a human life, and if the ice isn't thick enough to trek across you're risking just that. If you're cold, you'll spend more time thinking about getting warm, and less time focusing on catching panfish—a result none of us desires.

## Staying Safe

I enjoy the mystical feeling of walking on ice. There's something fascinating about knowing—figuratively speaking—we can walk on water. Unfortunately, we can also drop through, and while I've never experienced an unpleasant, icy plunge, it happens, usually to overzealous anglers during early or late ice, but sometimes during the midst of winter. Thus, safety is a primary concern, and safety guidelines must be followed. Here are some I live by.

First, be extremely cautious about driving vehicles on the ice. Ice thickness is rarely uniform, and I shouldn't have to mention discovering a thin spot and being sealed in a vehicle beneath an ice covered waterway is not fun. Nor should I need to remind you that even if you escape such a calamity, your monthly payments will now cover a water-logged, ruined vehicle and a bill from the local wrecking company for the service of raising it back to the surface.

I prefer to use a six-wheeler, four-wheeler or snow-mobile. These are lighter, less expensive risks, and easier

When unsure of the ice thickness, always carry a set of ice picks so in the event you do fall through, you can pull yourself to safety. (Courtesy Bob Hammes)

Commercially produced ice picks such as these offered by HT Enterprises, could easily save your life. To save money, a set of screwdrivers or wood dowels with nails inserted would work as well. (Courtesy Bob Hammes)

to escape should you fall through. They're also better designed for snow and ice travel. Should you choose to drive a car or truck on the ice, however, I recommend the following common-sense guidelines.

- Don't drink and drive. Alcohol slows response time and impairs your ability to react.

- Avoid ice heaves and fractures, unless bridged by an on-ice road maintenance crew.

- Avoid excessive speeds. Vehicles traveling on the ice produce shock waves that weaken and may even fracture the ice. This is especially dangerous when two vehicles are traveling close together.

- Leave your seat belts unbuckled, windows rolled down, heavy clothes off and a hand on the door latch. Each of these things saves precious seconds for escape in the event you break through.

Before running six-wheelers, four-wheelers, snowmobiles or even walking on ice, also consider the time of year and geographical location. Near my home in southeastern Wisconsin, we're usually ice fishing a month before folks in northern Illinois, while fishermen in northern Minnesota typically have a good month jump on us. Waters at higher altitudes generally freeze before lower ones. Proximity to large water bodies also has an effect: Parts of inland New York may have ice on the ponds and lakes, while those bordering the Great Lakes have none. Upper Michigan and Wisconsin might have ice on most lakes, while lower Michigan, at the same latitude but influenced by the so-called "lake effect" of Lake Michigan, might have none.

Depth matters, too. Ice may be several inches thick on a shallow lake, while a deep lake across the road might boast scarcely a fraction of a inch. What many anglers also don't realize is ice thickness is seldom uniform, even on an individual lake. Shallow bays protected from the wind and sun freeze faster than deep, exposed open-water areas. Snowdrifts may insulate the ice, slowing ice formation. Inflowing creeks, channels and springs create water movement, which inhibit ice formation. Shoreline water six inches deep can only support ice equal in depth, no more, while main lake areas may freeze considerably deeper. Pack ice, formed when broken chunks and blocks of ice blow together and freeze, can pose interesting problems because they invariably consist of various thicknesses. Animal activity, such as the movement of muskrats, ducks or geese, can prolong, impede or prevent ice formation. Aerators, placed to maintain oxygen for fish or protect man-made structures such as docks, may prevent ice formation entirely, even during the coldest temperatures.

Fishing reservoirs and flowages can also be treacherous because of fluctuating water levels. If the water rises, shore ice becomes flooded, leaving unsafe thicknesses

## Helping Someone Who Has Fallen Through The Ice

*If assisting someone who has fallen through, stand back and "extend yourself" to the victim. Throw a rope, extend an ice drill, chisel, or tie items such as belts or clothing together and extend them to the victim, without getting too close. Two people in the water can't help each other.*

*Most importantly, always respect the ice, and remember, "when in doubt, don't go out!"*

surrounding the shoreline. Falling levels cause steep ice heaves along shore, creating poor shore ice. Another danger involves cracks and pressure ridges. These are usually caused when ice expands as it thickens, creating large heaves. Typically, these are accompanied by open water and, given strong winds, may expand.

Later in the season, shore ice—the thinnest ice—becomes increasingly hazardous, as do shallow, dark-bottomed vegetated areas and ice surrounding objects such as downed trees, docks or large rocks exposed above the ice. Such objects absorb the sun's heat, transfer it to the surrounding ice and weaken the pack.

In summary, here's my recommended safety checklist:

- If traveling long distance to your fishing destination, call ahead for ice safety information before leaving home.

- Always travel on the ice in pairs.

- Walk slowly when unsure of the ice, checking ice thickness ahead with a heavy chisel.

- Wear a lifejacket or PFD (personal floatation device) when traversing ice you're unsure of.

- Carry a set of ice picks so in the event you fall through, you can pull yourself to safety.

- Carry a rope for throwing to someone in trouble, or perhaps your rescuer.

## The Quest for Warmth

Once you've checked the ice and ventured out, your next quest is staying warm.

Start by drinking and eating. Dehydration is a concern because moisture is quickly lost through perspiration and breathing. Loss of moisture to breathing may seem insignificant, but in cold, dry air, your body quickly moisturizes each dry inhalation, then expels it during exhalation. With your body continually drawing moisture from cells for this process, dehydration is imminent, causing slowed metabolism and resulting in inadequate heating function in your tissues.

To avoid dehydration, drink a lot of liquids, exclusively of the non-alcoholic and non-caffeinated variety. Alcohol cools the body by dilating capillaries and increasing blood flow to extremities where heat loss occurs. Caffeine is a diuretic, which triggers the bladder to release, causing loss of vital fluids. If you feel dizzy, listless and are suffering a nagging headache—signs of dehydration—try downing a glass of water, juice or non-caffeinated herbal tea. The symptoms may subside in a matter of minutes.

As for food, eat a lot and eat often. Fried, high-calorie fats provide more energy with less volume than other foods, plus burn slowly and steadily as opposed to carbohydrates, starches or sugars that offer quick bursts of energy and heat, but burn fast. Fried meats, potatoes with gravy or real butter and stews are good sources, and should be supplemented with heavy bread, butter, doughnuts, beef jerky, cheese, cookies, hearty meat or peanut butter sandwiches, instant oatmeal and hot, non-caffeinated beverages. Such a diet helps stimulate the duration of your body's metabolism and keeps your blood flowing, ultimately keeping you warmer.

## Clothing

In addition to fluids and diet, you must dress properly. Today's cold weather clothing—from underwear to coats—is lighter, warmer, better insulating and drier than ever before. If you're using the right combination of modern cold weather clothing, it's unlikely you'll become uncomfortable, even when spending extended amounts of time on the ice.

To understand proper dress, it's important to understand the body loses heat through three means: convected, conducted and radiant heat loss.

- Convection cooling takes place when the wind blows over your body, moving heat away with it. To minimize convective heat loss, reduce this effect by wearing wind-resistant clothing.

- Conduction cooling takes place when your skin comes in contact with cold, heat-conducting surfaces, such as a metal ice drill handle. Essentially, heat is absorbed from the skin into the cold surface. The best way to stop conducted cooling is to place an insulating material between the skin and the cold surface.

- Radiant heat loss occurs as we radiate heat. Most clothing materials don't stop this process, but rather reflect a small amount of radiated heat back toward the skin.

Because convective and conducted heat losses account for more than 85 percent of the body's total heat loss, most

**Layers of clothing will help insulate you from the cold because they trap layers of warm air. Bulky layers of lofty materials sandwiched between polypropylene undergarments and wind resistant outerwear work best. Depending on the conditions, add or strip layers to warm you up or keep you from perspiring.**

cold-weather clothing is designed to minimize the effects of convective and conducted heat loss, particularly in regions where body heat is lost in the highest percentages—the head, 40 percent, and the body torso and legs, 30 percent. While your hands, fingers, feet, toes, nose, ears, chin and cheeks are most susceptible to frostbite and must be adequately protected, heat for these areas originates from the body core and is mostly dispelled through the head, so let's begin by focusing on protecting these areas.

Start with a warm, well-insulated polypropylene lined stocking hat that has the ability to be loosened during periods of activity. Polypropylene allows moisture to be wicked away from the skin and hair, thereby keeping your head dry, and the ability to loosen the material allows you to release heat should you start to feel too warm. During periods of minimal activity, the hood from a hooded sweatshirt and/or hooded outergarment should cover your hat to help retain additional heat.

As for the body core, most people follow the layering concept, which means wearing multiple layers of clothing. This works because layers of warmed air are trapped between layers of clothing, holding heat close to your body and insulating you from the cold. But to achieve maximum warmth, this layering must be carefully assembled. If you don't wear enough layers, you'll get cold. Wear too many layers, and you may end up too warm and perspire. Perspiration means damp clothing, and since wet clothing conducts heat, it's a poor insulator. Furthermore, the evaporative process, being a cool-

ing one, draws heat from the body, especially when combined with wind and convective heat loss.

So while the layering concept is sound, you must remain "comfortably cool." If you get warm, the layer closest to the skin will become damp, which in turn migrates toward the outer clothing layers. As this happens, moisture encounters a temperature differential between each layer, making it relatively easy to reach it's "dew point," causing condensation and a build-up of excess moisture. If the temperature between layers reaches the freezing point, frost forms, and additional heat will be absorbed to convert the frost back to vapor.

Other drawbacks to multi-layered systems include:

- Often by the time you notice you're wearing too many layers and are too warm, you've already broken the perspiration barrier.

- The temperature range where clothing remains comfortable decreases substantially when the insulation becomes damp, because damp clothing is too warm when inside at room temperature and too chilling when outside at freezing temperatures.

- When layered clothes become wet with perspiration, it is often difficult or impossible to dry them without removing them.

Thus, the layering concept only works if completed properly. First, you must wear the right clothing in the proper order, based on the conditions and your activity level.

## WIND CHILL CHART

| Wind Speed (mph/kph) | Equivalent Temperature (Fahrenheit) To convert to Centigrade - C = 5/9 (F-32) | | | | | | | | | | | |
|---|---|---|---|---|---|---|---|---|---|---|---|---|
| 0/0 | 35 | 30 | 25 | 20 | 15 | 10 | 5 | 0 | -5 | -10 | -15 | -20 |
| 5/8 | 33 | 27 | 21 | 16 | 11 | 6 | 1 | -6 | -11 | -16 | -21 | -26 |
| 10/16 | 21 | 15 | 9 | 3 | -3 | -9 | -15 | -22 | -27 | -32 | -38 | -45 |
| 15/24 | 16 | 9 | 1 | -4 | -11 | -18 | -25 | -33 | -40 | -45 | -52 | -60 |
| 20/32 | 12 | 5 | -3 | -9 | -17 | -24 | -32 | -40 | -47 | -52 | -60 | -68 |
| 25/40 | 7 | 0 | -8 | -15 | -22 | -29 | -37 | -45 | -52 | -58 | -67 | -75 |
| 30/48 | 5 | -2 | -11 | -18 | -26 | -33 | -41 | -49 | -56 | -63 | -70 | -78 |
| 35/56 | 3 | -4 | -13 | -20 | -28 | -35 | -43 | -52 | -60 | -67 | -75 | -83 |
| 40/64 | 1 | -7 | -15 | -22 | -30 | -37 | -45 | -54 | -62 | -69 | -78 | -87 |

☐ Cold   ☐ Very Cold   ☐ Bitter Cold   ☐ Extreme Cold

Courtesy of Northern Outfitters

**In a still, windless environment, a "cloud" of warm air surrounds the body. Wind makes you feel colder because this cloud of warm air is quickly dissipated by the wind—creating the so called "wind chill factors" we hear so much about during winter. Wearing wind-resistant clothing that blocks this effect is imperative if you want to remain comfortable in bitter winter winds. (Courtesy Northern Outfitters)**

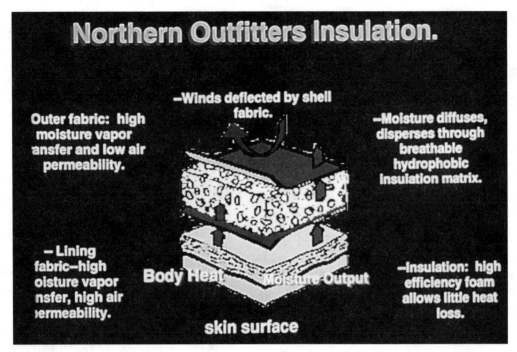

**Northern Outfitters Insulation.**

—Winds deflected by shell fabric.

Outer fabric: high moisture vapor ansfer and low air permeability.

—Moisture diffuses, disperses through breathable hydrophobic insulation matrix.

— Lining fabric—high oisture vapor nsfer, high air ermeability.

Body Heat    Moisture Output

—Insulation: high efficiency foam allows little heat loss.

skin surface

**(Courtesy Northern Outfitters)**

## The Three Ws

I refer to this proper layering concept as the "three Ws": Wicking, Warming, and Wind resistance. The wicking layer closest to your skin absorbs, then whisks trapped moisture away from your skin, keeping you dry. This can be accomplished using a variety of modern, man-made materials.

The second, or warming layer, resists heat loss by trapping pockets of warm air between your body and the cold outside air, providing insulation and warmth through layers of stabilized air. This is best achieved using layers of materials featuring very low heat-conducting properties near the skin. The more the material restricts air movement, the better the insulator.

Insulation that does not absorb water, or better still, insulating materials that can entrain moisture in vapor form and consequently expel it to the outside, are best. These layers should also be able to evenly distribute moisture in both vertical and horizontal directions, allowing adequate time for the diffusion of moisture through the insulation without significant heat loss. Materials utilizing strands of fiber, or better yet, small open air cells, create the most effective, insulating pockets of air.

The third, or wind-resistant layer, blocks the effect of wind. Wind makes you feel colder, because in effect, a cloud of warm air surrounds the body, but is quickly dissipated by wind—creating the "wind chill factors" we hear so much about during winter. However, be careful. True waterproof, wind-resistant layers don't allow wind to cut through the material, but don't allow moisture vapor to pass to the outside, either. While waterproof outerwear is good in mild, damp conditions, such materials cause serious problems in the cold because they don't allow adequate expulsion of moisture.

In the past, this was a difficult, if not impossible clothing combination to find. With today's modern technological advances in materials, however, the above has been achieved. Now, with winter clothing designs dramatically revolutionized, numerous exceptional choices in lightweight, dry, warm, comfortable, high quality winter clothing items are available.

Of all the products I've seen on the market, Northern Outfitters patented VAETREX clothing (an acronym standing for *Vapor Attenuating and Expelling, Thermal Retaining* clothing for *EXtreme* cold weather conditions) is among the best. According to the experts at Northern Outfitters, VAETREX works well because it provides superior ability to retain body heat, conducts very little heat away from the body by remaining lofty to stabilize an insulating layer of air, all while encouraging moisture suspension in vapor form and providing a means for both liquid moisture and moisture vapor transfer to the outside. Best of all, this, combined with very low wind permeability, are all comprised into one dry, lightweight, comfortable layer.

This is revolutionary. Modern ice fishing involves a great deal of movement and physical activity, and the ice angler's greatest enemy is multiple layers of restrictive clothing that slow blood circulation, and worse yet, often become too warm during periods of activity, quickly leading to chilling—all too common occurrences when wearing traditional materials like cotton or wool.

While cotton is warm and comfortable when dry, once you begin to sweat, it draws moisture against the skin—cooling the skin's surface and counteracting any insulating properties. Wool is an excellent insulator—and even stays semi-warm when damp—but dries slowly and becomes heavy and scratchy when wet, and any ice angler who has worn wool or cotton clothing while dragging ice tackle around a lake and drilling holes interspersed with periods of inactivity has certainly figured there must be a more comfortable way of doing things. After all, during periods of activity, you will perspire. When you stop to fish and become inactive, perspiration begins evaporating from the skin. Not only does this cause chilling, especially in wind, but also drains the body of energy.

This is where modern synthetic fabrics come into play. Rather than absorbing moisture and packing down, modern synthetic materials remain lofty, absorb water and transfer it away from the body to the outside of the fabric where it evaporates away. As a result, you stay warm and dry—even if you perspire—and you retain more energy.

So while conventional cold-weather clothing protection is based on the idea of warmth through multiple layers of insulation, top cold weather clothing designers know insulation is not the only requirement for efficient cold-weather protection. Managing the body's moisture is equally important, because even the finest natural or man-made fabrics can degrade in their ability to insulate when they become wet. If the moisture from perspiration is not removed or managed, clothing will be rendered useless as a thermal protector.

## Monolithic Clothing Systems

Back to Northern Outfitters. Building on a concept derived by the Eskimos and improved using modern physics principles, their singlelayer, or "monolithic" clothing systems are top of the line. The concept is simple, and best of all, consists of a single wicking, warming and wind-resistant layer designed to follow two fundamental laws of physics to expel moisture.

1) If moisture in the air is given limited opportunity to condense, it will remain suspended in vapor form.

2) Warm, moist air will flow across a temperature gradient to cooler, dryer air. The greater the gradient, the faster the flow.

Thus, the monolithic concept used by Northern Outfitters not only keeps you warm by insulating you from the cold and wind, but since moisture is not allowed to collect next to the skin or in the garment because it's removed from the moist, warm areas against the skin, suspended as moisture vapor and continuously diffused to the cold, dry outside air, you not only stay warm, but dry. Additional advantages of this monolithic system include the following:

- The single layer of clothing is lighter and less restrictive, allowing better circulation and freedom of movement, yet effectively wicks away moisture, keeps warmth inside and protects against wind.
- The clothing effectively and efficiently retains the body's natural heat.
- There is no moisture build-up or frost layers in the clothing.
- The clothing dries while being worn, using natural body heat.
- There is a wide external temperature comfort range. Your skin will not become damp, and you won't feel overheated when inside or chilled when outside.
- Less changing of clothes is required when activities require a person to move from the inside to the outside.
- Stripping layers of clothes during periods of activity isn't necessary, nor is storage, transport or access to extra clothing layers while inactive.
- While not waterproof, (waterproofing would destroy the ability of the material to wick moisture away to the outside) should the clothing, boots or mitts get wet, you simply pull them off, wring out the water, and put them back on. The outer layers of material will absorb any remaining moisture, keeping your skin dry and warm.

Essentially, this system creates the three W's layering system all in one dry, warm, comfortable layer.

To keep your feet warm, start with a pair of lightweight, unrestrictive PolarMax or Thermax polypropylene socks, then choose from the variety of high quality pack boots on the market. Companies such as Sorel, Red Ball, La Crosse and Polartech all produce excellent models featuring modern synthetic insulative materials.

Northern Outfitters also makes a boot using VAETREX technology, which keeps your feet dry, and thus warm. One final tip: the experts at Northern Outfitters recommend loosening boot laces when you're inactive to help maximize circulation. Just be sure to lace them back up when you're active so the boots provide proper ankle support.

As for the hands, I recommend polypropylene-lined mitts, not five-fingered gloves, although loose fitting fivfingered, polypropylene lined gloves can be worn under mitts as an additional warmth layer. Why mitts? They keep your fingers together instead of spreading them out and dissipating body heat. Of course, mitts should also consist of well insulated, polypropylene-lined construction. And always bring a second pair, just in case the first becomes damp.

Several companies make such designs, including Wells-Lamont and Northern Outfitters. The advantage of such mitts is you can place wet hands in them after baiting or handling fish, and with such strong wicking properties, the liners will dry on their own. Northern Outfitters VAETREX lined mitts can even be dropped in water, and if you simply wring them out, in a matter of minutes the wicking action will dry the liners.

## Other Factors

The other intrinsic factors affecting warmth on the ice include the quality of your blood circulation and your level of physical activity. Consider each when dressing. Blood circulation, for instance, varies between individuals—especially men and women. If your wife complains she's cold, she probably isn't kidding. Blood circulation in women is poorer than men, largely because they have smaller blood vessels than males.

As for the level of physical activity, think. If employing the layering concept and you'll be walking two miles to a secluded lake carrying all your gear, strip down to your initial layer and perhaps a light wind resistant layer, or you'll perspire and become chilled. Upon arrival, open the wind breaking garments for lake exploration and hole drilling, and when set up to fish—meaning the level of physical movement stops—add your insulative layers and close up the wind breaking layer, one step at a time as your body cools down and as dictated by the conditions.

In addition to adding or subtracting layers of clothing to adjust insulation, clothing can be loosened or tightened to adjust heat flow. Because heat rises, the human body acts as a chimney. Opening a flap somewhere near the neck or head, even wrists—can allow heat escape and a consequent cool down. The trick is to do so before perspiration becomes a problem. Otherwise, try modern clothing materials such as Northern Outfitter's VAETREX, and simply loosen or tighten clothing "vents" around the neck and wrists as necessary.

A couple final points to consider: Tobacco, or specifically nicotine, should be avoided, as it constricts blood capillaries, reduces blood flow to the skin and reduces warmth. And remember that alcohol dilates capillaries, thereby increasing blood flow and causing rapid loss of body heat through the skin. Other problems include cosmetics, lotions, perfumes and colognes, which increase the possibility of frostbite because the alcohol content decreases skin temperatures.

## Clothing Summary

When traveling from place to place on the ice consider wearing a PFD, carry warming and nourishing food and drink, dressing properly using modern clothing technology and the three W's system, always being prepared to add, remove, loosen or open layers of dry clothing as necessary to suit your body and activity level, and avoid using cosmetics.

## Ice Shelters

On especially cold days, you might also want to consider the advantages of an ice fishing shelter.

Permanent "shanties" offer protection from the cold, so you can concentrate on your fishing. They're also nice for taking out kids, beginning anglers or guests new to the cold, and for overnight stays. I've also used them when fishing for long periods during extremely cold weather, using a portable shanty to move around, and the permanent shelter as a warm home base.

While all you really need is a sturdy, well-ventilated enclosure with a window and a heating device, I've even seen some pretty elaborate "shacks" in recent years, some two-storied, complete with carpet, woodstoves, tables, beds, generators for electricity, refrigerators, televisions, satellite dishes, even portable toilets.

Permanent shanties can be rented or purchased pre-built, but if you wish to build a permanent fish house, design it carefully. Be sure the design fits in your truck or trailer, or build a base with an attached axle assembly. Be sure the unit features adequate room and organized hole set-up for the number of people you want to house, the desired or required number of windows, and proper ventilation. Vents should be provided near the ceiling and floor, or you risk carbon monoxide poisoning.

Of course, when using a heater or woodstove, set the controls and chimney to reduce the danger of fire. Also

---

### Winter Clothing Checklist

❏ *Polypropylene long underwear*
❏ *Polypropylene socks*
❏ *Polypropylene-lined pants*
❏ *Multiple layers of polypropylene-line T-shirts or light sweaters*
❏ *Hooded sweatshirt*
❏ *Light, lined windbreaking jacket*
❏ *Hooded snowmobile suit, or better yet, two-piece bibbed Gore-Tex snowpants and hooded coat*
❏ *Quality pair of heavy-duty pack boots*
❏ *Quality pair of polypropylene-lined mitts, plus at least one spare pair*
❏ *Warm, polypropylene-line knit stocking cap*
❏ *Facemask or scarf*
*OR:*
❏ *Polypropylene long underwear and socks*
❏ *Northern Outfitters-style liner, parka, hooded coat or wind anorak and pants, and baraclava*
❏ *Polypropylene-lined hat, socks, pack boots and mitts*

**Permanent "shanties" offer protection from the cold so you can concentrate more on your fishing. They're also nice for overnight stays, or trips involving the kids, beginning anglers or guests new to the cold.**

be sure to check laws on license, permits and building codes requiring windows, roofing designs, trailer safety standards, lights, removal times and name labeling—all of which vary from state to state and area to area. I also recommend use of a carbon monoxide meter. These may not be cheap, but what's a life worth? Sadly, a few seasons ago a group of Wisconsin teenagers were asphyxiated in a permanent shanty equipped with a space heater—deaths a detector may have prevented.

Once on the ice, slip wood blocks between the frame and ice, or the unit will likely settle into the pack and freeze down. Be sure to loosen or move the unit every ten to fifteen days to prevent freeze down, especially during warm periods or later in the season; and be responsible enough to remove these blocks after each move rather than littering the lake.

## Portable Shelters

The problem with permanent shacks is if you're not positioned over fish, mobility is limited. In today's modern world of mobile ice fishing, permanent shelters play little, if any, role. Don't get me wrong—permanent fish houses properly located over a good spot or set up by a winter guide service over a productive location are terrific. And if you want to play cards, watch football, cook out or spend an extended weekend on the ice, they're the best way to go. But if you're on your own and following modern, mobile ice fishing approaches, you have the choice of sitting in the open within a comfortable, portable shelter that blocks the wind and offers protection from the cold.

And why not? With today's lightweight, portable enclosures, there is no excuse for not going ice fishing—

**When resting a permanent shanty on the ice, slip wood blocks between the frame and ice, or the unit can settle into the ice and freeze down.**

no matter what the temperature. Most importantly, portable shelters provide most of the advantages of a permanent shelter: A wind barrier reducing convective cooling; ample opportunity to heat the air around you, reducing conductive and radiant cooling; plus the opportunity to neatly organize and store your gear during transport and while fishing—without the reduced mobility of a "permanent" fish house. For these reasons, portable shelters are becoming increasingly popular.

But choosing a unit today isn't easy. Ten years ago, you could choose from perhaps a dozen models, today, there are many. So how do you go about choosing one?

I recently asked Mark Gostisha of Frabill portable ice shelters about the primary functions of a portable shelter.

"Their primary function is simply to keep you dry, dark and out of the wind," Mark commented. "I suppose this could be accomplished with a refrigerator box and a $3.00 tarp, but today's portables offer a variety of advantages and benefits anglers should be aware of." He then proceeded to list the following considerations for anyone contemplating a new shelter purchase.

• Portables should be sturdy and close tightly so minimal snow is picked up during transit, yet should be lightweight for easy pulling or towing.

• Portables should feature molded plastic, flat floors.

**With the protection offered by today's advanced clothing and lightweight, portable shelters, there is no excuse for not going ice fishing, no matter how cold the temperature or how strong the wind.**

Wood is heavy and disintegrates in wet, freezing conditions. Flat floors eliminate the awkward hinge joint positioned in the center of the shelter.

- Canvas and nylon materials are more durable and quieter than ripstop polyethylene. Removable material is also nice for mending damage, or drying and storage during the off-season.
- High quality, self-contained steel frames and material fastened to the floor or base are necessary to make set-up easy, even when wearing gloves and setting up in blowing winds.
- Windows are important for watching outside lines, and drapes help darken the tent so you can "sight fish" finicky biters.
- Arched doors make entering and exiting in heavy clothes easier. Also look for high quality, self-repairing coil zippers.
- Portables tall enough to allow standing and stretching are most comfortable.
- Be sure fishing holes are large enough and spaced wide enough to be easy to fish with the intended number of anglers.

Another increasingly popular portable design is the so-called "portable fish station," designed for the mobile, on-the-go ice angler fishing alone, or perhaps with one other angler. Key features here include:

- A comfortable, built-in seat, to maximize mobility and comfort.
- A deep base, important for gear storage and, when towing, preventing kicked-up snow from entering the shelter.
- A base offering adequate space to safely store your auger, tip-ups, electronics, bait and other ancillary gear during transit, and conveniently place while fishing.
- Canvas or nylon material, preferred for durability and quietness.
- Multiple roof positions, including closed, windbreak and open. For maximum convenience, this should be performed without taking off or adding pieces to the frame with each use, even in strong winds.

Keeping such things in mind will make selecting the right unit an easier task, given the number of portable models on the market today.

## Portable Heaters

A variety of portable heaters in an array of sizes and heating capacities are available. Some even offer accessories that allow heaters to double as cookers or portable stoves.

---

### Questions to ask when shopping for a portable ice shelter

*Is the shelter made of durable, quality materials and workmanship?*

*Is there a manufacturer warranty?*

*How much does the unit weigh?*

*Is it easy to set up?*

*Is the unit self-contained, or are there any loose parts that may get lost?*

*How many people will be fishing in the shelter, and how much room is needed for people, equipment and gear?*

*Does the floor plan suit your needs?*

*Can you fish effectively in it with your preferred equipment and methods?*

*Is there adequate room to set the hook using your preferred rod length?*

*Are ice anchors included?*

*Is the lighting and number of windows satisfactory? Are they draped?*

*How many doors are available? What type of zippers are used on them?*

*If you plan to use heaters, does the unit have adequate ventilation?*

*How compactly does it fold up?*

*Is the shelter easy to transport, carry, or tow?*

---

The primary concerns for the buyer involve choosing a unit that will adequately heat the size portable you're using, safely. A small one person portable may be warmed adequately with the help of a simple camping lantern, depending on the outside temperature, wind velocity and type of material the portable is made of. Canvas for example, tends to dissipate heat.

Larger shelters require larger heaters, but guidelines are more easily established for a typical insulated, permanent house. They are as follows:

| SHELTER SIZE | RECOMMENDED BTU'S |
|---|---|
| 6' x 8' | 15,000 |
| 8' x 8', 8' x 10' | 20,000 |
| 10' x 10' or larger | 30,000 |

If using these heaters in a portable, you'll want to oversize slightly to compensate for the non-insulated walls. For example, in a 6-foot x 8-foot portable, you might want to use the 20,000 BTU heater.

As for safety, make sure all connections are tight and the unit is properly vented. Watch for gas leaks, and be sure to keep any heating unit away from shelter walls, gear and loose clothing. Preferably choose models with built-in heat shields, be sure you have adequate ventilation, and as I recommended for use with a permanent shelter, carbon monoxide detectors are a good investment.

# Chapter 2

# *The Modern System: Concepts for Putting the Location Puzzle Together*

Years of experience have taught me that piecing the winter location puzzle together can be challenging.

There's a lot of water out there, and it comes in many forms, including rivers, river backwaters, ponds, small and large natural lakes, flowages, reservoirs, even Great Lakes bays. Each of these waters offers unique under-ice environments and conditions perpetuated from a variety of physical, chemical and biological conditions, and each of these factors vary at least slightly—sometimes significantly— each time you fish, over the years, through each season, throughout each day. And each panfish species responds and relates to these sets of conditions in its own unique way.

Sure, a sunfish is closely related to a bluegill, and in many respects a brook trout is similar to a rainbow trout. Yet they are different species with different preferences, habits and responses. Consistent success depends on learning how these individual species relate to each unique environment. By learning about the specific species we want to catch, and combining this knowledge with the ability to skillfully recognize and define the environment these fish are found in and analyzing the conditions they're subjected to, it's possible to adapt strategies for locating your target fish more consistently.

In this chapter, we will review basic physical, chemical and biological factors and how they influence general winter panfish location, movements and migrations. Once we've outlined some general patterns, we can then apply this knowledge to use of lake maps and electronics; and more specifically, target several popular panfish species, eventually using this system to establish more specific primary winter seasonal and daily panfish location patterns, movements and migrations.

## How to Begin Assembling the Puzzle

The trick to patterning winter panfish comes through evaluation. When you catch a fish, ask yourself where, what, why and how. Where are you fishing? What type of lake are you fishing? Why was the fish there? How far has the season progressed? What kind of structure and cover

are the fish relating to? How deep are you fishing? What time of day is it? Is the sky bright and sunny, or overcast? What is the water clarity? Was the fish on the bottom or suspended? Did you hook just one fish, or several? What size were they? If you've caught several, did fish bite continually or just periodically? Did they bite over an extended period of time or a short time? Did you catch a mixture of two or more species? What were they feeding on?

Even if you don't catch anything, ask similar questions. You can learn from reviewing these conditions and the results, too.

I look at each experience as pieces of a jigsaw puzzle. As you begin assembling the puzzle, establish the "corners and edges," reviewing and assembling the obvious factors—then work your way toward the more complicated inner workings, one piece at a time. You'll gradually see the overall picture come together. Too few ice anglers bother to assemble information and consequently don't learn from experience. Instead, they head to a lake with a pre-existing notion of where they will fish, then fish there, regardless of what happens.

Consider this: Two winters ago at the end of a bright early winter day, I met two ice anglers at a public launch. Stopping to inquire how they'd done, they proceeded to explain they'd heard the ice was thick enough to walk on, and believing the stereotype that panfish hold in shallow shoreline cover during early ice, they proceeded to their favorite lake—a small, shallow, weedy, clearwater dishpan style lake with little structure—and set up in a shallow, vegetated bay. An hour later, after catching nothing, they packed up and drilled holes in another similar area, only to experience the same thing. After a couple of similar moves and several hours of fishing they gave up, determining the panfish weren't biting.

What they didn't know is while fishing the same lake the day before, I noticed few panfish holding shallow because of the passing of a severe cold front and heavy recent snows. Instead, I found large schools had moved out of the shallows and suspended over deep water adjoining

Whenever you catch a fish, ask yourself why, where, what and how. By carefully evaluating the situation, you will often be able to narrow down the reasons for success, establish a pattern, and increase your day's catch. (Courtesy Reef Runner Lures)

these typically productive first-ice bays. In two hours of fishing these deep schools, I accumulated a nice catch of panfish. To confuse matters, the very same morning on a nearby deeper lake—which was still largely open and featuring only a thin layer of ice formed recently on some shallow bays—I'd taken a limit from shallow shoreline cover.

The problem here? Preconceived notions of where panfish should be. Top location patterns vary from lake to lake and species to species. To be successful, anglers must recognize this, then maintain open minds. It's okay to have some preconceived notions about fish location and patterns, after all, we must start somewhere. But we must also maintain open minds.

## A New Strategy for Success

Now let's repeat the above scene with versatile, open-minded anglers. First, reviewing an atlas, they recognize their target lake is small and shallow, and that a larger, deeper lake exists across the road. Driving past both lakes, they notice a full parking lot at the shallow lake's access, and note the deep lake remains open through the mid-section and the lot is empty. However, they also notice ice has formed on some shallow bays—just enough to walk on.

Aha, first ice action at its prime! They know few ice anglers have devoted time to fishing this lake because the ice has just formed. Fishing pressure has been nil. So, instead of fighting the crowds and "transition" panfish that have likely moved in response to the weather or perhaps even begun mid-winter patterns by moving away from the clatter atop the ice, moving deeper into cover or deeper water and becoming less active, they choose to fish the deeper, less-pressured lake. There the panfish haven't been disturbed and are likely following more active, classic first-ice patterns.

Once on the ice, they also discover the deeper lake features a slightly stained water clarity, whereas the shallow lake across the road is clear. Thus, the bright sunlight likely won't have as severe of an effect on panfish in the deeper lake. Also noting that although the weather has been cold and bright, it has also been stable for three days, they conclude panfish might move into these shallow bays during twilight periods, simply because there's a lot of food and cover there. Besides, after three days of likely being semi-dormant, these panfish are probably hungry.

So they head back to shore and review a lake map and local conditions over a long lunch, follow this with a visit to a local sporting goods store, then head to the deep lake at 3 p.m.—and catch more panfish in two hours than our other shallow-lake-angling colleagues did all day.

Bottom line? Good ice anglers, regardless of where they fish, continually evaluate and ask questions. What is the lake type? Where are active panfish likely to be found given the time of winter and day, and when are they most likely to be active? Once a fish is caught, they'll ask why the fish are there. Is it structure, cover, food, oxygen, or a combination of the above? And if panfish are attracted to a specific structure, why that structure and not another one? Were these fish holding within weeds on the deep, shaded side, or the shallow sunny one?

Determine why, and you too, will learn to pattern winter panfish.

## "Thinking Like a Panfish"

I always crack a smile when people talk about panfish being smart, or thinking.

Let's be realistic. A panfish is a panfish, not a rationalizing human being. They have small brains, and respond by instinct. Panfish cannot think, rationalize, review situations or determine the outcome of their actions. Yes, they most certainly can be conditioned to respond or not respond to various stimuli—I've seen hatchery-raised fish follow a man on shore carrying a pail of fish pellets. I've also seen schools of panfish holding beneath the ice bite on purple plastic strips, and after catching several, witnessed the remainder become skeptical. But when I would switch to pink, they would strike again before slowing down and stopping—until I switched to chartreuse, when they'd resume biting. If these panfish were smart, such strategies wouldn't result in success. The fish were not rationalizing, they were only becoming conditioned to specific stimuli.

Consequently, because panfish can't think, if we can determine panfish responses and reactions to certain sets of conditions, we have the upper hand, because we have the ability to rationalize and conclude that these panfish will likely continue such trends under similar sets of conditions. Maybe we can't always fully explain why, but we can predict how panfish might behave based on repeat observation.

Consider a late ice movement toward spawning grounds, a relatively easy pattern to decipher. Based on lengthening days, these fish instinctively move toward shallow spawning grounds sometime between mid-winter and late-ice. If we can identify the spawning grounds and areas where mid-winter panfish hold prior to making their spawning movements—usually the deepest available water adjoining shallow spawning grounds—and what path they use to move between the two areas, we can increase our odds of locating them repeatedly under the same annual conditions. Similarly, predictable but lesser daily movements may also occur throughout the winter. Figure them out, and you won't be left in the cold.

First, we can rationalize panfish will move into specific areas at specific times, spending transition time between them in dormant, semi-active and active feeding states. So in this instance, if we can locate the specific patterns panfish use between the mid-winter depths and the spawning grounds, then identify what conditions stimulate movement, how fast panfish move along them, how

# Evaluating Lake Type

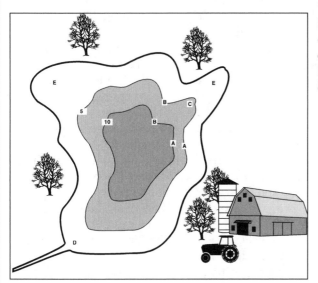

Left: In a small farm pond, structure is minimal. Depending on the pond, features such as drop-offs (A), turns in bottom contours (B), slots of deeper water extending shallow (C), inlets and outlets (D) and shallow bays (E) are often the only distinct features panfish can relate to.

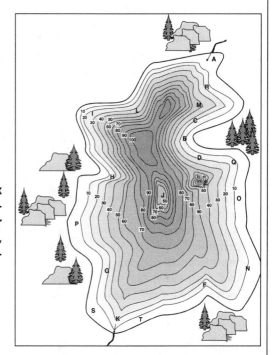

Right: Larger, deeper natural lakes often feature more complex and diverse forms and varieties of habitat, structure and cover, including inlets (A), points (B,F,G,H,L), turns (C,D) sunken islands or reefs (E,J), slots of deeper water into the shallows (I,M), outlets (K), shallow flats (N,O,P,Q,R,S,T,). With more complex structure availability comes more complex winter patterns.

Left: In a small, shallow natural lake, you'll find more distinct fish attracting structures, such as shallow bays (A), points (B), sunken islands (C), deep holes (D), drop offs (E) and bars or shoals (F). Also try to find the most convenient access points (G) closest to your intended destination.

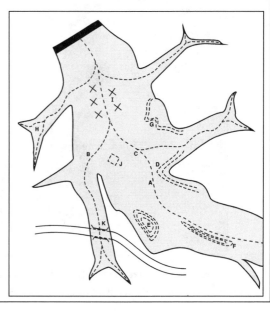

Right: Like natural lakes, reservoirs (in some areas, they're called "flowages") come in a variety of sizes, shapes and depths. They also offer structure that is unique to reservoirs, including: The main river channel (A), secondary river channels (B), intersections of river channels (C), points (D), sunken islands, reefs and rises (E), shoals lining the old riverbed (F), bars (G), shallow coves (H), flooded wood and stumps (I), old building foundations (J) and submerged roadbeds and bridges (K).

far they will go, and where, when and how long they will remain in active feeding states, we are more likely to pinpoint active panfish and increase our winter catches. We should also make an attempt to identify the specific sets of conditions stimulating each movement and feeding activity, by carefully evaluating potential hotspots.

This is best accomplished by applying the "deadly dozen" formula to the situation.

## Evaluating a Hot Spot

Begin by evaluating factor number one, determining the lake type best matching your target species preference. Is it a pond, shallow natural lake, deep natural lake or reservoir? Once identified, examine the lake's physical qualities such as maximum depth, water clarity and bottom content breakdown. Are the conditions favorable to good fishing for the time you plan to fish? Then move on down the "deadly dozen" line by contacting a local fisheries office to confirm the population cycle is high or on the rise.

Next, begin reviewing what types of habitat, structure and cover are available. Lake bottom configuration and irregularities, whether simple features such as drop-offs; classic structures such as points, bars, reefs, rock piles, channels and shoals; secondary structure and microstructure, cover such as weeds, wood, rocks, docks, fish cribs or current; or more complex, less visible attributes such as temperature stratification, springs or oxygen gradients—each demands consideration.

And remember, not all structure is created equal. Any location where two or more of these factors meet or overlap are the highest-percentage locations. For example, find a rocky or gravel drop-off reaching from a deep, muck-bottom hole likely to hold mid-winter panfish butting up against a sand bottom, weedy secondary point extending along a vegetated, sandy main lake point leading to a shallow spawning flat or bay and you're on the right track.

Also ask your local biologist to note primary forage bases and where they're likely to be found. Panfish might relate to specific spots and depths along that point, simply because that's where the forage is congregated. Of course, this may vary with lake type, how far winter has progressed, time of day, inter- and intraspecies competition and the weather, but given the specific set of conditions, make an effort to predict where your target panfish might set-up home areas, and where and when possible movements to and from them might occur.

Once again, this can be a challenge of huge proportions, so let's start at the beginning and break things into the simplest possible terms. Start by checking with local biologists, guides and anglers to identify target lake types in your area featuring a population of fish of the species and size your want to catch. Now knowing the fish are present and must be shallow, deep, or somewhere in-between, locate a productive structure, such as a long, shoreline point connecting a shallow flat to deep water. Along that point, we must determine, specifically, which secondary structures and cover types the fish are likely using as home bases within these depth ranges, based on how far winter has progressed, the time of day and the conditions. We must also determine if any type of movement or migration between

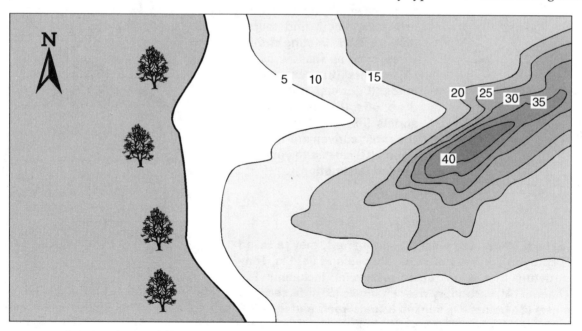

**When searching for the best structures, focus on structures leading from shallow to deep water, because deep water offers more environmental stability for winter panfish.**

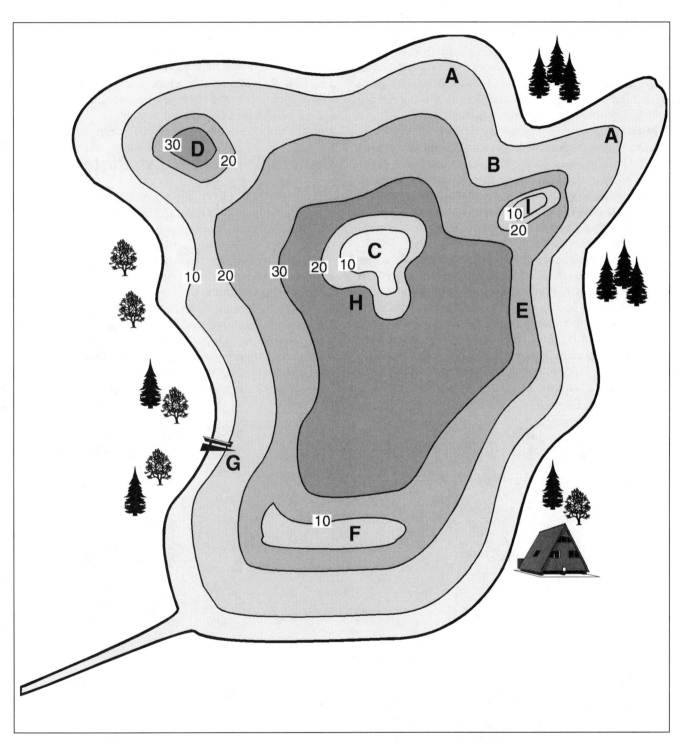

Knowing fish-attracting structures exist, we should try to determine which ones our target species is most likely to be using during the time we're fishing. Bays (A) might be great shallow water spawning areas early or late ice, but hold few panfish mid-winter. Deeper structures such as points (B), sunken islands (C), deep holes (D), bars and shoals (F) and rock piles (I) might be more productive during mid-winter, depending on the species being sought.

these various depths is taking place, and when.

For the sake of definition, let's call shallow water anything less than 6 feet deep, and deep water as any depth over 10 feet. During most winters, panfish prefer deep water, simply because they're cold-blooded and heavily influenced by environmental conditions. Thus, deep water is used most often, because it's most physically and chemically stable, and most protected from environmental changes. I've also found the bigger the panfish, the more important deep water is.

In fact, if your target is trophy panfish, they'll likely be found in the deepest available water in the home area you'll be fishing, most of the time. So if our point exists within the right home area and extends from a shallow, 4-foot-deep flat toward a hole more than 10 feet deep that is also the deepest hole in the area, not only is there a good chance that panfish will relate to it, but larger panfish might be present as well.

With your target panfish species potential deep water mid-winter holding area and spring spawning locations established, begin considering movements. Start with basic movements within and between shallow and deep water and where they might occur. Then, secondarily, consider how local conditions might affect them. If the days are getting longer but you're fishing well before ice-out, start by fishing deeper water. If the ice is beginning to darken and the spawn isn't far away, try shallower.

Don't forget the influence of weather. If a cold front passes and brings bright, high skies, panfish will generally move back toward deeper water, whereas mild, hazy conditions might draw them in. Such knowledge combined with a mobile, open-minded approach, should give you an opportunity to locate active panfish.

Again, we will look more at specific panfish species and how they relate to structure given various conditions in future chapters. For now, let's review some general winter patterns, based on how far winter has progressed and some basic influencing variables, beginning with first-ice.

## General Winter Panfish Patterns

During late fall, most panfish move into deeper, more stable water. As the ice forms—the so called "first-ice" period, there are typically short, scattered movements from deep water autumn holding areas toward cover and food-laden shallows. Given a combination of suitable shallow water structure, cover, food, minimal fishing pressure and cooperative weather, these panfish are likely to remain in the shallows as a home area— longer with extended periods offering the above conditions, shorter with less. As the season progresses, cover and forage often become diminished, and fishing pressure takes its toll. Yes, panfish may make occasional movements back and forth from deep to shallow water

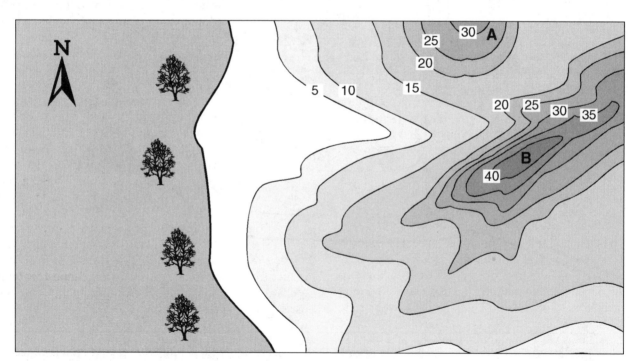

**When evaluating a potential winter panfish holding structure, look not only for features leading from shallow to deep water, but also the deepest water in the area. The edge closest to the deepest water will usually draw the most fish. Here, the side of the structure adjoining area B would have the greatest potential, especially for larger panfish.**

**Always search for paths panfish might follow from deep to shallow water, then spend time drilling holes along that path attempting to intercept the fish. Also note the water and weather conditions when you finally locate an active school. You might be able to establish a pattern.**

throughout the winter, but as a whole, mostly small and scattered panfish remain shallow.

During mid-winter, larger concentrations of panfish tend to relate to deep water flats, drop-offs and mid-lake structures, starting with such features adjoining productive first-ice areas, and as the season progresses, gradually moving deeper. However, movements between the two areas may occur. Panfish holding in a deep hole adjoining a long point, reef or bar leading to shallow water offering cover and food will, given the proper conditions, make movements along the edges and breaklines, onto the top of these structures—perhaps even move up and scatter into the adjacent shallows. The degree and duration of these movements will vary with the conditions.

For example, if fresh, green, oxygen-producing weeds persist in the shallows throughout mid-winter offering

cover for plankton to live and grow, baitfish will move in. Should a path be available for panfish to follow from deeper mid-winter haunts to these shallows—and weather, light intensity and other factors are suitable—this combination of cover and food is likely to periodically attract panfish back into the shallows throughout the winter. If one variable is missing—say the weather brings a cold front and bright sunny skies—panfish may still become active, but simply not move all the way into the shallows. Instead, they may—depending on the severity of the cold front and degree of brightness—make only a slight movement toward the shallows, stopping on a combination of structure and cover along their migration route, or under very severe conditions, become active directly within their deep-water haunts.

By late-ice, most panfish begin feeling an instinctive drive to move toward shallow spawning areas and again use shallow-water areas more regularly, but drop into adjacent deeper water if conditions dictate. Again, the distance and degree of these movements vary with the conditions. As spawning time approaches, not only will a movement toward these shallows occur, but likely there will be an all-out migration of actively feeding deep-water schools into the shallows—causing the traditional, classic "late ice bite."

## High-Percentage Locations

These movements are based on instinct, so if we can rationalize and identify where and when such movements and migrations will occur, we increase our odds of locating and patterning active winter panfish. Yes, the process can be complicated, but for now, let's stick with basic facts.

To increase consistency, we must fish high-percentage areas offering the greatest combination of features, or locations likely to attract the largest numbers of concentrated, active panfish under the broadest variety of conditions due to their versatile array of location options.

Applying the deadly dozen variables, we know high-percentage areas are locations offering the best combinations of structure, secondary structure, bottom content, varied cover types, food and oxygen for the weather and water conditions, and depth adequate to protect these schools from dramatic changes in environmental conditions—which we also know are structures usually close to the deepest available water in the area. Just keep in mind this may not necessarily be the deepest water in the lake you're fishing, but the deepest water available near the high-percentage area.

Say your lake features a maximum depth of 50 feet. While possible, it's unlikely panfish will be stacked on the bottom in 50 feet of water, even given the most severe conditions. It's more likely panfish will be positioned in or near the deepest water available in the area. In a structurally diverse lake, this might consist of an elongated shoreline point or bar extending from a shallow feeding

**To increase your consistency, you must fish "high percentage" areas, or locations likely to attract the largest numbers of concentrated, active panfish under the given conditions.**

flat into 35 or 40 feet of water. In a smaller lake, it might be a bay mostly 4-6 feet deep, sporting a hole running 10-12 feet deep within it. In either instance, be sure to check these areas out—you're likely to find panfish holding and moving in or around these deeper pockets and holes.

## Migration Routes

The next trick is determining where and when these fish move between shallower and deeper water—and determining if these are simply temporary movements, or seasonal migrations. Specifically, what paths are the panfish using to get back and forth, when do they move, and are the movements daily or seasonal?

While panfish can't think, they seldom move haphazardly, either. By instinct, they follow the safety of migration routes leading from deep water into the shallows, and often, the same paths back into the deepest water. Depending on the environment, these routes may be along the edge of a weedline, edge of a depth break or structure such as a point, reef, hump, underwater river channel or edge of a bottom content change. But whatever it is, the path will usually run between the deepest water in the area toward productive shallows, and will consist of a distinct edge differentiating it from the surroundings.

Once a path is located, the next challenge is to determine when, how frequently and how far the fish move. Start with when and how frequently. If panfish are moving through daily or holding in a certain location during early morning, are they also coming through again in late evening, or are the movements occurring under the cover of darkness? Are the fish making partial or secondary movements during late morning and early afternoon and stronger runs early morning and late afternoon? If so, specifically when and how often do activity levels peak? Are these patterns occurring only during a certain portion of the winter or all season long?

Also note how far these movements occur. If the migration route leads between a 3-foot-deep shallow flat and a 40-foot hole, and is 200 feet long, are the fish moving all the way into the shallows and dispersing—the strongest runs—or are the movements you've noted on a smaller scale where panfish are only moving to the edge of the shallow flat before returning, or only coming part way up? Are these regular daily movements at certain times of the year, and how does the degree of movement vary given specific conditions?

I've often noted under mild conditions and overcast skies panfish move onto shallow vegetated flats and feed heavily, but during mid-winter or brighter, more unstable daily weather conditions, panfish move up the migration route, but a shorter distance. And given a severe cold front, panfish may simply move down the route into deep water, then hold there, and while not moving far, become active within the deep water during the same times that under better conditions they were typically moving shallow to feed. As a knowledgeable winter panfish angler, it's up to you to discover such patterns on your target waters.

Why is this important? Most of the time, panfish are not aggressive, but rather, only become active during certain times—and this primary activity is often centered around specific areas, depending on the conditions. These activity periods usually occur on shallow feeding flats, but might happen on what I call "holding areas" along migration routes. This might consist of a secondary point, a patch of dense weeds along an otherwise sparse weedline, a series of stumps along a submerged river channel, fish cribs placed along a rocky breakline or a rock pile—basically, anything different providing cover and likely to attract forage may constitute a holding area.

Also bear in mind that although migration routes can be huge and holding areas can be a challenge to find, migration routes can also be small. On a large, deep natural lake, elongated points, bars and reefs several hundred feet long may act as migration routes, and secondary structure such as a finger might constitute a holding area. On a large reservoir, the route might be the junction between a main and a secondary river channel several miles long, with submerged roads and flooded bridges, building foundations or stumpfields constituting holding areas.

On a small, shallow lake, however, the weedy fringe of an eight-foot-deep pocket the size of a car in the midst of an otherwise three-foot-deep vegetated flat might constitute a migration route, and a larger, or more dense clump of weeds, change in vegetation type, subtle depth or bottom content change might constitute a primary holding area. Still, primary fish activity will likely be focused around specific holding areas on the edges of these routes, and it's up to you to find them.

## Identifying Fish-Holding Locations

Many anglers will ask how to identify these spots, and the answer is to simply search them out. Recently, two anglers explained that they were fishing crappies on a local lake, had found a beautiful point leading from an expansive shallow flat to a deep water pocket and were marking suspended crappies there, but had no success consistently catching fish there. This sounded like an interesting place to evaluate, so after confirming with local biologists the lake supported a population of crappies of the size we wanted to catch and identifying primary forage bases, I went to their lake and immediately

began evaluating the area, based on the immediate weather and water conditions.

First, was the nearby deep water the deepest water in the area? Was there any secondary structure or microstructure available? Cover? Secondary cover combinations holding the desired forage? What was the water clarity, bottom content? Was there any potential migration route from deep to shallow water? Where? And what about potential holding areas and their locations?

Further investigation found that yes, the deep water nearby was the deepest available in the area. I also identified a small, hook-shaped, mud-bottom, vegetated finger extending out about half way between the deep water and the shallow flat—a holding area supporting good quantities of plankton and baitfish. Repeated fishing has shown this to be an excellent crappie spot late morning and early afternoon during periods of stable, overcast weather when crappies are moving from the deep hole toward the shallow flat.

So why weren't my friends catching fish? Quite simply, I confirmed crappies use this migration route, as my friends had noted, but were only moving on it during periods of stable weather, and feeding mostly on the secondary finger—otherwise they quickly moved through and didn't focus on feeding. By simply fishing along the point, these anglers periodically were able to tempt fish to strike—but without fishing the secondary finger during the right times, were unable to do so consistently. Concentrating our

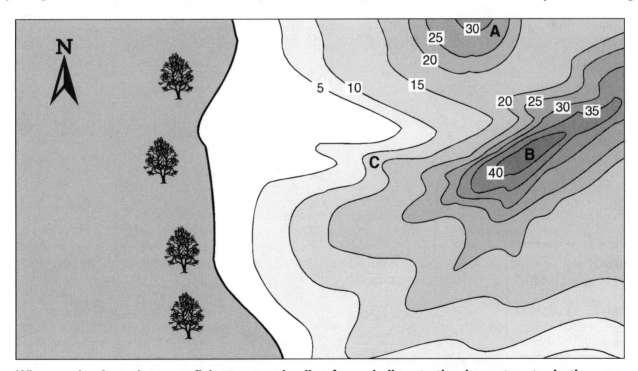

**When evaluating winter panfish structure leading from shallow to the deepest water in the area, look for secondary features such as turns, points or fingers. Here, the secondary point and turn (C) would constitute the best "combination" feature likely to draw the most and largest winter panfish.**

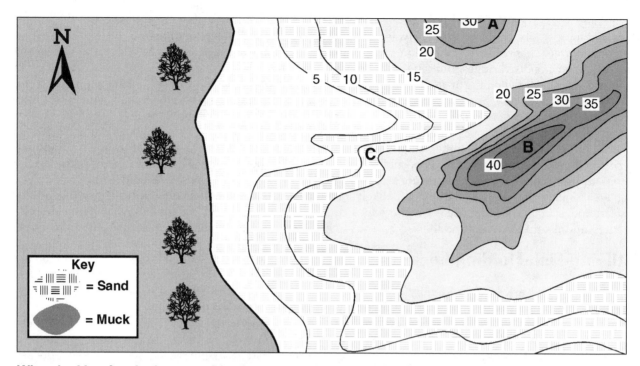

When looking for the best combination structures, look for details, starting with bottom content. Here, the secondary structure off a high-percentage structure leading from the shallows to the deepest water in the area *and* sporting a distinct bottom content change would increase the area's potential as a winter panfish holding location.

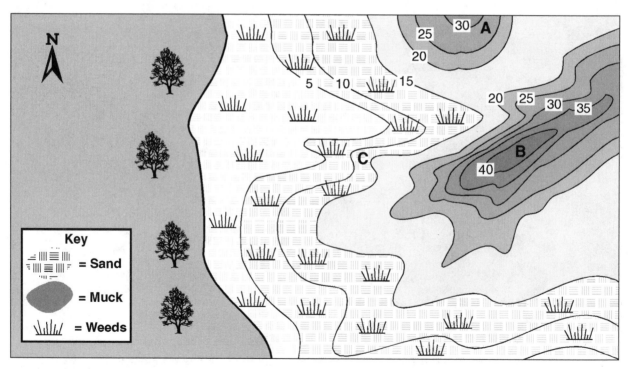

Add cover such as vegetation, and you increase an area's "combination" features, again increasing the structure's potential to attract and hold winter panfish.

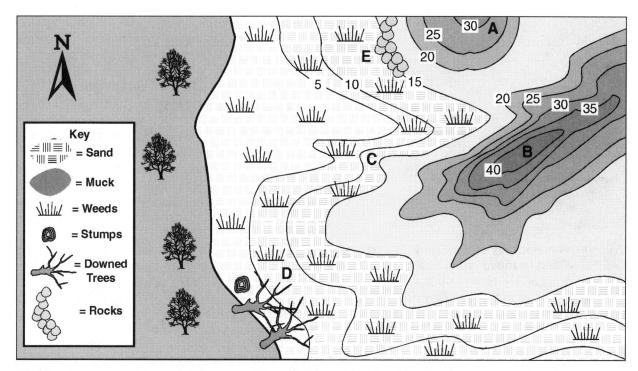

High percentage structural features with a variety of cover types such as vegetation, submerged wood and rocks further increase an area's potential. The edges of two differing types of cover—for example, where wood meets vegetation (D) or rock meets vegetation (E)—are especially productive.

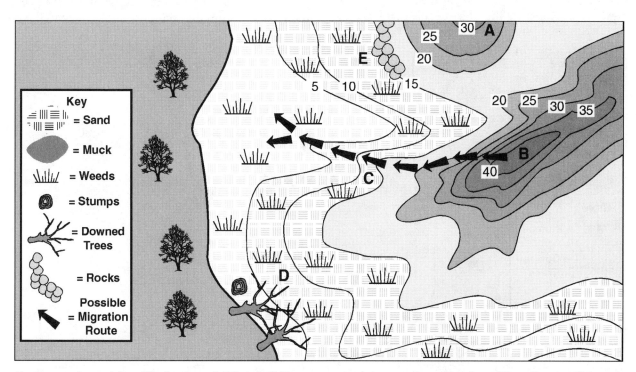

Once you have identified potential fish holding structure, your next effort is to identify possible migration routes between deep water and the shallows. Winter panfish likely will follow a path along a combination of structural edges, depth contours, bottom content changes and cover leading from deep water toward the shallows.

**Panfish can't think, but they seldom move haphazardly, either. Be willing to move often, searching for the paths they're most likely to be using as they move from the deepest water in the area toward productive shallow-water areas.**

efforts in this holding area during periods of movement, however, we've been able to do well, repeatedly.

We also found that under periods of stable weather, these crappies would move onto the shallow flat and disperse, feeding heavily, and that during severe cold fronts and high, bright skies, they would typically hold along the weedline lining the deep hole, or suspend over the deep water. Simply fishing the edges of this point as they

had been—without targeting the secondary point holding area, or, depending on the conditions, fishing the flat, weedline or deep hole— resulted in poor catches.

## Deciphering Daily Patterns of Fish Movement

Consider another example. Two anglers head to a local lake before daybreak, drill holes above some shallow green weeds, and are fishing just as the sun cracks over the horizon. For two hours, they catch bluegills with consistency, then the action stops. They continue fishing hard all day, but get no consistent action again until late in the afternoon. Why?

The fish simply could be sitting there all day and becoming active only early and late in the day—but unless we're fishing a shallow, weedy river backwater, pond or lake, this is unlikely. More likely, these bluegills had moved into the shallow weeds early and late in the day, implying they might be moving into deeper water during midday. These anglers should have located the deepest available nearby water and the migration route between the shallows and the depths. They probably would find themselves catching bluegills during mid-morning and mid-afternoon on holding areas along the migration route, perhaps would have caught fish from deeper water during midday, and still could have taken good catches from the shallows early or late in the day.

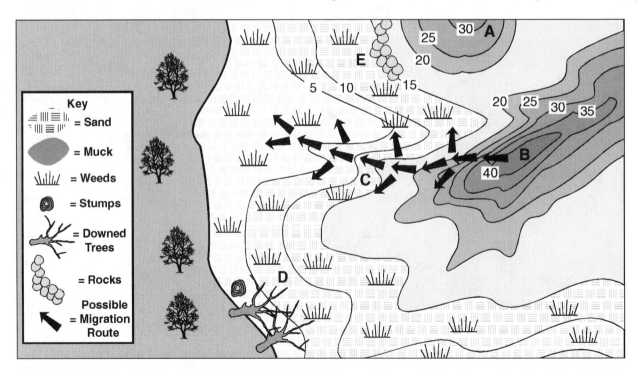

**Once you've identified a potential migration route, your next goal is to determine how far the fish will move along the route given the time and conditions you're fishing. Over time, you will be able to note distinct patterns and the conditions causing movements.**

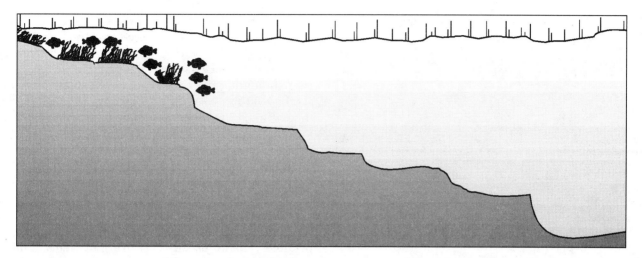

**Winter panfish movements along a migration route vary with the conditions. Provided suitable cover, forage and oxygen are available, and given a cloudy, overcast day during a warm front, winter panfish may move along a migration route into shallow feeding flats and disperse. This would be an example of "ideal" conditions, a time when most ice anglers experience good catches.**

Again, these daily movements might not only vary in timing, but seldom will be the same distance or length. The same two anglers might return the next day after the approach of a cold front and fish the shallows, catching nothing, simply because the bluegills didn't move into the shallows. However, by identifying the migration route, they could follow it down toward deeper water until they encountered fish, and more importantly, active fish—something that would vary with weather and water conditions—conditions these anglers would have to identify and evaluate.

Under ideal conditions featuring cooperative weather and light penetration, good structure, cover and food availability, these fish might move far into the shallows, spread out for long distances and remain there for lengthy periods of time. During such conditions, many ice anglers will do well. Under good conditions not offering this ideal situation, these fish might simply move toward mid-depth areas, hold tighter to the migration route and stick close to the safe cover offered by holding areas of dense cover. Here, only anglers fishing close to this cover along the migration route would catch fish consistently. And given poor conditions, the fish may not move at all, but simply hold deep and require an entirely different approach.

Recognizing that such movements are occurring and then trying to decipher just where, when and how the fish are responding will unquestionably lead to more consistent winter panfish catches. You—unlike the crowds—are aware that fish are responding to the given conditions, and are trying to determine exactly how and why.

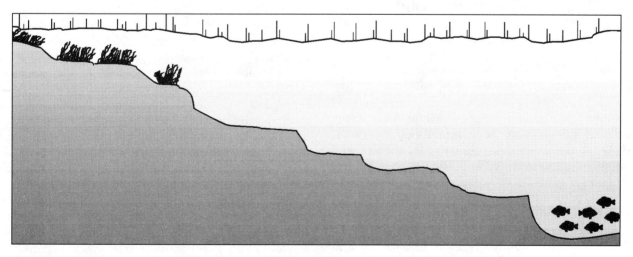

**Given a bright, sunny day following a cold front, most winter panfish are likely to move into the deepest available water at the base of the migration route. Some small fish may linger in the shallows, but the highest percentage fishing will probably occur deep.**

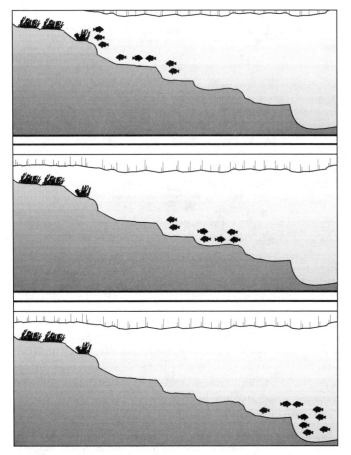

Panfish movements along a migration route vary with the conditions. Most of the time, winter panfish will hold somewhere between the two extremes portrayed in the previous figures. If light penetration is reduced and sufficient cover, food and oxygen are available in the shallows, panfish may hold just outside shallow flats (Top). Given lesser conditions, they'll hold slightly deeper (Middle). A day or two after a severe cold front, they may make a slight movement toward the shallows (Bottom).

Remember, panfish adapt to their environment based on lake type, habitat, structure, cover, depth, forage, oxygen availability and light penetration, and these adaptations are often made through slight adjustments in location and position along established migration routes. Some panfish species adjust faster than others, and some are more sensitive to particular changes and therefore react more strongly. It's up to you to find out which ones, why and how on your target water.

As pointed out earlier, the greatest conditional changes take place in the shallows, where most ice anglers like to fish. But where folks like to fish and where they'll actually catch them are usually two different things. Temperature, light and oxygen concentrations can vary dramatically throughout the day in the shallows. Small fish hiding in the shallows—unless the changes are extreme or severe—may not be bothered much by such variations. But larger panfish are—and because the least changes take place in deeper water, panfish holding deeper are not only usually larger, but also spending less time adjusting to such factors, thereby allowing them more time to focus on feeding—meaning potentially greater "catching" for us.

## Temperature Less Important Than Other Variables

Notice through this entire discussion I haven't given much regard to water temperature. This is because temperature variance usually isn't that great beneath the ice. Secondly, panfish are cold-blooded. So, other than the fact their metabolism is slowed, the cold water doesn't affect them adversely. However, as we've already established, shallow water does demonstrate dramatic swings in light penetration, oxygen availability and activity on the ice—all things that affect panfish location, movement and positioning, whereas deeper water is more stable and less susceptible to such variables. Consequently, panfish are often more "comfortable" in deeper water. While movements and feeding activity in deep water panfish may be limited—namely because they move there under adverse conditions—we also know these fish still must feed, and if we can determine when, they can be caught.

Given severe conditions, deep water panfish may not move at all. But, I have found that although they won't move, they will become active at the same time they would otherwise move given better conditions, and are catchable, even in deep water. Otherwise, feeding activity in these deep water panfish may be accompanied by a slight movement toward, or into, more productive shallower water, depending on the conditions.

Again, panfish don't think, and they don't move shallow because they think food will be there. They simply instinctively move when they get hungry and adequate food isn't available where they're holding. As they move, they follow established migration routes, and when they encounter food within a depth range offering "comfort"—comfort levels depending on the conditions—they stop to feed.

Thus, by evaluating the conditions when feeding occurs, we can determine how far they move and how long panfish will remain active in particular areas given the noted conditions, thereby patterning them.

So we come back to what we've already discussed: Always locate the deepest water available in the area and identify possible migration routes from the depths to the shallows, then evaluate and learn through experience the conditions and locations causing the strongest and longest migrations of active fish for the time you're fishing. By

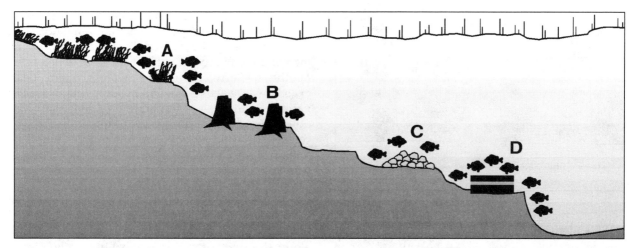

**Most migration routes offer distinct features to which panfish relate. This may be vegetation (A), submerged wood or stumps (B), rocks (C), fish cribs (D), or some other more subtle feature such as a depth contour, bottom content change, or transition in oxygen concentration. Such locations are "holding areas" for migrating fish.**

doing so, you will place numerous pieces of the puzzle together and learn to increase your consistency greatly.

## More on Structure, Migration Routes

Be careful where you begin such searching for productive locations and their associated migration routes. Again, not all structure is created equal. A lot of productive looking structures simply don't extend all the way down from shallow feeding flats to the deepest available water, thereby forming a good migration route. Or, they might extend down, but not offer adequate cover, holding areas or perhaps connect to only a small, steep breaking flat not supporting much cover or food. All the above would likely constitute less-than-ideal conditions. And as we already know, determining primary migration routes can already be tough enough without conducting your research activity on the wrong structure. Be sure your structure extends from the deepest available water to a vast, cover-laden flat offering cover, oxygen and food.

And don't forget to consider the deadly dozen variables and how they come into play. Take lake type, for example. On a river backwater or a small natural lake, the deepest water in the area might consist of little more than a 12-foot hole within an otherwise shallow water bay or flat. In a large, deep lake, it might be a 40-foot hole adjoining a gradually breaking shoreline point. On a river, flowage or reservoir, this might be the deeper river channel adjoining a point extending from a shallow flat. Exactly when, where, and how far along these features panfish movements occur is dictated by the structure, water and weather conditions.

In addition, some structures might be shallow, some deep. Some might have gradual drops, some steep—some with stair step-style breaks, others sudden. Some will be elongated, some round. Some will have hard bottoms, some soft, some a mixture. Some will feature turns, bends, fingers and irregularities along their edges. Some will extend from shallow feeding flats to the deepest available water in the area, some won't. Some will feature cover such as rocks, weeds, or stumps, others don't.

We've already established that the best structures offer the best combination for the conditions you're fishing. But rather than dive into this complicated scenario, simply understand that panfish follow these structures, particularly those featuring cover, and such conditions will determine where, when and how long panfish will relate to various structures and cover.

Structures can be abundant, large and found at a variety of depths. I can't tell you specifically which ones and where to fish, but I can tell you it's important to establish top patterns by strategically moving around to locate the particular structure, secondary structures, cover, migration routes and holding areas panfish are using—and if you continue following this mobile, open-minded approach every time you fish, even as panfish continue moving seasonally and daily, you'll learn to better understand where and when to find active panfish, even during tough conditions.

## Positioning

Once the proper combination of features and active panfish have been located, consider the fish's position on their holding area. Are they holding directly on the bottom

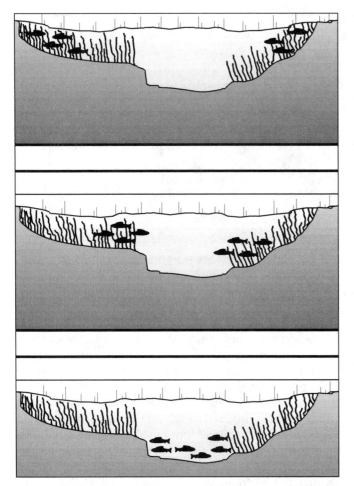

While migration routes are often large, on smaller ponds and lakes migrations and movements may occur on a smaller scale. Under ideal conditions panfish may move shallow (Top). Given a lesser situation, they may hold along weed lines or the fringes of deep holes (Middle). Under severe conditions like a massive cold front, fish may drop into deep pockets and holes (Bottom).

or suspending? If the sun is bright, are they holding on the sunny or shaded side of the feature? If current is present, are they facing it or hiding behind a current breaking feature? This will often vary with the time and conditions you're fishing, but be aware of such different positions and note the fish's responses. Often, you can drill holes in various spots, fish them, then note specifically where your target species is holding—and most active—given the conditions. You'll soon note characteristic movements, times and patterns vary by species, and discover specific areas most likely to attract certain species under specific conditions—even those of predictable sizes.

Frequently, small panfish are most likely to hold higher on the feature, while larger panfish hold slightly deeper. Such positioning might be intensified during

severe weather conditions or intense light penetration. Less significant, more difficult to understand, positioning moves may be caused by predator/prey movements, forage movements or lack of oxygen in the depths, respectively. Just be aware of them. Learning exactly where active fish will position themselves under various conditions is imperative to consistent success, especially when conditions get tough. In fact, the key to consistently finding active panfish under tough conditions not only involves separating good-looking structure from truly productive structure and cover, but carefully evaluating positioning details.

Under good conditions, I like to locate potentially productive areas, identify possible migration routes and holding areas—then look for panfish to be holding along the first, or primary breaklines adjoining deep water. This is where most panfish hold the majority of the time. I especially like cover-laden primary breaklines leading from deep to shallow water in a stair-step fashion as opposed to sudden, steep breaks. And if these stair-step breaklines offer irregular, cover-laden secondary features like smaller turns, slots, fingers and points gradually leading into various depths—holding points—the better the chance they'll hold and attract panfish. Combine this with suitable features, cover and adequate oxygen concentration within the preferred depth range for the time you're fishing and near the deepest available water, and you're likely to find active panfish using them. And don't forget to identify likely holding areas and the fish's position on them.

Just remember, if the conditions are poor, panfish will likely drop to the secondary breakline; if favorable,

How deep panfish hold along a migration route is largely dependent on the available structure, water qualities, and most importantly, weather conditions. Bright, sunny days following a cold front often send them deeper where they're not very active, while hazy, overcast days like the one portrayed here tend to draw them into the shallows where they feed aggressively.

Temperature, light and oxygen concentrations can vary dramatically throughout the day in the shallows. Smaller fish appear not to be bothered much by such changes, but larger fish are. If your catches seem to be running on the small side, it's not a bad idea to try deeper water. (Courtesy Reef Runner Lures)

change current flow, shoreline development and construction of causeways, bridges, fish cribs or other man-made structures may change bottom configuration and depth—all of which may change movements and migrations. Be mobile and versatile. Locate the right locations during periods when weather and water conditions are favorable on the best seasonal structure near the deepest water available at the right time, and you may established patterns that will work for you year after year—just be aware they are subject to change.

This can be further complicated by conditions such as local weather. Of all the deadly dozen variables, weather is the most tricky and most out of our control. It has a major impact on making conditions unstable—thus causing fish movements and changes in activity level.

When a cold front passes, bringing high, bright skies, panfish typically move into cover lining primary migration routes and follow it down to the deepest available water where light penetration is reduced and environmental conditions are more stable. These movements may be modified and less intense in lakes featuring dark water, thick ice, heavy snow cover or a combination thereof. Regardless, changes in panfish movement, positioning and activity will likely take place until the temperature stabilizes and at least some cloud cover returns following passage of the front.

Now take this a step further. The lasting effects of cold fronts may last one to several days, depending on the severity of the front and the number of days required to gain some cloud cover. If a minor cold front quickly passes and mild, overcast days with light snow return, panfish may become active and start moving in a day or two. However, if several major cold fronts move through in rapid succession, keeping the days bright, movement and feeding activity may be minimized several days in a row.

they'll move up the migration route into the shallows. Again, check panfish position on the structure. Are they on a particular holding area at any particular depth? On the left or right side of the structure? Is it shaded or sunny? Are the fish preferring edges featuring hard bottom, soft bottom, or bottom content changes? Are they along the base of the cover near bottom, or suspended along the edge? How high? If you're on a steep break, are there temperature or oxygen breaks the fish may be relating to? Is a current present, and how are they positioned in relation to it? The more details you can discern by answering these questions, the better.

## The Effects of Time and Weather

Keep in mind that while established patterns may be repeated from winter to winter, they can change. Stumps in a flowage or reservoir may rot away, dredging may

Combine a mobile approach of searching for the features, cover and oxygen in the preferred depth range for the time you're fishing near the deepest available water, and you're likely to find active panfish.

It's important to establish top patterns by strategically moving around to locate the particular structure, secondary structure, cover and migration routes panfish are using for the time you're fishing. Bright, sunny conditions like the ones shown here will tend to drive fish deeper. Don't be afraid to drill holes in search of them!

If you're fishing during a cold front and have a choice of lakes, pick a deeper one with some water color. Water conditions will allow a slightly higher degree of fish movement and have less impact on activity levels, despite the cold front. The general guideline following cold fronts is the lighter the conditions, the less movement, less activity and tougher the fishing. The darker it is, the easier.

Obviously, you can surmise panfish will not always be active. Even during ideal conditions, no panfish feeds all the time, and because their metabolism is slowed, it takes time for food to digest, so they don't have to feed often. Still, I've caught perch with a couple of good-sized minnows sticking out of their mouths. Panfish may have already fed, yet you can still make them strike if you fish with the right presentations in the right manner.

This brings us to another facet of catching winter fish, presentation, a topic we'll touch on in the next chapter. For now, understand that if you're able to identify these factors and how panfish react to them in your lake environment given various conditions, then place them together in a workable system, you will learn to locate active winter panfish with more consistency, and with experience, learn to build on these basics and fine-tune solid, strategic location approaches, making you a better winter panfish angler.

### Summary: Piecing the Location Puzzle Together

Let's review the main points:

- Panfish utilize survival instincts to respond to weather and water conditions. They are likely to use structures and associated breaklines offering the best combination of features, cover and forage—especially those featuring smaller breaks or "holding areas" they can relate to and use as rest areas along the way. How far they will travel any given day varies with seasonal and daily conditions.

- When conditions are poor, panfish may not move to even the first major breakline. When favorable, they may move far beyond, into the shallowest areas on or adjoining a structural feature, then hold there for several days. Evaluate the conditions and find the right combination of structure, secondary structure and cover for the time you're fishing. When you catch several panfish in a specific area, ask yourself: Why were the fish there? What led them there? Where did they come from? What spots along the migration route might be likely to hold the school, even if only temporarily? How are they positioned on these features?

- The best combinations of structure and cover are most likely to attract and hold panfish—but these aren't necessarily large and distinct. On smaller, muck bottom "dishpan" lakes, look for dredged boat channels, deep pockets on shallow vegetated flats, "runs" dug by beavers through shallow weeds, changes in bottom content, weedlines—even slight bottom contour changes, which may appear like Mount Everest to a fish.

- Different species may be holding on different types of structure at any given time. Bluegills might be holding on a hump with a tall weedline, while perch are holding along the base of a hard bottom/ soft bottom transition at the base of a deep underwater bar. Don't make the mistake of mixing the patterns of various species. To reduce inter-species competition, panfish usually follow distinctly different patterns.

- Even a single species may be in two or more locations at the same time—even on the same lake! Some bluegills in a deep water basin might be holding deep along a 17-foot weedline, while in an adjacent shallow basin, they might be holding shallow on a weedline bordering a 6-foot hole. To combat such behavior and complications, be mobile and versatile.

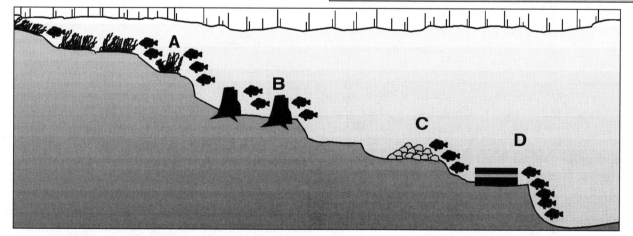

**Once migration routes and holding areas are identified, pinpoint where and how panfish are positioning on them. Here, all the fish are holding on the deep edge of the holding areas, and facing one direction. They could simply be relating to the deep edge—or this might happen to be the shaded side, or the side protecting them from a current flow. Winter panfish might also position themselves at a particular depth or along a particular form of cover such as vegetation (A), submerged wood (B), rocks (C), or fish cribs (D).**

# Chapter 3

# The "Right Combination, Total Approach" Modern Ice Fishing System

*E*ven if you've never ice fished before, you should now have a pretty good grasp of where to locate winter panfish in a variety of lake types. You should also have an understanding of seasonal and daily movements, corresponding migration routes and changes that may occur because of local weather and water conditions. The next step is learning how to find these areas and establish viable patterns.

This is accomplished by combining the variables influencing winter panfish location with another important concept, winter lake stratification—then tying everything together through use of lake maps and electronics. Combine this with a willingness to be mobile and versatile, and you'll understand general winter location and presentation patterns, or what I call the "total approach" to modern ice fishing.

## Winter Lake Stratification

In summer, lakes stratify with the warmest water on top and coldest on bottom, and a layer between that cools quickly—one degree centigrade for every foot of depth.

In fall, shorter days, less direct sunlight and colder air reduce surface temperatures until they become colder than the water below. As it becomes cooler, it becomes heavier and sinks. This process continues until surface water cools to 39.2°F., water's heaviest state. Now the surface layer and middle layer dissolve, and with the help of fall winds, lakes mix to a uniform temperature of 39.2°F.

When surface water cools below 39.2°F, the maximum density and heaviest state of water, it becomes lighter and rests on the 39.2°F water below. When the surface reaches 32°F, it freezes. Frozen water molecules expand by approximately 10 percent, becoming less dense and consequently floating on the liquid water below. With an insulating layer of ice now covering the surface, surface water is 32°F, the water temperature just below the surface is slightly higher, and as you go deeper the water warms gradually until it reaches bottom, where the heaviest water pools at 39.2°F.

Some anglers believe this causes panfish to go deep, toward the warmest water—so they fish within a few inches of bottom, and catch fish—sometimes. Remember, temperature is not a primary factor in winter panfish position. Cover, food and oxygen are more important. Green vegetation, for example, provides cover, security and food for panfish, and through photosynthesis generates oxygen. At times, fishing green vegetation near the bottom can be a key to catching winter panfish.

Consider first ice, when ice and snow cover are relatively thin, sunlight penetration is good and plant life is

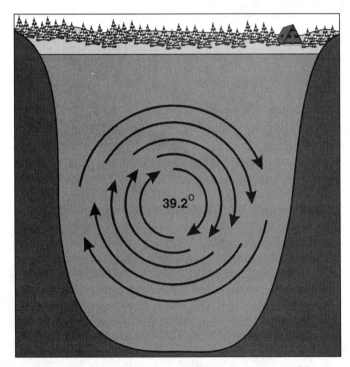

**As air temperatures cool surface water to 39.2°F—the temperature water is heaviest and most dense—surface water sinks, dissolving summer stratification, making the lake a uniform 39.2°F and renewing oxygen concentrations throughout the lake.**

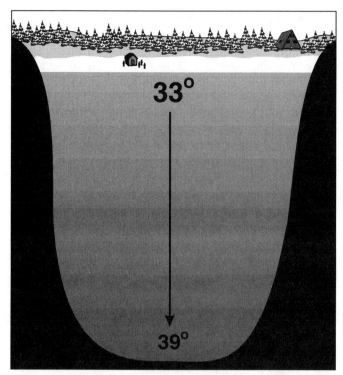

**Following fall turnover and the formation of ice, winter stratification results in the coldest water just beneath the ice (32°F) and the densest, warmest water (39.2°F.) pooled on the bottom.**

fishing on bottom—where the water is warmest but cover, forage and oxygen levels have dwindled—would likely be inappropriate.

At the same time, water just beneath the ice supports oxygen-producing plankton that also act as a food source—but such areas are closer to bright light and usually offer little cover. As winter wears on, foregoing their desire for deeper, warmer water and cover, panfish often abandon the oxygen-reduced shallows and oxygen-deficient depths, and begin relating to any remaining green vegetation on shallow flats or mid-depth main lake structures or they suspend over deep, main lake basins where life-sustaining oxygen and forage are available. You'd think with panfish so concentrated, catches would be easy. But since this oxygen layer rarely provides the preferred combination of cover in which to hide and ambush forage, these fish seldom feed aggressively, and you'll have to present specific techniques to catch them.

Right before ice out, the situation changes again. Cracks and openings develop in the ice, allowing relatively "warm" meltwater to enter. Recall that because ice is approximately 10 percent less dense than water, it floats approximately 10 percent above the actual water level. During mid-season, the weight of water and snow may actually push the pack below this level, and as longer days and warming sun cause melting, the icepack is relieved of this weight and eventually "pops" back up above water level. This causes warmer, oxygenated water to flow through cracks and openings, drawing panfish.

In addition, sunlight penetration increases. This effect is especially prominent near shallow bays, where many panfish species stage to spawn. With added sunlight causing vegetation and plankton to rebound in the shallows and causing warmwater runoff to slip under the ice, panfish eventually move shallow again and become active.

Of course, this is a simplified example of general winter panfish movements. Nature is much more complex. Because winter water temperatures remain essen-

abundant. With the autumn mixing of the water just completed, both shallow and deep water support high dissolved oxygen levels, so panfish often hold near bottom where there is a favorable mix of temperature, cover, food and oxygen.

During mid-winter on many waters, however, ice thickens, snow cover increases and light penetration decreases, reducing weed growth and oxygen production in the shallows. Now sealed by ice, the water is not mixed, and deep water oxygen is often used up. Now,

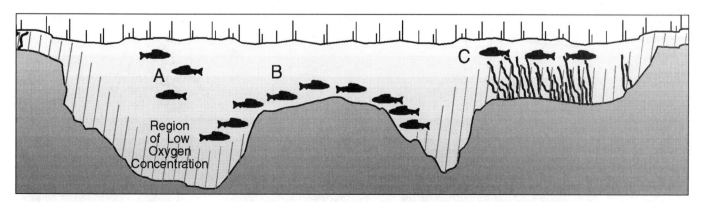

**During mid-winter, high-percentage structures—such as sunken islands (B) or vegetated points (C)—intercepting the zone of highest temperature and oxygen concentration and offering cover and food are most likely to attract and hold the most panfish. If such features aren't available, winter panfish may suspend over deep, open water (A).**

tially equal, temperature doesn't generally have a substantial bearing on where you'll find panfish. But consider this possibility: Could panfish relate to winter's slight temperature breaks as they do more prominent summer stratification? While seemingly far-fetched, panfish may relate to subtle temperature breaks, say, perhaps, from 34 to 35 degrees. It is unlikely, seeing as these breaks aren't very pronounced, but these could affect winter panfish positioning.

Temperature also becomes significant if you pinpoint an inlet or underwater spring—spring water, for example, remains a constant 50-some degrees year-round, considerably warmer than the 33-39°F surroundings. These "spots on the spots" often consist of minute qualities seldom noticed by most ice anglers, but they are critically important to consistently locating active winter panfish. Such areas also offer the possibility of additional cover, oxygen and forage, creating high-percentage winter panfish areas.

Maintain a sharp eye. Search for structure and migration routes, then locate specific microstructures and holding areas offering the best combination of features falling within the strata most likely to support a combination of cover, food and oxygen for your target species during the time you're fishing.

Just keep in mind numerous unique patterns exist. Some panfish may not relate to obvious structure—especially during less-than-ideal conditions. They might hold on subtle, deep water features or suspend over deep, open water, spots many ice anglers pass up, thinking it takes too much time, effort and work to pinpoint these isolated deep water schools.

Mistake.

Deep water panfish may be heavily concentrated, less stressed by environmental conditions and less affected by activity on the ice and fishing pressure. In fact, large concentrations of active, deep water panfish such as yellow perch, white bass and cisco often go untouched—yet are very catchable. This is because they're protected by depth, and likely to remain active barring barometric changes, storms, cold fronts or heavy activity on the ice.

You might feel such fish are difficult to find. Yet thanks to today's accurate lake maps and modern electronics, it's not difficult to find and fish several deep water schools in a relatively short period of time.

## Lake Maps

The process of finding good ice fishing locations begins long before you're on the ice. Again, you must consider the lake type, its depth, structure, water clarity, the weather and the species you're targeting—then review a lake map.

Reviewing lake maps and marking high-percentage locations based on the lake environment, weather and water conditions is crucially important to consistent success. If your map is a good one, it will show depth, structure, bottom content and vegetation types, allowing you to identify potential fish-holding locations before heading onto the ice and enabling you to concentrate valuable time in high-percentage locations.

Assuming you've talked to a biologist or local angler to confirm the lake offers a good population of the species and size you want to catch, this "homework" process should involve the following:

1. Choose an accurate, well-marked lake map, preferably one featuring tight depth contours for better definition, plus recent fisheries survey information, fishing tips and pointers from knowledgeable anglers, and a listing of lake characteristics.
2. Identify the lake type—river backwater, natural lake, flowage, reservoir, Great Lakes bay, etc..
3. Review the outlaid lake characteristics such as maximum and average depth, water clarity, primary bottom contents, cover types, forage and fish species present and their interrelationships.

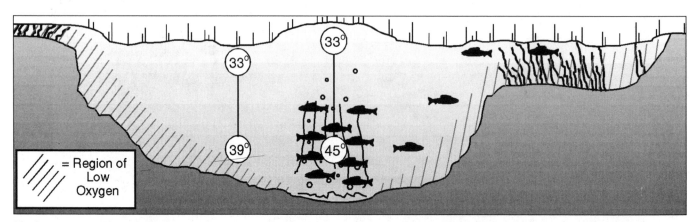

**Underwater springs bring a continual supply of relatively warm water and replenish oxygen, drawing winter panfish. Such areas may also harbor additional fish-attracting cover and forage, creating "high-percentage" locations.**

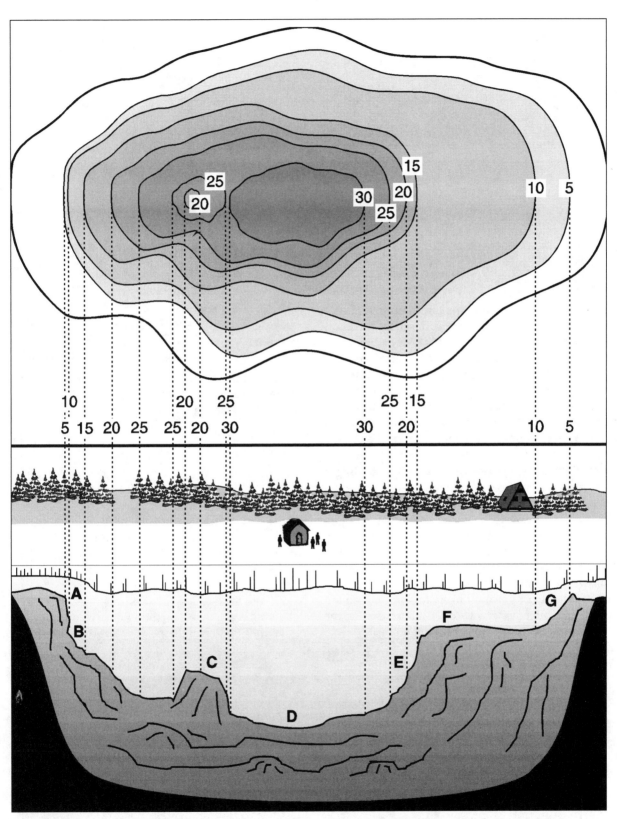

Lake maps are indispensable tools, because they take 3-dimensional lakes and place them on 2-dimensional paper. Areas such as shallow bays (A,F,G), drop-offs (B,E), sunken islands (C) mid-lake flats (D) are transformed into a series of connecting depth contour lines, allowing enterprising anglers to visualize the bottom layout and structure hidden beneath the ice.

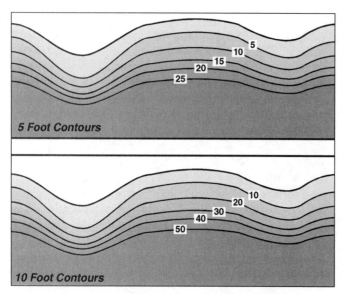

5 Foot Contours

10 Foot Contours

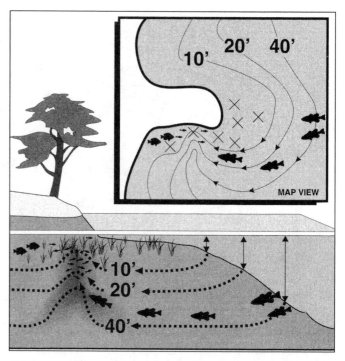

**A lake map illustrating a shoreline bar, its depth and the cover present. Many maps also reveal bottom content. (Courtesy Fishing Hot Spots)**

**Lake maps may feature different depth contours of 1, 2, 5, 10 or 20 feet. On a lake 10 feet deep, 20-foot contour intervals would be useless, 10-foot contours wouldn't show any detail, 5-foot and 2-foot contours would be better, and one foot intervals would be better yet. On a deep lake, however, 1-, 2- or 5-foot intervals would make a complicated map, especially around steep breaks. Yet within reason, the closer the contour intervals appear, the better the map detail.**

4. Locate the highest percentage structures by finding those featuring the desired combination of natural structures, secondary structures, depths, bottom content changes, cover, cover combinations and edges, inlets, outlets and current breaks, plus manmade cover like fish cribs or submerged roadbeds—all within the desired depth strata and adjoining the deepest water in the area.

5. Identify the structures most likely to produce fish for the time of winter and day you're fishing based on the lake type and depth, weather, sunlight intensity, water color, your target species' forage preference and the locations most likely to offer them given the time and conditions.

6. Locate the deepest water in close proximity to these preferred structures, and any adjacent shallow water feeding flats, then identify potential migration routes between these points and potential holding areas and feeding locations along them.

7. Note the day's wind direction—yes, even in winter, wind has an effect on the ice and the water beneath, and panfish will usually be positioned on the windward

**Although some structural features may be visible above the ice, most require the use of lake maps to positively identify their location below.**

**Lake maps reveal structures beneath the ice, along with secondary structures, bottom content, cover and cover combinations, man-made cover including fish cribs—even their GPS coordinates. Productive areas can then be marked, labeled and saved as waypoints for ease in relocating them when you wish to return. (Courtesy Fishing Hot Spots)**

side of most structures.

8. Identify the nearest access points to these locations;
9. Review where you intend to fish and how deep so you can surmise what gear you'll need. If the water is clear and features only light cover, lighter tackle may be necessary. If the water is dark and you'll be fishing heavy cover, heavier rods, lines and lures might be required.
10. On larger waters, enter Global Positioning Systems (GPS) coordinates to your GPS receiver, then use a compass or GPS and scale on your map to determine the direction and distance from your access point to the preferred structure. Perhaps even use the map scale, GPS receiver and anticipated speed of movement to determine the actual amount of time required to move to your anticipated initial location and between secondary ones.

Once you're on the ice, you can use the combination of your lake map and GPS to move efficiently to your target location, and use your sonar—your underwater eyes—to visualize what's below you and mark unmapped locations.

But back to lake maps. For best results, purchase a high quality commercially produced map, review it carefully, and after making some mental notes, meet with knowledge-

able local anglers to glean additional information. If they're willing, have them mark areas they feel have the most potential for the time you're fishing. Combine this information with your own thoughts based on our winter panfish system, and you're almost ready to set out on the ice.

Before finalizing your initial strategies, remember each water body has a different size, maximum depth, variety of structural features, water clarity, bottom configuration, bottom content, prominent vegetation type, cover, nutrient concentration, forage base, and variety of fish species. You might find similar lakes, but you'll never find two that are identical. Carefully consider all the variables and how they might affect winter panfish location on your target lake before interpreting what you see and pre-planning your approach.

The key isn't necessarily to determine where fish will be, but to eliminate water unlikely to hold panfish, helping you pinpoint where they're more likely to be, based on the conditions and time you're fishing.

**While use of a compass and lake map can help accurately locate structure with little investment, this is the hard way of navigating on ice, considering development of GPS, which demands no time-consuming manual calculations to determine direction and distance to a specific location. (Courtesy Lowrance Electronics)**

## GPS on Ice

While using a compass and lake map can help accurately locate prime fishing areas with little investment, this is the hard way of navigating on ice—especially considering the development of Global Positioning Systems (GPS), that demand no time-consuming manual calculations to determine direction and distance to a specific location.

GPS is not only fast, but accurate. Coordinates for targeted locations are simply taken from your map, entered as "waypoints" on portable or hand-held GPS receivers, then recalled at will, allowing you to move directly to the intended location and return to the same coordinates, repeatedly. When you locate potential waypoints, give each a number, record that number on your map, and store this number along with the reference name, prominent structure, cover and forage present along with other notes in a waterproof, tearproof logbook such as the one available from Strikemaster Ice Augers. Anytime you wish to fish that location, simply review your lake map, recall your waypoint, press the "Go To" button, and watch as the receiver provides a "map" on the plotter screen indicating the direction and distance to the requested waypoint. Some units also provide your speed of travel—thus providing your estimated time of arrival.

If you find a new or secondary "hot spot" while on the ice, simply push the "save" button on the unit, which will automatically store your present coordinates in the unit's electronic memory. You can then add information

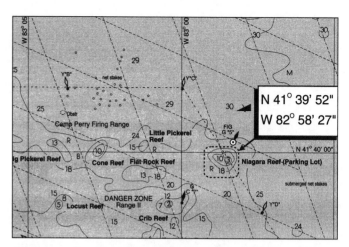

GPS coordinates are invaluable, time-saving tool anytime you're fishing a large or expansive lake and want to locate specific high percentage structures quickly and efficiently. Here, the coordinates for "Niagara Reef" are clearly marked. (Courtesy Fishing Hot Spots)

to your logbook, such as the time you were fishing, the species caught there, and productive presentations used. Exchanging waypoints and such information with other knowledgeable anglers can also be a productive way of communicating specific hot spots.

GPS technology has the capacity to read out to thousandths of a minute in latitude and longitude—a distance of approximately six feet. However, for the protection of our country, the military deliberately scrambles civilian signals through a process called selective availability. GPS satellites therefore broadcast two signals, a commercial Standard Positioning Service (SPS) for civilian use, and a Precise Positioning Service (PPS) exclusively for military access. If this "dithering" process is shut off, GPS has the potential to direct you almost right back to your intended location—but as it stands, getting within three hundred feet of your initial waypoint is considered good. Several companies use a technique called Differential GPS (DGPS) to somewhat compensate for military interference and increase accuracy, but still, this signal is not as accurate as the military's PPS.

Regardless, GPS saves time by efficiently moving you near your pre-planned locations quickly—and this can be important, particularly when searching for panfish on expansive flats, large lakes, flowages, reservoirs or Great Lakes bays. And with today's models offering in-use charge adapters for connecting to an ATV or snowmobile, better receivers with improved sensitivity, better accuracy and faster satellite lock-on, well, you simply can't go wrong.

## Sonar

Once you've found the targeted area using your GPS, you'll want to visualize the structure's layout and pinpoint high-percentage combinations of secondary cover,

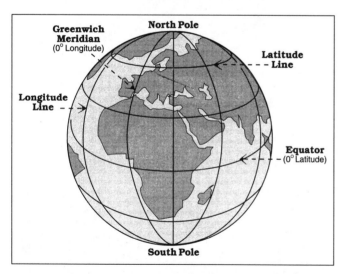

Lines of latitude and longitude encompass the Earth. The precise locations where these lines and their fractions read in "minutes" and "seconds" intersect are called coordinates, which can be saved electronically on Global Positioning Systems, so you can locate them repeatedly with the mere press of a button. (Courtesy Fishing Hot Spots)

By entering the coordinates of your intended destination, GPS receivers guide you to your listed waypoint. Once there, the unit will "zero out" or beep, indicating your arrival. If you find a new or secondary "hot spot" while on the ice, simply push the "save" button on the unit.

Before leaving shore, enter the coordinates or waypoint number for the location you wish to go, then press the "to go" button. The GPS receiver will provide a map on the plotter screen indicating the direction and distance you must travel to the requested waypoint.

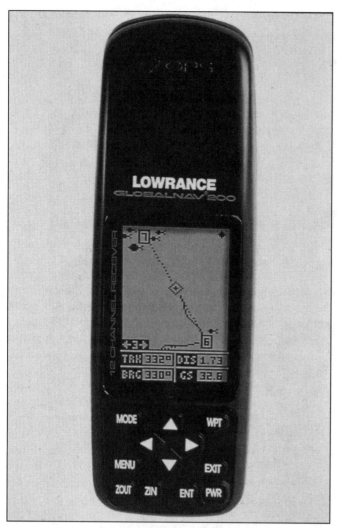

**GPS saves time by efficiently moving you near your pre-planned locations quickly—and this can be important, particularly when searching for panfish on expansive flats, large lakes, flowages, reservoirs or Great Lakes bays. (Courtesy Lowrance Electronics)**

depths, structures, bottom contents, secondary cover, forage or fish—I wouldn't even know specifically what depth my bait is off bottom—and I certainly can't efficiently monitor fish activity levels or responses to my presentation. In other words, sonar—flashers and Liquid Crystal Graphs (LCGs)—is arguably one of the most valuable tools a modern ice angler can use.

## Liquid Crystal Graphs

Let's start with liquid crystal graphs (LCG). Today's LCGs are dramatically improved over the models first offered to fishermen, and function much better than ever before. Thanks to features such as Lowrance's "Clearvision" they're easier to read in bright sun. And, a growing number of vertical pixels combined with today's "zoom" features—magnifying images several times—offer greater resolution, more-detailed pictures and more easily readable images than ever before.

Additional features, such as Lowrance's "Greyscale" also enhance the ability to determine bottom topography and secondary cover, and help separate fish from the bottom. Other options include side-scanning transducers for taking readings to the side as well as straight down, split screen for viewing two different areas at once, zoom screens for zooming in on specific depth sectors, even modules capable of incorporating GPS functions into the unit—all features flashers don't offer.

Split-screen zoom features are especially helpful. Say you're fishing 40 feet of water and you've located a school of perch directly on bottom. With the press of a button or two, you can split the screen into two windows, and have the left side of your screen showing the entire vertical column, and the right side "zoomed" in on the fish. You'll see the overall picture on the left hand side of the screen on the 0-40 foot range scale, so you're

forage and fish. Provided you know how to set your unit and interpret the appropriate signals, sonar enables you to decipher depth, bottom type, cover, forage and fish—even estimate the species, approximate size, the depth they're holding, their activity levels and responses to specific presentations.

Electronics concepts were covered in book one of this *Hooked on Ice Fishing* series, but let's review the basics to make sure we're fully covering winter panfish patterns.

The process begins with choosing the type of sonar you prefer. Most "modernized" ice anglers are now using some form of electronics—or while they may opt not to, at least understand the advantages of using high-tech navigation and sonar devices. I know I'd be lost without them. Without sonar, I can't easily find precise locations,

**Most veteran anglers prefer to use flasher sonar, because they report in "real time" and can be manually fine-tuned to best suit specific sets of winter fishing conditions.**

covered in the event additional fish come through at another depth. By utilizing the zoom feature and splitting the screen into two windows, you can also program the unit to reveal only a specific sector of this column, say the 30-40 foot depth range, on the second window.

Not only does this feature allow you to zoom right down into the area where your lure and the fish are holding, but also focuses the entire, broad-face pixel width into a small area of coverage, providing better resolution and hence, more detailed coverage. Say you're in 30 feet of water using a unit featuring 30 vertical pixels, or one pixel per foot resolution. Zoom in the entire screen from the 15 to 20 foot range, and you'll now have six pixels per foot resolution—significant difference.

## LCG Limitations

There are drawbacks to using LCGs on ice. For example, the fluid operating the crystals can freeze. The situation can be avoided, however, by keeping the unit warm, turning the unit and screen light on and leaving them on to generate heat while fishing, keeping the battery at maximum power, and—something many folks don't realize—purchasing a nitrogen-packed unit or a unit featuring industrial grade fluids. There are actually two types of liquid crystal fluids, consumer grade and industrial grade. Consumer grade doesn't have the freeze-resistant capability of the industrial grade fluid, which while costing more, is tested freeze resistant to -40°F. For ice fishing, try to purchase units packed in nitrogen and using these higher grade industrial fluids.

Another concern for LCG ice fishing applications is their automated settings. Turn them off. These are set by the engineer's interpretation of the "average" situation

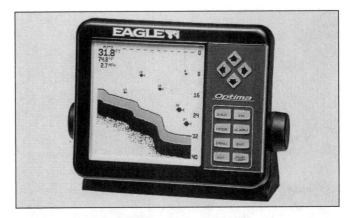

**Special LCG features, such as Lowrance's "Greyscale" enhance the ability to determine bottom topography. (Courtesy Lowrance Electronics)**

the average angler will be fishing—and being an ice angler, you're not an "average" angler. Be sure to use the manual sensitivity, chart speed, gray scale and screen darkness settings so you can customize your picture to the situation. One of the keys to improving response time with an LCG is to increase the scroll speed. This can best be accomplished by turning off these automated features and maximizing the chart speed setting. You can also help achieve an exceptionally fast scroll speed by turning off the digital sonar—the feature that provides the digital depth reading. Simply put, faster scroll speeds adjust the pulse widths of the transducer, improving resolution and making it easier to mark baitfish, plankton and fish and to note fish movements and responses.

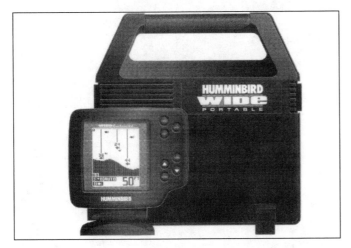

**Sonar acts as your underwater eyes and allows you to better visualize what your map and GPS have revealed. Liquid Crystal Graphs (LCGs) are perhaps the easiest to read for beginning ice anglers new to sonar.**

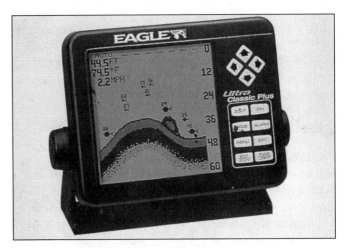

**Today's LCGs feature many improved qualities, including larger screens, easy-to-use keypads, increased numbers of vertical pixels for improved resolution, and thanks to some clever engineering, are more user friendly than ever before. (Courtesy Lowrance Electronics)**

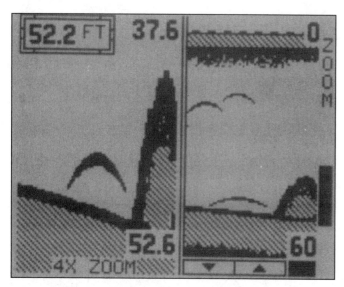

The zoom feature on LCGs, as demonstrated on this Lowrance unit, allow you to magnify images beneath the ice for better visualization. Here, a fish relating to a bottom feature is shown on the 0-60 range on the right side of the screen, and is magnified for better visibility on the 37.6-52.6 range on the left.

As you can see, an important consideration with using LCGs on ice is response time. While some LCG manufacturers claim signal send-out and return are instantaneous, the symbols representing signals are generally slightly behind "real-time," instantaneous flasher responses. Yet technology is getting closer. The experts at Lowrance now offer a "FasTrack" feature, a vertically oriented flasher-style reading alongside the liquid crystal display screen. These readings are almost instantaneous, just like a flasher—meaning this is closer to real time. If you lift your lure, it will move almost instantaneously on this display, similar to a flasher. And by making the adjustments we've just reviewed, you can get closer to the "real time" feature of the traditional flasher.

## Flashers vs. LCGs: A Comparison

When you work a bait below a flasher, you will see the lure's response and movements simultaneously—not with a moment's lapse like you will with a liquid crystal graph. Most liquid crystal graphs feature a slight delay—even the best units set on their fastest chart speed feature a somewhat slower than instantaneous response.

Better results have been attained with "real time" direct-drive liquid crystal circuitry. One of the first such units marketed as an ice fishing LCG was Zercom's Real-Time Sonar RTS. The biggest advantage with this unit is that thanks to direct-drive liquid crystal circuitry—meaning transducer signals are instantly presented on the screen

instead of being delayed as they are with traditional multiplexing pixel circuitry—the entire screen presents an instantaneous flasher-style readout. Set on the 0-15 foot range (creating more available pixels per foot) your lure and fish look immense and are easily tracked.

Why is this so important? Consider fishing panfish in shallow water such as a river backwater. Again, given more available pixels per foot, your definition is outstanding—and readouts are instantaneous.

Some ice anglers will point out that the liquid crystal graph "history" is beneficial. Should you look up just as a fish quickly moves through while using a real-time flasher, the image would be gone. You'd never know it was there. On an LCG, however, there's a slight delay in signal response, so the image remains on the screen briefly even after the target has passed, simply because objects appear elongated on an LCG. The pixel furthest right is almost instantaneous, the further left you go, the older the signal. That's the pixel "history" I'm referring to. In other words, if you look down a split second after the target has passed, you can still see the mark briefly thanks to the elongated target display, providing a second chance to bring your bait to that level and work the fish.

Others will also argue instantaneous responses don't matter much anyway. When jigging active panfish, they'll say that simply knowing you've located fish at a specific depth and precisely where your bait is relative to them is enough to get action. Even with a momentary, delayed signal response, you're still getting this information.

Perhaps. But at times, evaluating specific jig movements and immediate fish response is imperative. Drop a jig down a hole in clear water, and watch how fast a bluegill

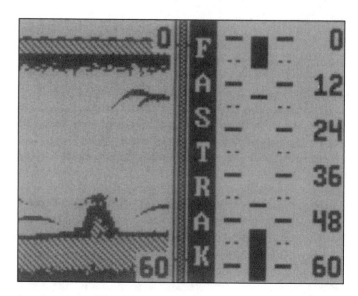

Lowrance's "FasTrack" feature allows you to visualize the bottom using the LCG picture, yet also splits the screen to reveal a flasher-like view on the right.

can inhale and expel a tiny ice jig, and you'll see what I mean. Instant feedback simply lets you make split-second decisions about what you must do to trigger and hook fussy panfish.

This is where the advantage of a flasher comes in. Flashers provide instantaneous readouts—meaning any movement of your lure or fish showing on your screen is happening—at exactly that depth and moment below. Other general flasher advantages include manual sensitivity settings, meaning you can adjust and fine-tune your sonar to the point you can read even a tiny micro jig—even be able to tell if a maggot is stripped off the hook!

Most manufacturers won't set the automatic sensitivity modes on LCGs this precisely, because the average operator wouldn't be able to see fish easily. But when you're fishing panfish with a tiny micro ice lure, it's like trying to sense a stealth bomber on radar. The thin, knife-like edge—especially of a hook or vertical ice jig, is difficult for the pulse of an electronics unit to pick up. But set correctly, a good flasher can and will show these fine tar-

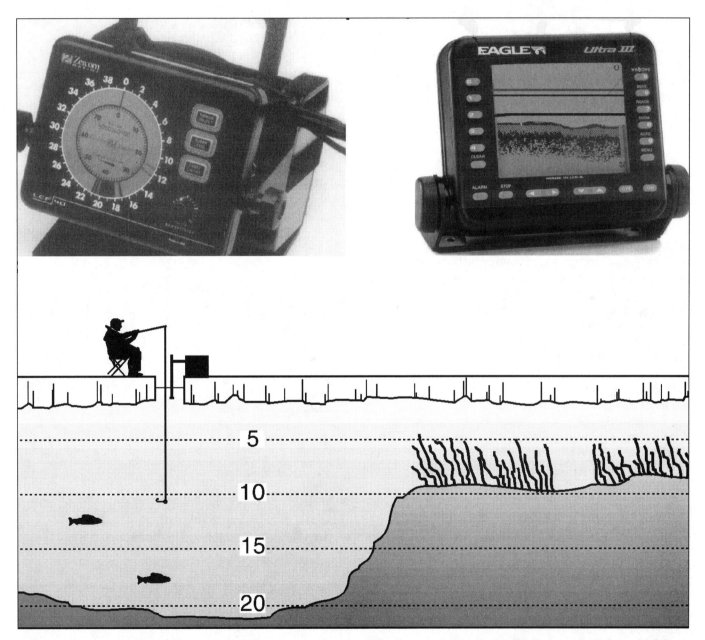

A flasher and an LCG reveal the same information, just in different ways. Here, the flasher on the left and LCG on the right reveal two fish—at 12 and 17 feet—and the angler's lure at 11 feet. Note how targets appear as elongated lines, rather than objects, on the LCG. This is because you're stationary, and the target is being repeatedly marked.

Thanks to direct-drive circuitry, Zercom's Real-time Sonar RTS provides a liquid crystal display with the traditional "flasher only" instantaneous response time. (Courtesy Zercom Marine)

gets. This is why so many ice experts prefer fully adjustable flasher style sonar.

Flashers provide the ability to finely control your resolution. Unless automated control settings are turned off—if this option is available on your Liquid Crystal Graph—automated control settings will spontaneously adjust gain as the computer chip deems necessary. Even in "manual" mode, slight compensations are made beyond user control—making focused readings difficult.

When you set the gain and suppression on a flasher, however, even pulses are maintained—an important characteristic, because automated changes slow transducer pulse, decreasing resolution and making precision readings like measuring fish response time or marking fish close to bottom almost impossible. Once you adjust your gain and suppression on a flasher, however, there are no needless automated changes.

Remember, you're stationary when ice fishing, so depth remains the same. Unless you move to another hole, there's no need for further adjustment, in fact, this is a disadvantage because it virtually eliminates consistent resolution.

Flashers are also more cold weather compatible, thanks to direct-drive circuitry. Instead of receiving pulses from the transducer, sending them through multiplex drivers and a series of liquid-filled pixels like most LCGs, the direct-drive digital signal circuitry of a flasher sends pulses directly to a neon bulb, LED or direct-drive liquid crystal display.

## Flashers

One of my favorite models is Vexilar's color monitor flashers. Units such as the famous FL-8, which really

began the modern era of ice fishing electronics and its successors like the FL-8SLT, feature a neon flasher bulb that pulls sensitivity levels in three colors. Sensitivity is easy to read, because signals in the center of the transducer cone appear in red—indicative of a strong signal—orange, an intermediate signal—and green, a weak signal. This is much akin to watching a meteorologist showing the strength of a storm system, using color as a guide to intensity, with the darker colors indicating stronger intensity. The only difference is that while television stations can use virtually any color of the spectrum to show intensity, the neon LED bulb on the Vexilar series flashers are limited to three colors—but this still creates ease in interpretation, and makes objects easily identifiable.

Units without color readouts indicate signal strength by the width of the signal—thicker being stronger and thinner being weaker. This also shows on Vexilar's color readouts, but the color creates an easier standard to go by, making interpretation of strong, intermediate and weak signals and as you'll soon see, monitor fish activity levels much easier.

Just don't abuse this setting. To many anglers adjust their sensitivity so their lures appear in deep red—which is overkill. What you want is to make your lure appear green or green with an orange fringe. By turning the sensitivity weak on the bait, any slight reduction of the signal shows. In other words, if a fish appears near the bait

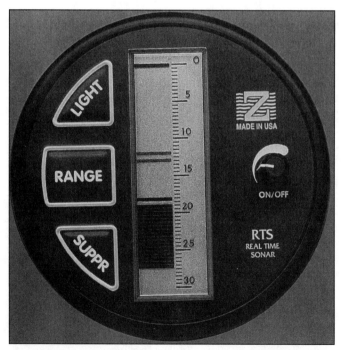

The clean, easy-to-read screen on the Zercom RTS is nice, and works especially well in shallow water on the 0 to 15-foot range because your lure and any fish appear large and are easy to read. (Courtesy Zercom Marine)

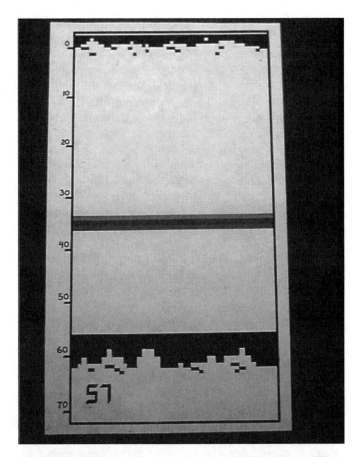

**When ice fishing you remain in a stationary position, so on a liquid crystal graph, objects are repeatedly marked, and therefore appear elongated, as shown here, where my lure is positioned at a depth of 35 feet.**

and steals the waxworm off your hook, the green line will thin or the orange fringe will disappear. This is more difficult to see if you're sensitivity is set too high and the lure and bait appear thick and red.

More importantly, if the unit is properly set a fish will appear green as it enters the cone, will turn orange as it approaches your bait, will be red when right on your bait. This allows you to tell if a fish is approaching or moving away from your bait, and by watching how slow or fast the changes occur, reveal how active they are. To date, Vexilar is the only manufacturer offering this convenient feature in a flasher.

The Vexilar's resolution is also good. The FL-8SLT, for example, features 530 LED segments. If you're on the 20-foot scale each of the 530 segments represents about one-half inch of depth—hence the high level of detail.

Flashers are also available in direct-drive liquid crystal displays. This might seem like a contradiction, using the terms liquid crystal and flasher in the same breath, but note I said direct drive liquid crystal display—not multi-plexing liquid crystal graph. Zercom's Clearwater Classic was the first unit to incorporate such technology.

Zercom claims the Classic, which reads like a flasher but utilizes LCD technology, is so sensitive that a tiny micro ice jig can be seen in 40 feet of water. The Clearwater Classic's was improved upon by its successor, the Clearwater Pro, which features electroluminescent backlighting, battery charge indicator, greyscale for bottom determination and reads well in sunlight.

The Clearwater series also features Time Variable Gain (TVG) that always shows true bottom and displays fish equally at all depth ranges, making secondary cover such as weeds easier to read, and giving you the ability to easily mark and differentiate fish or other objects among them by simply adjusting the sensitivity. In addition, the Clearwater Series offers features like super sharp gray scale display for easy recognition of bottom content, weeds and other structure, fish holding tight to bottom—and with Zercom's backlighting system, readings will show up even in bright sunlight, and marks indicating your lure show up clearly whether you're fishing just beneath the transducer or fishing just off bottom.

Electronically, the Clearwater series features fast cold weather response time, low battery current draw, 1,000 watts of power, and target separation of 2.5 inches for seeing fish, including those holding tight to bottom. This engineering has led to an entirely new category of high definition sonar: high definition liquid crystal flashers.

But the technological advances don't end here. Desiring to build better direct-drive liquid crystal units for ice

**Flashers such as this Zercom Clearwater Classic provide instantaneous readouts, meaning any movement of your lure or fish showing on your screen is happening at exactly that moment at the depth indicated. (Courtesy Zercom Marine)**

**Zercom's Clearwater Classic flasher, the first flasher to offer a direct-drive liquid crystal display (LCD). (Courtesy Zercom Marine)**

fishing, and understanding the basic ice fishing advantages of flashers, Zercom Engineers improved and advanced flasher technologies and incorporated them into the LCF-40 liquid crystal flasher. Like traditional flashers, the LCF-40 operates on real time. When you lower your bait, thanks to the "direct drive" circuitry, you'll see it dropping instantaneously. On many LCGs, multiplex drivers operate 10 or 20 pixels each, one at a time. Zercom's direct drive liquid crystal display (LCD), features one driver per pixel, meaning pulses from the transducer are immediately received by each individual pixel, instead of being sequentially transferred through several. Mathematically, this makes Zercom's response time faster. In fact, the display responds instantly—so you can see precisely how fish react to your motions—instantaneously. In addition, Zercom uses a special military-grade fluid that remains tractable down to -50°F. On many liquid crystal graphs, fluids aren't designed for such extremes, and the combination of multiplex drivers and reduced fluid speeds result in delayed signal response.

Like its Clearwater series predecessors, Zercom's LCF-40 also offers Time Variable Gain (TVG). This patented feature insures targets remain consistent in relative size: Big fish appear bigger than smaller ones, regardless of depth. On standard flashers, larger fish appear as smaller marks in deeper water. The shallower they come, the bigger they look. There's no way of determining relative size...unless multiple fish pass through at precisely the same depth. Resolution is also consistent on Zercom flashers—once set, targets can be picked up close as 2.5 inches from the bottom.

Another Zercom feature is Greyscale, which allows each LCD segment to operate independently. Benefits? When small fish appear, they register light, while larger fish appear dark. With TVG, this remains constant

throughout the entire vertical column, not just the horizontal plane you're fishing, enabling you to differentiate relative target size from just under the ice to bottom. The combination of these two features also allows you to precisely evaluate a fish's response to your presentation. Fish on the outside edge of the cone appear a light, "fuzzy" gray, become solid gray as they approach the middle, then turn dark when they reach center. Nice, because you can tell when fish move into the cone toward your lure, or out, away from the lure—and with TVG, you can monitor both their position and size.

The LCF-40 also offers 1,000 watts of power, making readings in deep water clearer and allowing fabulous target separation. It's not difficult, for example, to discern fish moving through light weed growth on the bottom, or see fish holding tight to the bottom. In fact, instead of having two small perch holding on the bottom look like one larger mark, the LCF-40 will show two distinct marks. This power, combined with TVG, also results in no "surface clutter" along the first few feet of your screen—outstanding when fishing shallow. And with all this power, Zercom units feature low current draw, 50 milliamps compared to a typical 350 milliamps. Obviously, with seven times less current draw, batteries last seven times longer. Zercom engineers claim their units will run 100 hours on a single charge, although daily charging is encouraged to prolong battery life.

Such power can—in any unit mind you—result in such outstanding sensitivity that interference can sometimes become a problem, particularly when multiple anglers are using such electronics in close proximity, and I suspect one of the coming innovations in ice fishing flashers will be better receiving units that can offer maxi-

**Zercom's LCF-40 direct-drive liquid crystal display flasher. The unit features one driver per pixel segment, meaning pulses from the transducer are immediately received, providing an instantaneous readout. (Courtesy Zercom Marine)**

Sonar comes with various cone angles. Narrow cone angles concentrate the most power within a smaller area, making it easier to determine the precise depth fish are holding. Wider cone angles cover more area and thus see more fish, but you won't be able to determine precisely where they're holding.

mum power with minimum interference. We can all eagerly await the new models featuring such advances!

One final note: Flashers offering easily read screens are a big bonus, especially when fishing in bright sunlight or at night. Most flashers and LCGs read well at night because of their neon bulb, LED or lighted liquid crystal screens, although I must admit Zercom's liquid crystal display is among the most highly visible in bright sunlight at virtually any angle and pleasant to use. Electroluminescent backlighting is also available on some units, providing a pleasant, evenly dispersed light across the entire screen for night angling.

Leading manufacturers of electronics products—those that are serious about providing equipment for ice anglers—are developing new technologies and features that will make electronics use more effective and user friendly. Look for many of the models listed here to be improved upon as technologies advance.

The evolution of modern electronics is fully under way.

## Cone Angles

This brings us to cone angles, which determine the amount of water being covered by your electronics. No matter what unit you choose, cone angles come in various sizes, but you must understand what the advantages of various cone angles are in order to select the unit that's right for you—and correctly interpret what it's telling you.

I prefer units featuring narrow cone angles, because their power is more concentrated within a smaller area, making it easier to determine the precise depth fish are holding. Although wider cone angles cover more area and allow you to cover more water and more fish, those located on the outside edge of the wider cone are so much further from the cone center they may appear slightly deeper than they are really holding—hence, you won't know precisely where they're positioned.

This is why today's "3-way" or "Sidefinder" style electronics have so many beneficial ice fishing applications. These units actually feature three narrow-cone transducers. One points left, one right, and one straight down. On most of these units, you can employ any one alone, or all three in a composite picture to create a wider cone angle—thereby allowing the benefits of either a narrow or wide cone angle. Some of these units even provide a depth cursor that indicates the exact depth of suspended targets, which takes some of the confusion out of reading marks when operating wider cone angles.

Still, for most applications, it's best to utilize the center narrow cone to concentrate power and achieve better target separation—especially on bottom—then take advantage of the wider cone under special circumstances, such as when fishing wandering schools. If a school starts moving away from your current position, you can check the general direction it's moving by enlarging your cone angle. Simply relocate the school using the side cone, move toward them, then switch back to the narrow cone as you jig, repeating the process as necessary. Although you won't be able to pinpoint specifically which direction the fish are heading you'll have a general idea which way to move, and you'll find the benefits of this strategy tremendous.

If this all sounds confusing, start from this point: A wide cone angle is often suitable for use in less than 40 feet of water because you can see more fish. Your resolution may not always be as great, but it's good for fish finding. A narrow cone angle, however, like tightening the spray nozzle on a garden hose, allows you to channel the same amount of output into a smaller area, providing more power so you can see smaller objects more easily, or any object better in deep water.

## Batteries for On-Ice Electronics

One recurring problem with using electronics on the ice—GPS, LCG or flasher units—is battery power and life. Given harsh, cold conditions, batteries are more prone to trouble. Standard, heavy-duty batteries lose power quickly in the cold, and aren't adequate for operating elec-

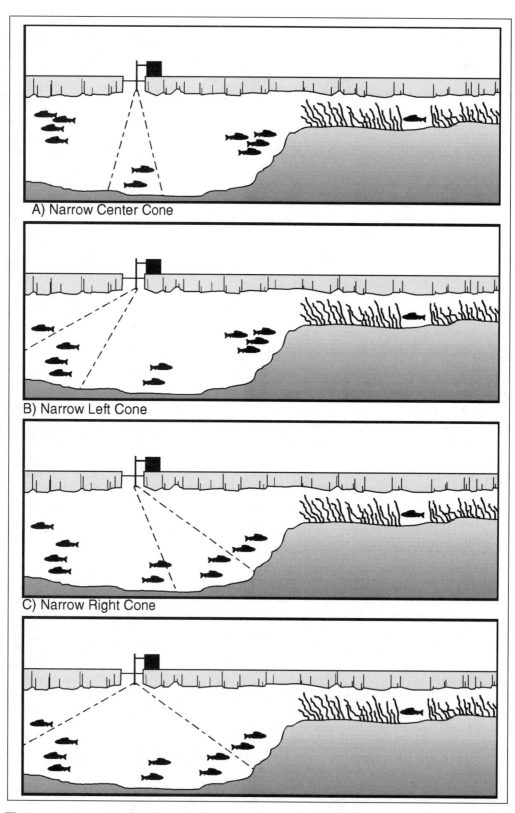

A) Narrow Center Cone

B) Narrow Left Cone

C) Narrow Right Cone

**Three-way transducers feature three narrow cone transducers, one pointing left, one right, and one straight down. You can employ any one alone, or all three in a composite picture to create a wider cone angle—thereby allowing the benefits of both narrow and wide cone angles all in one unit.**

tronics for long-term field use. For increased reliability at a relatively low cost, start with alkaline batteries,

When using a hand-held GPS, for instance, alkaline batteries are your most affordable bet. The more expensive nickel-metal hydrate or lithium batteries are better if you want to invest in batteries offering the best thermal characteristics. Some nickel-metal hydrate batteries also offer recharging capabilities, charge quickly, and feature no "memory", meaning they can be recharged at any capacity from near dead to fully charged without reducing the capability of the battery to receive a full charge.

As for sonar, lantern-type batteries, even alkaline models that offer greater longevity in cold temperatures, don't have the power and "endurance" to handle operating electronics in cold weather for extended periods, and they're difficult if not impossible to recharge, making them expensive. Motorcycle batteries are a step up, but are bulky and heavy and, if tipped, will leak acid. Despite these disadvantages, motorcycle batteries feature longer ampere hours—so by using a motorcycle battery, you'll somewhat sacrifice longevity and convenience for larger capacity.

To prevent cold-weather battery problems, my preference is the 7 amp sealed lead acid power pack gel-cell type batteries. They're relatively small and lightweight, generate excellent power, and are capable of operating power-draining flasher-type sonar units for 16-24 hours continuously, an LCG for 30-40 hours continuously, and liquid crystal flashers like the Zercom LCF-40 100 hours or more continuously.

Gel-cells feature a thick, putty-like electrolyte solution inside. This is pressed between the battery plates and doesn't flow or leak if tipped. However, like an acid battery, they function best when standing up. Like standard acid batteries, gel-cells are also subject to freezing. Although power is drained faster, if you're packing in to a distant fishing location, 1.2 or 4 amp gel-cells are much smaller and lighter. A fully charged 1.2 amp gel cell should provide power for a full day's fishing, and a 4 amp will provide a good 60 hours, or several days, of usage. By the way, a cold battery loses one third of its capacity in cold temperatures, so larger, fully charged batteries provide the most power.

When it comes to charging, the engineers at Zercom Marine recommend charging your batteries after every seven or eight hours of use. Charging on a trickle charger is normally good for a satisfactory charge—however, don't overcharge your unit. Your charger should be a high-quality, 15 volt "smart charge" unit, and a volt meter should be

**If your sonar unit doesn't feature a self-aligning transducer, you must set your transducer perpendicular to the bottom manually to receive an accurate picture of what's below. The best way to accomplish this is by gluing a leveling bubble on top of the transducer.**

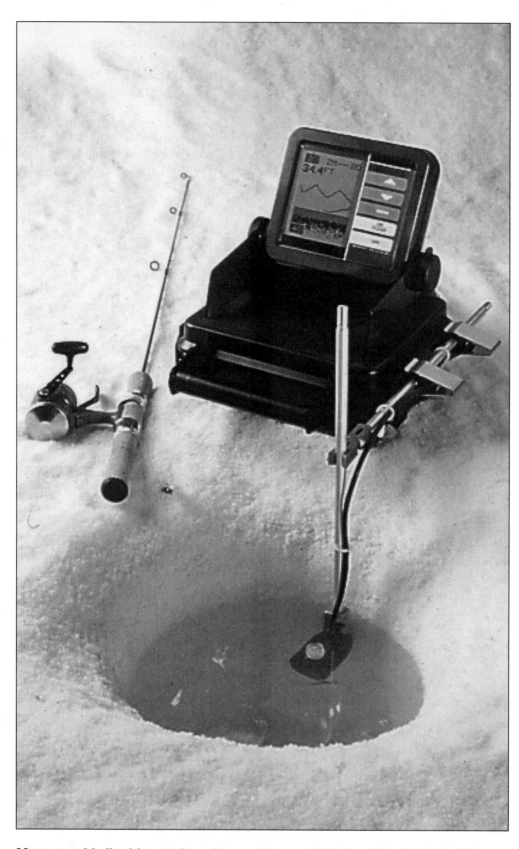

**Most portable liquid crystal graphs come in compact, hard plastic protective cases which double as transport boxes on the ice. (Courtesy Lowrance Electronics)**

used to monitor the charge. When the charge reaches 14.5-14.8 amps, discontinue the charge, or you'll risk permanent damage to the battery. Vexilar produces a charger that automatically shuts off at 14.5 volts, eliminating the chance of overcharging.

As for maintenance, placing your battery on a regular charging schedule as recommended by the manufacturer will double its life. Remember to always charge batteries before storing. Periodic supplementary charges during storage are a smart idea to prevent "sulfating." Finally, keep your batteries clean by occasionally wiping them with a water- or alcohol-dampened cloth.

## Transporting and Preparing Your Sonar

Once you've chosen a battery and unit featuring the desired cone angle, you'll need something to transport them. You can build your own case; otherwise commercially produced boxes such as Vexilar's P-160 or Winter Fishing Systems "IceBox" are perfectly suited for transporting electronics on the ice. Vexilar and Zercom, prominent manufacturers of popular flashers used for ice fishing, also offer sonar kits that include the carrying cases, sonar units, battery, battery indicators and chargers all in one package.

Most portable flashers and LCGs are available in compact, hard plastic protective cases. Just be sure your chosen model is compatible with today's gel-cell batteries. Lowrance, for example, offers a "Porta-Power Pack", a self-insulated battery compartment that will accommodate either gel-cell or D cell batteries.

The next step before heading onto the ice is correctly setting up your unit. Have your battery adequately charged, and be sure your transducer is set perpendicular to bottom. This provides the most power and best readout, and means all distances from the center of the transducer cone are equally distant. Many modern sonar units designed specifically for ice fishing now feature suspended transducers that automatically right themselves. If not, set the unit on a level surface, adjust the transducer perpendicular to the ground using a level, then glue a leveling bubble on top of the transducer. Some sonar units include such a bubble, if yours doesn't, check with a local sporting goods dealer; they should know where to get one.

Finally, be sure the transducer and power cords are properly and tightly connected to the unit, wipe the face of the screen clean with a damp cloth, plug in the transducer cord and power connectors to the battery. You're now ready to step on the ice.

## Setting Your Sensitivity

Once on the ice, you'll need to occasionally correct your power settings.

Start by dropping your lure down halfway to bottom and turn your sensitivity all the way down. You

**By properly setting your sensitivity, you'll be able to read the bottom, your lure and fish. Here, the depth is 18 feet, there's a fish holding a foot off bottom, and another fish is holding at 12 feet. The mark at 11 feet represents my lure. (Courtesy Zercom Marine)**

won't see much. Turn it up slowly, and the bottom will show up. Turn it up more, and you'll see your lure. It's not that the lure didn't exist previously, it just wouldn't show up at the setting where you had your unit set. Turn up the sensitivity, and fish may appear. You've now turned up the amplification enough to show something that's been there the whole time, but didn't show up at your previous setting.

The lesson? You must control such settings, and continually adjust them to best fit your situation. One limitation of electronics is knowing what they're telling you; another is setting them so they tell you what you want to know.

This is especially important when other anglers around you are also using sonar. Because they're operating at or near the same frequency, your unit is shooting electronic pulses and waiting for their return, and also is receiving misdirected pulses from other nearby units, causing interference. This is much like being in a room with several radios. Operate just one, and you can hear it distinctly. Turn a second radio on locked onto a different station, and it's harder to focus. The more you add, the more difficult it becomes to sort. Ditto for sonar.

Vexilar has helped reduce this problem by offering patented, interference reducing circuitry on its FL-8SLT. The simple press of a button changes the signal, reducing interference. If two or more people are fishing close together—say in a fish house—by pushing the button an equal number of times you can synchronize the pulses.

The closer you get, the less interference that will occur, because pulses from both units are operating at the same frequency. The more times you press the button (up to a possible eight) the more interference will be reduced, although each press also slows the pulse rate, pulling you away slightly from real time readings. This must also be adjusted if you move or change depth ranges.

Otherwise, the best way to reduce interference is to go to a smaller cone angle—which concentrates your power and signals into a narrower field—then make yours "loudest." Other factors that help reduce interference include having the most powerful transducer and battery, carefully adjusting your sensitivity, and fine-tuning your suppression settings. Together, these things add up to the greatest "volume." To reduce interference problems, purchase a unit with a powerful transducer, keep your battery charged and set the sensitivity properly as described above. If interference persists, you'll need to adjust your suppression. The higher you set the suppres-sion, the less interference you'll get—but the harder it will become to mark fish.

## The Sonar Advantage

Let's review the sonar advantage, beginning with shooting reading directly through the ice. The most compact, simple sonar product I'm aware of is made by Strikemaster. Called "Polar Vision," the unit provides a great way to find depth. A hand-held unit about the size and weight of a medium size flashlight, the unit provides easy to read digital depth readings. A similar unit, the LPS-1, is made by Vexilar.

In either case, simply clear surface snow or slush away from clear, solid ice below, squirt down some water—I prefer heated saltwater, it doesn't freeze as easily—and using a squirt or sport drink-style bottle, make sure the bottom of your transducer is completely immersed in water. Place the transducer level on the clean surface to establish a seal. Properly sealed, the units will read depth. With repeated readings, you can easily pinpoint fish holding structure.

Understand that several differences exist between using this technology in summer and winter. First, no transducer will provide a reading if you're shooting through slushy, mottled or air-bubbled ice. Transducers can't obtain signals when interfered by objects or air. Secondly, when shooting through the ice, your unit will disregard the presence of ice and tell you only how deep the water is. In other words, if the ice is two feet thick over 10 feet of water and you shoot through it, the depth will read 10 feet. But if you drill a hole in the same spot and re-check the depth by placing the transducer in the water-filled hole, the screen will read 12 feet.

The difference? Water now occupies the space where two feet of ice once was, and the sonar reads the water where it didn't ready the ice previously. This may not seem important, but I've seen many anglers who mark the depth on certain structures in summer become needlessly confused by such discrepancies after the ice forms. Remember to account for them when shooting through the ice.

You can also obtain readings through the ice using more complex sonar units like flashers and LCGs. Simply form a seal of water around the transducer, and adjust the sensitivity until you see bottom clearly. Although the Polar Vision sounds an alarm and flashes the depth when fish move into the cone, the advantage to using standard sonar is that the unit will reveal not only depth and fish, but bottom content, presence of cover and forage. Like the Polar Vision, however, readings cannot be shot through slushy, mottled, or air-bubbled ice. Under such conditions, you will need to drill holes to obtain readings.

Either way, once you've obtained a depth reading, mark the depth next to each hole, and continue this pro-

**Strikemaster's "Polar Vision," a hand-held sonar unit about the size and weight of medium-size flashlight, provides easy-to-read digital depth readings. By shooting these readings through the ice, you can find structure and fish without even having to drill a hole.**

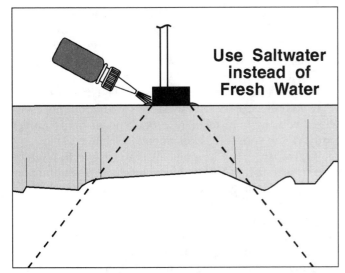

**Use Saltwater instead of Fresh Water**

If the base of the transducer is completely immersed in water, sonar can read depth directly through the ice. Use saltwater, which is more resistant to freezing. Taking readings at multiple locations, you can determine the outlay of the structure below without having to drill a hole.

cess by taking multiple readings. By marking the depth and moving strategically—all while referencing your lake map—the bottom configuration, including structure, will be revealed. Once the structure is outlined, begin looking for unique features or irregular contours in association with each productive structural element. A finger on the edge of a submerged hump, a hook on a point, a weededge near a dropoff—all would be primary fish-holding areas—and all can be revealed simply by using sonar.

Continue taking readings, referencing your map while doing so, and you'll eventually locate various structures and their orientation. Once you've uncovered a good piece of structure, look closely at your readings on those unique features or irregular contours; you should also be able to determine depth, secondary structure, bottom content, presence of cover, forage and fish—all important variables in pinpointing high-percentage locations.

Bottom will simply appear as the depth at each reading, and by combining various depth readings with personal knowledge and lake map interpretation, you'll be able to determine and visualize the placement and orientation of various structures and secondary structures. Furthermore, hard bottoms will register thick and dark and feature a "double echo" on a flasher, while soft, thin, dim readings are indicative of a soft bottom. The figure on the previous page shows a depth of 10 feet, and a second echo at 20 feet, indicating a hard bottom condition. On an LCG, the bar graph for sensitivity will read high in soft bottom areas, and low over hard bottoms.

If present, weeds and other forms of cover will also appear—usually as batches of fine lines or stacked markings forming columns attached to and rising from bottom. Plankton and baitfish look similar, but will generally show up as suspended scatterings or "clouds" of fine lines or dots separated from bottom. When inside your transducer cone, your lure will also appear as a distinctive moving "blip" or line at the depth you're fishing that moves as you lift or drop your lure.

Notice on the illustration below how marks between the 10 foot bottom and the surface have appeared. These are fish, and hopefully, one of the marks represents your lure among them. If such locations aren't holding fish, mark them as waypoints on your GPS and make reference notes, so if you wish, you can come back and try them another time. Such areas may hold panfish under a different set of conditions.

Once fish are found, accurate depth control will often make the difference between no fish and a limit, so before

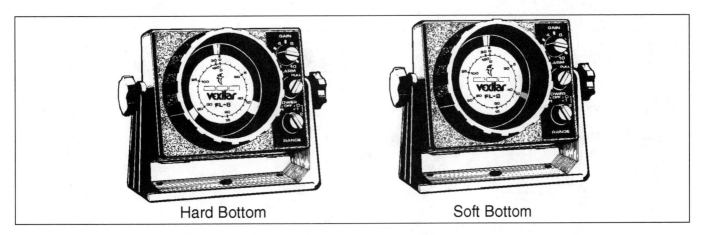

Hard Bottom                    Soft Bottom

Bottom content can be deciphered using sonar. Hard bottoms will register thick and dark and feature a "double echo" on a flasher, while thin, dim readings indicate a soft bottom. On LCGs, the bar graph for sensitivity will read high in soft bottom areas, and low over hard bottoms.

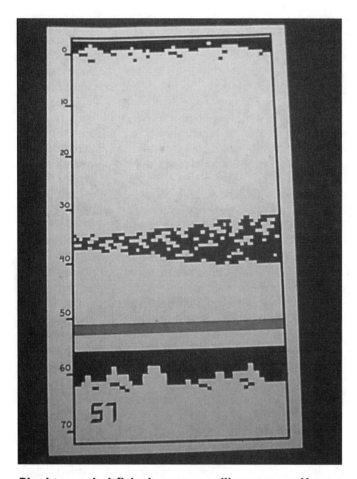

**Plankton or baitfish show up readily on sonar. Here, a cloud of plankton appears, suspended off bottom between 30 and 40 feet deep over 57 feet of water. The bar at 52 feet is my lure.**

you begin jigging, measure how many inches of line your reel picks up per revolution of the handle. Mark the line at your rod tip with a marker, turn the handle 360 degrees, and measure the distance between your mark and rod tip. Now you'll know precisely what distance every turn of your reel handle moves your lure. This, combined with what your electronics show you, lets you know precisely where your jig is in relation to bottom—or more importantly, where your lure is positioned in relation to fish.

Obviously, your lure or bait is most effective when placed near fish. When you work a bait in conjunction with sonar, you can't help but increase your odds of being in the right place at the right time. It's simple. If you can see fish on your screen, you can lower your lure to them, and seeing your lure in relation to bottom and where fish are coming through is vital to success.

How would an angler fishing in 30 feet of water and not using electronics be able to consistently catch fish suspended 15 feet down? I've had several instances where someone was fishing next to me, I was catching fish and they couldn't get a bite. Reason? Depth. They were fishing bottom, and the school was suspended. Without electronics, they were at a total disadvantage.

There's no excuse for not seeing fish, as they create obvious marks. If you're using an LCG that features a "Fish ID" style readout, fish will register as conspicuous fish shapes, some units will even provide the precise depth the marked fish are holding. Otherwise, single, faint lines suspended off bottom and away from surface clutter are representative of suspended fish on the outside edge of your transducer cone, while thick, bright lines are fish suspended directly inside the cone. Fish on or near bottom and away from surface clutter are representative of suspended fish on the outside edge of your transducer cone, while thick, bright lines are fish suspended directly inside the cone. Fish on or near bottom will appear as thin lines barely separated from the bottom signal.

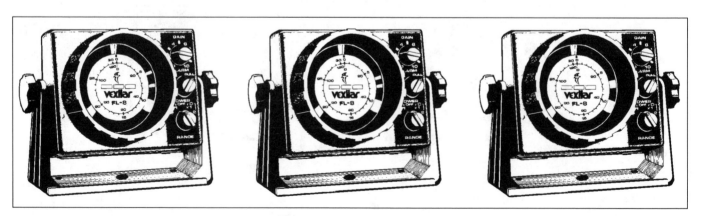

**Sonar will not only reveal depth, structure and bottom content, but fish as well. Here, three readings reveal fish in 10 feet of water over a hard bottom. At left fish have been marked at 6 and 8 feet. The center screen shows fish at 6 and 7 feet. The screen at right shows two fish close together between 7 and 8 feet.**

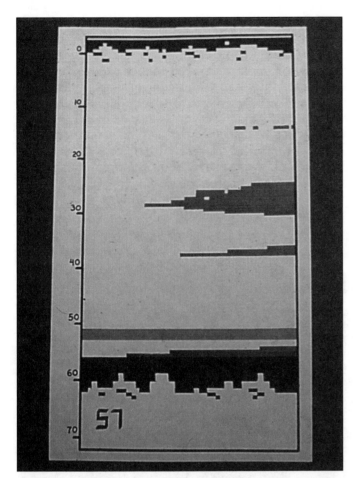

**Unlike plankton or baitfish that show up as loose "clouds" of suspended material, schools of panfish will show up as dense conglomerations. Notice how my lure is positioned just off bottom, away from the fish. Using sonar, I can now adjust my lure to the fish. By simply fishing on bottom without electronics, I'd likely miss catching anything from this hole.**

You can even estimate the size of the fish by the height of the signal. Sonar measures the distance of an object from the transducer, thus large objects closer to the transducer will register smaller in length than objects of the same size located farther away. In addition, you're stationary, which enhances this "lengthening" effect—another situation demonstrating that thickness, not length, indicates size. It may seem as though I'm dwelling on this point, but that's because I've seen too many ice anglers mistakenly believe that long marks are large fish, when actually they're just marking fish holding high or stationary directly within the cone.

Also, by looking at the depth, bottom content, structure, secondary cover and position of various numbers and sizes of fish, you can begin to pattern them. Interestingly—to a degree anyway—you can also surmise the species being marked by noting their position. For exam-

ple, perch often hold near bottom, while crappies, cisco and stocked trout tend to suspend.

Consider the consequences of these advantages carefully. Using our understanding of high-percentage winter panfish locations, lake maps and GPS, we move efficiently to predetermined high-percentage locations. Once there, sonar allows us to mark depths, locate drop-offs, rises and breaks. By taking multiple readings, we can determine structural layout, bottom content, secondary cover such as weeds, rocks or sunken timber, forage—even fish and their relative size. From here, it's possible to discern what depths, bottom contents, structures, cover and forage the fish are relating to; and by identifying your bait and placing it in relation to marked fish, observe their reactions, making changes in lure styles, sizes, colors and actions until a winning combination is surmised.

Obviously, electronics can do more than just read depth or help you find structure and panfish. Using this technology, you can actually start piecing location patterns together—at times, without having to drill a single hole!

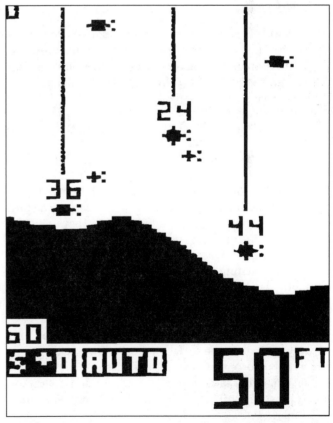

**Liquid crystal graphs also show fish. Some even offer features such as "Fish ID" that show the fish and the depth they're holding. Keep in mind that because you're stationary, fish will appear as long bars on your screen. Many experts recommend turning off such features because this will help speed up your scroll speed and improve your signal's response time.**

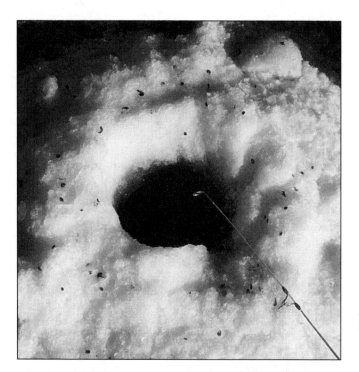

Using sonar is one way to find productive areas harboring forage. Here, the freshwater shrimp were so thick and high under the ice pack they actually washed out within the ice trailings from my hole drilling.

## Monitoring Fish Activity Levels

Watching a fish strike is always an interesting experience. It's fun to watch a fussy bluegill suck in a tiny jig, a trout dart out from under an undercut bank to hit a nightcrawler, a bass kiss a topwater plug, or pike smash a spinnerbait. And whose knees wouldn't shake as they witness a musky crush their bucktail on a "figure eight" at boatside?

Most anglers enjoy watching fish strike, not only because it's exciting to see and adds to the fishing experience, but also because it's possible to judge the approximate activity level of the fish, based on how hard they strike and how often they hit.

The above examples are all open-water scenarios, and are only evident on the surface or in shallow or clear water where fish are obvious to the naked eye. How can ice anglers enjoy the same type of experience and determine how panfish are striking if they aren't visible under the ice?

Sonar!

It's important to understand the use of electronics for finding high-percentage locations and schools of panfish, because knowing how you're positioned in relation to a school is of key importance. Yet to fully appreciate the applications of electronics for ice fishing, you must also understand electronics are equally valuable in determining panfish activity levels and monitoring presentation

responses—and when properly set, these units can accomplish this feat. You simply need to know what to look for.

For instance, it's best to find tightly clustered schools of panfish as opposed to scattered ones, because concentrated schools are more likely to be feeding, active fish. Schools of "squiggly" or "fluttering" marks near suspended forage are especially good indicators, as they designate groups of actively feeding fish moving in and out of our transducer cone, appearing and disappearing from your screen as they do. If you run across this situation, drill a hole and quickly drop your lure to the school, then watch your electronics with an eagle eye to confirm they're feeding.

This can be determined by monitoring how the fish are positioned and how they react to your lure. Are they

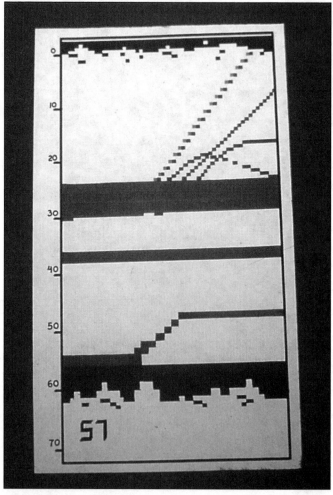

"Squiggly" or fluttering marks near suspended forage and fish are good indicators of actively feeding fish. Here, I've caught a fish from a suspended school and brought it to the surface, while three other fish followed. A couple of other fish are holding about 37 feet down. Another fish was positioned on bottom, rose a few feet, and stopped at about 48 feet.

**Strategic use of sonar is dependent on a working knowledge of reading lake maps, plus properly setting the sonar and interpreting what it's telling you so you can visualize the bottom configuration presented on the lake map.**

reacting slowly, spooking easily and short-striking, or are they aggressively chasing down your lure and completely swallowing the offering? Do they want the bait moved fast or slow?

Once such questions have been answered, you can adjust your lures and techniques according to the mood and activity level of the fish. For instance, if the fish spook easily, lighten up and work smaller and slower baits more gingerly. If they're aggressive, work larger, more aggressive flash or jigging lures, and work them hard. Also experiment with lure style, action, color and live bait tippers. Do they show any preferences? If so, make adjustments in your presentation accordingly—your extra efforts should pay off.

However, if the fish are producing firm, scattered marks in one suspended position or hugging bottom and won't react to various presentations, they're probably sedentary, non-active fish. Always try fishing them, but if they don't respond within 10 minutes, don't get hung up

trying to trigger these inactive fish. Instead, move on in search of an active school, and consider coming back to try them again later.

The only way to consistently and efficiently find productive structures, mark active panfish, accurately track their movements and systematically monitor their activity levels—in other words, pattern the fish—is with sonar. Yet strategic use of sonar is dependent on a working knowledge of how to read lake maps, plus being able to properly set and interpret what your unit is telling you. Otherwise, even the best state-of-the-art electronics will be of little use.

So next time you ice fish, don't make the mistake of randomly drilling holes. Instead, do your homework. Read up on the species you're seeking and the lake you plan to fish, carefully review a lake map before you begin searching for primary structures—preferably during the fall when you can "run the lake" and mark high percentage locations and plot waypoints on a GPS unit most effectively. Then, choose an LCG or flasher best suiting your ice fishing needs and, learn how to use its features to their fullest capacity.

You'll soon discover how the proper use of electronics on the ice will increase your number of successful "hardwater" fishing trips, because the culmination of all these efforts means you'll see exactly what's below you in terms of structure, cover and forage—helping you locationally pattern winter panfish. And monitoring and knowing what's happening below you in terms of fish position, movements, activity levels and responses will help you pattern the fish presentationally—providing you with a better, more complete understanding of *total* winter fishing patterns.

## Assembling Location and Presentation Patterns: The Total Pattern

Going this far has already placed you among the top 10 percent of the ice fishing crowd, but you can take yourself even further. With an integral knowledge of how to use electronics, you can establish both location *and* presentation patterns: The total pattern.

As we've already established, the best way to determine total winter patterns begins with examining a detailed lake map, then, taking into account how the species you're seeking will instinctively respond to factors such as lake type, how far the winter season has progressed, time of day, weather, primary forage bases and predator/prey relationships, you can locate the best looking locations using maps and electronics, then begin targeting panfish in the most productive areas—in effect, deciphering productive winter patterns.

Following such a practice repeatedly, you'll soon notice productive winter panfish patterns repeat them-

An on-the-ice strategy involving the use of lake maps, sonar and a mobile approach will help you target the most productive winter patterns. Note the zig-zag pattern of my footprints, a pattern I often use to help cover water.

How deep is the forage, and how are the fish positioned in relation to it? How deep are the most active biters? Are they holding along a major migration route? Do specific holding points exist active fish are relating to? When?

Sonar will allow you to determine these answers. Be thorough and always decipher complete location patterns. Every lake is different, featuring different water clarities, bottom contents, prominent vegetation types, nutrient concentrations, oxygen contents and so on. Again, you may find similar lakes, but you'll never find two that are identical. Therefore panfish within any two given lakes generally aren't doing the same thing at the same time.

In fact, even populations of the same species in the same lake won't necessarily follow the same location patterns, because while their needs and natural instincts are the same, various schools are exposed to different conditions, causing them to move throughout the winter period, daily—even hourly. A weather change, movement of forage, increase in fishing activity or simply the sight of a passing pike can break up established patterns and lead to the development of new ones. This means numerous winter panfish patterns exist—often, simultaneously. But frequently one stands out, and it's best to search for clues that will reveal the most productive patterns.

This is important. If your goal is a trophy, large lakes generally offer more trophy potential than small ones, because there's a greater amount of water for fish to hide, feed and grow—but because there's so much area to cover, high-percentage hot spots holding active fish can be more difficult to find.

The best method for defining specific patterns is to record productive locations on your lake map and GPS as you find them, along with other pertinent information, including the date, time, weather conditions, prevalent bottom content, forage base and cover. Such references will help you establish repetitious annual location patterns that create degrees of consistency few other anglers can match.

A major difference between "good" ice anglers and "experts" is that experts spend hours pondering over maps and carefully considering potential hotspots—carefully considering the lake they fish, the species they're seeking, the prevailing weather, and the time of year. At times, experts may invest more time looking at maps, thinking about the predominant conditions, and drilling holes than actually fishing. But once they're in the right location, the action is fast and furious, and they often leave the lake with more fish than the person who spends all day fishing in just a mediocre spot or two. The secret? Spending quality time fishing within the highest percentage areas with the highest percentage presentations.

Just as you can locate microstructure on several good structural features in the right depth range holding forage and active schools of your target species to interpret top proper location patterns, you can also pinpoint the

selves on single bodies of water. But don't stop here, consider the big picture! If you find a large school of active panfish several years in a row on a gradually sloping shoreline point covered with cabbage weeds stretching from deep to shallow water, there's a good chance you'll find them in similar locations throughout other areas of the lake. However, they seldom will follow the same location patterns from one body of water to another. A shallow, weedy, bowl-shaped lake may not present distinct structural elements like a deep, structurally diverse one, but may feature distinct weedbed pockets or stumpfield edges that become primary structural locations.

To decipher winter patterns consistently, you must note as many important details as possible. What lake type are you fishing? What's the prevalent weather pattern? Predominant bottom content? Cover type? Is there a well-defined "edge" in the form of a weedline, change in bottom content, depth, cover or other variable that may be causing the fish to hold there? Is there a specific forage present?

**Shallow, weedy, bowl-shaped lakes may not present distinct structural elements like a deep, structurally diverse one, but may feature distinct weed bed pockets or stumpfield edges that become primary structural locations.**

most productive presentation patterns. Panfish behave differently in winter—at times they may even settle into semi-dormant states. Yet these fish must feed, and they bite throughout the winter, even aggressively at times. Ice pros understand this, and realize the secret to consistent winter catches begins with capitalizing on these periods by determining precisely when and where they will occur—in other words, they pattern the fish from a location perspective.

However, *total* winter panfish patterns are based on two fundamental principles: the locations where panfish will likely be most active, which we've already covered—and the most suitable presentations needed to catch them, or presentation patterns. Just as top ice pros must analyze each situation and decipher the best location patterns, choosing the right presentation isn't a random process, either. Because all panfish species are unique and respond differently under various conditions, experts must select their presentations carefully to best suit the targeted species, based on their instincts and senses, the lake being fished, the prevailing weather, depth being fished, water clarity—even the habits size and color of the target species primary forage bases.

In deep or dark water environments, for example, panfish can't see well and instinctively rely on their sense of hearing, smell and ability to sense vibration to find food. Therefore aggressive jigging presentations with vibrating blade baits and larger, high profile, bright colored lures and baits with rattles or fins are often helpful for attracting fish and creating consistent catches. Ditto for phosphorescent colors, because you're doing every-

**Sonar will help decipher winter location patterns by revealing depth, structure, secondary structure, bottom content, presence of cover, forage and fish.**

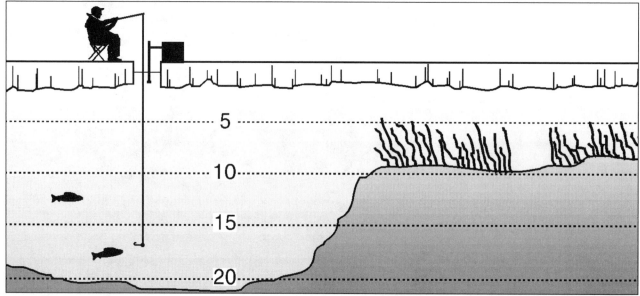

**Once you've located panfish, your goal is to lower your lure to the depth they're holding. In this case, the fish are suspended, and if they aren't actively chasing food, fishing directly on bottom would bring poor results. Using sonar, you can adapt your jigging to the depth fish are holding, increasing your chance of a hook-up.**

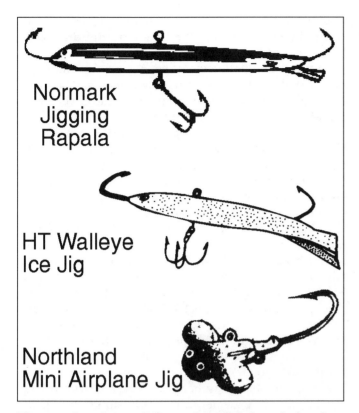

**Three swimming style lures that glide in a circle when jigged, great when winter panfish are active are competitively chasing down lures—something you can see on your sonar.**

Still, watch their response carefully on your sonar. If the fish spook or strike at the lure halfheartedly, try switching to less active jigging lures and motions, or baits with more subtle actions, styles, sizes and colors to determine which ones draw the most strikes. To prepare for these situations, it's a good idea to rig several rods and tip-ups with a variety of lures and rigs. Then, like a successful golfer who chooses various clubs given different situations, you'll be able to change quickly to presentations best suiting the situation you're confronted with, and adjust your presentation to the conditions at hand.

This is important, because no two plankton, minnow, or insect species look and act exactly the same. Some are short and fat, some are long and skinny. Some rest on bottom, some swim slowly up then drop in vertical movements, while others make quick darting horizontal movements or a combination thereof, and these motions may vary given the lake type, time of day and light intensity. So experiment with various lure weights, sizes, colors, designs and jigging actions, trying to match the hatch, using balanced tackle. The extra effort often pays off.

This is where consistently successful anglers stand out. Given such conditions, knowledgeable anglers utilize a mobile approach, take numerous electronic readings and keep an open mind while experimenting with a variety of presentations in numerous, high-percentage locations. By sticking it out and analyzing each situation right down to

thing possible to help the fish find your bait. Of course, adding live bait is helpful, as this adds natural scent, taste and texture to the lure in any environment, rounding out the appeal to each of the fishes primary senses.

In clear water, oversized noisy lures and unnatural color schemes may actually spook panfish. In such instances, more-subdued, realistic-sized, naturally moving, naturally colored baits are more likely to catch panfish. These fish rely on their sense of sight to feed successfully, and because they have ample time to examine your bait, you must make them believe they're looking at something real. Again, a touch of live bait is usually a plus, but should closely resemble the natural forage in composition, size and color.

However, as with location patterns, successful formation of top presentation patterns goes beyond such basics, because for best results you must locate schools, then determine the primary prey of these schools and their activity levels. When you find a school, start by determining the prey they're likely relating to, then begin fishing larger, more active lures such as swimming and vibrating lures. After all, active fish will strike almost anything, and larger, louder, fasting moving "action lures" are the quickest way to attract and catch active biters.

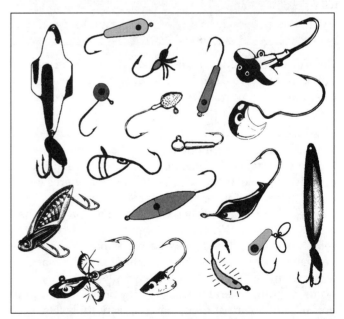

**Winter panfish aren't always active, and if you note this response to your presentation, try something different to see what will make them strike. Not all forage looks and acts exactly the same, and the same is true for lures. Find ones that are easy for panfish to locate and closely resemble the natural forage in size, shape, color and action.**

**Careful adjustment of the sensitivity on your sonar will allow you to decipher winter panfish patterns in quick order.**

able to certain presentations much of the time. Don't just randomly drill holes and haphazardly drop your bait down just any hole. Rather, pay attention to location details and be mobile in your approach, until you pinpoint these high-percentage locations for the time and day you're fishing—then be versatile in your presentation to determine their vulnerability.

I usually start by trying tiny ultralight presentations, then gradually working larger lures and presentations with more active jigging motions (or vice versa, depending on the conditions and the species being sought) until I determine fish activity levels and the most efficient presentation for catching them.

However, if nothing happens after 10 or 15 minutes, move! It's always tempting to fish long and hard when a school is found, but finding fish doesn't mean you'll actually catch them—as many frustrated ice anglers will attest. So don't get caught up in this Catch-22, it completely defeats the purpose of this efficient ice fishing approach. Rather, fish wisely and efficiently, stay mobile—and whatever you do, always search for the most active fish.

Do this at several high percentage waypoints, and it's unlikely you'll strike out on every one. Just remember, one waypoint may hold nothing, another nothing but inactive fish, while a third is bustling with activity—or you might simply catch a couple of fish from each area. Find the active fish on each, stay with them as long as possible, and when they move or become inactive, move to the next waypoint. Such efficient processes lead to consistency, and by doing so, you'll gain invaluable experience, and over time, learn to consistently pinpoint high-percentage panfish-producing locations and top producing presentations. You'll save valuable fishing time and become an increasingly more

the tiniest detail, you'll often discover panfish feeding on certain prey items or utilizing specific depths, and consequently, be able to piece together loose patterns even under the most agonizingly tough conditions.

Yes, there will be times you encounter panfish that just won't bite. When this happens, move along in search of more active fish, but always mark the area so you can return. Remember, the school may be inactive at the moment, but they must eventually feed. This may occur an hour, several hours, or a day or two later, but if you remain aware of their changing activity levels, you could end up catching a limit from just such a school.

Whatever the conditions, the challenge is to successfully work out the most productive patterns by carefully and systematically observing groups of location and presentation variables, then monitoring them as they change and panfish responses vary. After all, most panfish can be found in certain places and vulner-

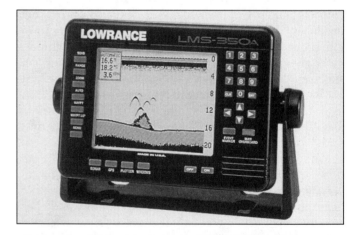

**Modern sonar such as this LCG will help you determine productive winter patterns more easily by allowing you to collect up-to-the-minute information regarding the most productive location and presentation patterns. (Courtesy Lowrance Electronics)**

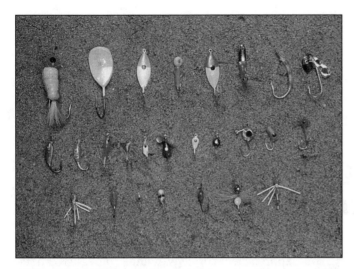

**Since all panfish species are unique and respond differently under various conditions, you must select your presentations based on your target species instincts and senses, the lake and depth being fished, weather, even the habits, size and color of the target species' primary forage bases. A wide variety of ice lure styles, designs and colors are available.**

We've covered many basic total winter patterns, and we've learned how to apply this knowledge to finding winter panfish. Now we need to explore how individual panfish species respond given various conditions. We will learn how to apply our system to determine how specific panfish species respond and relate to various lake types, weather and water conditions. We will discover the value of a mobile, versatile approach for determining their reactions and activity levels. We will learn to match the presentation with the current conditions to maximize success. And we will identitify the proper timing for incorporating these strategies. The results will be more consistent winter panfish catches, even when many other anglers are coming ashore with empty pails.

efficient ice angler, with a better understanding of winter panfish location, behavior and activity levels on various lake types given a variety of conditions.

Don't just randomly walk out onto the ice and sit in place waiting for panfish, and don't casually use electronics without fully interpreting what they're telling you. Many ice anglers don't realize it, but we're living in a historic age. The present day ice fishing scene is much like the open water fishing scene years ago. Think about it. You'd be hard pressed to find a serious crappie tournament angler in today's world of fishing that doesn't attempt to move from spot to spot, trying to determine the predominant location pattern. These anglers attempt to match the correct presentation—be it a slip bobber and minnow, tube jig, spinnerbait or crankbait—to a particular summer crappie pattern to obtain the best results.

It's fairly easy to find ice anglers that have never considered winter location patterns. Unfortunately, there aren't a great many frontiers left in open-water fishing, but there are many in ice fishing—and those anglers who explore them now are in for a real treat.

So join in. After all, if you study the panfish species you're seeking, learn to read the water, interpret lake maps, properly use electronics to pinpoint the primary winter locations of actively feeding winter fish, then top this with the best producing presentations, you're sure to latch onto some productive patterns—and some awfully nice winter catches as well.

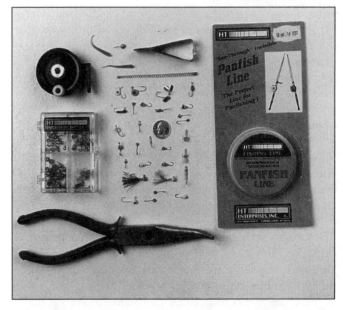

**I usually start by experimenting with tiny ultralight presentations involving light lines and tiny lures, then gradually work larger lures and presentations with more active jigging motions (or vice-versa, depending on the conditions and the species being sought) until I determine the fish's activity levels and the most efficient presentation for catching them.**

# Chapter 4

# *Understanding Sunfish and Bluegills During Winter*

*I*ce fishing.

It seems all ice anglers experience the same strange propensity each season. As icy winter gales blast crinkly brown leaves hanging delicately from dormant trees, loosening them from their bases and sending them skipping across the frozen ground, we start getting anxious.

About the time we begin scraping frosty windshields on still, icy mornings, witness the tranquil sight of snowflakes lightly gracing the frigid air during the first freezing days of winter and sense the advent of sub-zero nights, some intrinsic, unquenchable desire drives us to freshly frozen lakes, where we suddenly feel an overwhelming, uncompromising desire to boldly trod where no one else has gone before. On this initial trek, we crave the strange captivation of walking onto our favorite ice-capped waters for the first time, seemingly enjoying the icy sensation that comes from that apathetic, apprehensive thrill of uncertainty as the ice adjusts to our weight and crackles warnings through the expanse of heavy winter air.

As dedicated ice anglers, we know bluegill populations haven't been disturbed much throughout the fall, and understand that during the first-ice period, bluegills eventually find their way onto productive, cover-laden shallows, drawn in number by the sheer abundance of cover and forage. Furthermore, we know while enjoying this lavish extravaganza, these fish are going about their everyday business of feeding aggressively—at times almost carelessly, scarcely noticing the eminent development of ice thickening above their heads.

And us? We're there to capitalize on this favorable situation by quietly creeping across a shallow ceiling of ice, boring holes to accommodate our tiny ice lures and baits to trick these fish. In short, we're there to catch bluegills—and often justly rewarded. After all, first-ice bluegills are typically not only unwary and actively feeding, but heavily concentrated and easily accessible along shallow shoreline coves, bays, flats and points, and many first-ice anglers come off the ice with heavy five-gallon pails.

But approached correctly, winter bluegills can be caught throughout the winter. The secret to catching winter sunfish and bluegills consistently revolves around an understanding of the primary locations active fish will most likely be found and why, then determining the best presentation for coercing them into biting. Don't succumb to the notion that once a few seasoned ice anglers reveal productive locations all you must do is follow well-traveled trails out from shore toward temporary cities of shacks, vehicles and anglers. To limit the amount of time spent searching for sunfish and bluegills, remember the system: learn the habits of each species, review a lake map prior to setting out, and considering all the predominant variables, begin searching for high-percentage locations. Then, using your electronics, set out to pinpoint them, and using your knowledge, stay with sunfish and bluegill as they move throughout the winter season. If you do, you'll likely be able to experience the excitement and productivity of first-ice action—right through the entire winter.

But first, the fish.

**Sunfish and bluegills feature short, compressed body designs, allowing them to make fast turns to capture fast moving prey—or make quick, short turns for fast, evasive maneuvers to escape from larger predators.**

**The secret to catching winter sunfish and bluegills consistently revolves around an understanding of the primary locations active fish will most likely be found and why, then determining the best presentation for coercing them into biting.**

**The best bluegill populations grow in clear water environments featuring moderate weed growth. Although large populations often develop in waters featuring heavy weeds, the protection offered by them ultimately results in stunting.**

### Pumpkinseed Sunfish

Pumpkinseed sunfish—arguably the most strikingly colorful of all winter panfish—have greater distribution throughout the ice fishing belt than most sunfishes, and their tolerance of cool water makes them among the most commonly winter-caught sunfish. Pumpkinseeds thrive in shallow, dense vegetation, and generally travel in loose schools through shallow, vegetated areas, although larger individuals may be found in deeper water holding in small groups over rocky or vegetated structures. They feed most actively during the day. Diet consists primarily of plankton and insect larvae, although crustaceans, snails, clams, worms and small fish may also be consumed. Table quality is delicious.

### Longear Sunfish

While longear sunfish are runners-up to the pumpkinseed for the most beautifully marked of all winter panfish, their distribution is somewhat limited throughout the North American ice fishing belt. Being largely a river species, longears aren't typically caught by ice anglers, although some wide, slow-flowing rivers and

impoundments on them have made longears accessible to hardwater anglers. Longear sunfish are usually found in shallow water cover and don't move much. Diet is very similar to the pumpkinseed, although the longear's preference for warmer water means they generally don't feed as actively in winter. Table quality is very good.

### Redear Sunfish

Because the redear's northern range of distribution cuts across the southern border of the North American ice fishing belt, they are not a common ice fishing catch. Diet is very similar to the other sunfishes, although they demonstrate a preference for snails. Habits are much like the other sunfishes, and table fare is good.

### Bluegills

The best bluegill populations grow in clear water environments featuring moderate weedgrowth. Although large populations develop in waters featuring heavy weeds, the protection offered by them ultimately results in stunting.

Feeding slows dramatically in water below 50°F, but the bluegill's winter diet includes plankton, insect larvae, plant materials, leeches, fish eggs, small crayfish and small fish. Smaller bluegills prefer shallow vegetation offering plankton and insect larvae as a food base. Larger bluegills are known to hold deeper than their smaller counterparts, and turn more to a crustacean and minnow based diet.

Given ideal conditions, bluegills are limnetic during the day, feeding on plankton in open water, then moving into shallow littoral areas during twilight periods to graze on plankton, eat insect larvae and other available prey—although this varies depending on competitive species. When bluegill encounter no other competing panfishes, shallow water plankton and plant materials make up the primary forage; when competing with shallow water species such as pumpkinseed and green sunfish, they will tend to suspend over deep water pockets or holes and feed on open water clouds of plankton. Highly prolific, bluegills easily overpopulate and stunt. As table fare, bluegills are highly respected.

Green sunfish are a close relative of the bluegill (in fact, they frequently hybridize with them) and are a common quarry of shore-bound summertime anglers. But, they are not frequently caught through the ice and their winter habits are very different from the four species just profiled. For that reason, green sunfish are discussed briefly in their own section in Chapter 13.

## Primary Winter Location Patterns

Because sunfish and bluegills are typically willing biters, if you can locate them you'll likely catch some. The search begins with lake type, and no discussion of winter bluegills would be complete without special coverage of one of the largest winter bluegill resources:

**Sunfish and bluegills are typically willing biters, so if you can locate them you'll likely catch some.**

**First ice in natural lakes will find sunfish and bluegills in shallow, protected dark-bottomed channels, bays and flats, where cover and forage is abundant.**

River backwaters. To the untrained eye glancing across acres of vast, frozen backwater areas, the scene may appear intimidating. However, veteran ice anglers know that weed lines, pockets, stump fields and "deep" holes you find in backwaters produce excellent bluegill action.

For best results, fish deeper, cover laden areas influenced by slight current flow, as these areas hold forage, and the moving water supplies a fresh supply of oxygen. However, be cautious—moving water can erode ice. Other factors also influence fish movement and distribution, including water level, ice and snow thickness, current flow, oxygen counts—and how far winter has progressed.

First ice in river backwater systems finds large concentrations of sunfish and bluegill in shallow, weedy sloughs and backwater ponds. Provided cover, food and oxygen remain adequate, the fish will remain there throughout the winter. Should any of these variables dip below preferred levels, the fish will move toward spring holes or current-influenced sloughs and channels. Late ice, they move shallow again in preparation for the spring spawn.

First ice in natural lakes will find sunfish and bluegills in shallow, protected dark-bottomed channels, bays and flats where cover and forage is plentiful. As winter progresses, sunfish make only slight movements based on environmental constraints such as ice thickness, sunlight penetration and oxygen availability; bluegills make movements toward deeper weed lines. Larger individuals may even break out onto deep, hard-bottom, mid-lake structures such as points, sunken islands and rock reefs.

Late ice, cover, food and oxygen supplies increase in the shallows; sunfish and bluegills return to primary break-lines adjoining spawning bays and gradually move back into the shallows, where they feed actively.

Patterns on flowages and reservoirs are similar, although first-ice movements are toward cover-laden boat channels, creek arms or coves. Mid-season movements are onto gradually sloping flats and points featuring cover in the form of vegetation or flooded wood. If cover, forage and oxygen levels aren't suitable, movements toward deep structures, especially those in close proximity to the main river channel, are likely to occur. Late ice will find these fish returning to shallow, cover-laden spawning coves.

Daily movements occur throughout the winter on any lake type. Weather and changing light levels are primary triggers. Events such as cold fronts may drive sunfish and bluegill into heavier cover or toward deeper water, slowing progressive movement along migration routes toward the shallows. Yet while such circumstances

**During first ice, productive patterns inevitably revolve around shallow water areas supporting a plentiful food source.**

**First ice creates fabulous opportunities for anxious anglers. Here, a friend couldn't wait for safe ice, and used a downed tree to access some early ice 'gills.**

may slow movement and feeding activity, sunfish and bluegills are not as sensitive to light as some panfish species, and some feeding is likely to continue.

Let's review each of the phases of the ice fishing season in detail and explore how sunfish and bluegills behave at different times throughout the winter.

## First Ice Magic

Each year the turbulent, stormy days of late fall and early winter that have caused waters to roil and froth in the midst of bitter autumn gales are suddenly stilled by a silent, mysterious process that enchants the winter night.

This mystical process begins as sub-freezing air suspends gracefully over the water, stealthy robbing the water of energy until the surface temperature slumps below 32°F. Suddenly, like kernels of popcorn in a popper, a few molecules of water along the shore will yield to the penetrating cold by freezing and expanding, beginning a series of chain reactions that radiate and spread, ultimately forming a thin film of ice that expands softly across the lake in the immense blackness.

The next day, in the gray, subdued light of early morning, faint wisps of smoke will rise from the chimneys of cottages surrounding the lake, and the sharp scent of burning ash from some distant, soothing warm woodburner will hover in the tranquil, arctic air that whispers above this unique frozen desert, where tiny grains of loose snow glide freely across the desolate, slick surface.

Several such mornings will pass, and as the blanket of ice thickens, ice anglers will watch anxiously as they begin spooling their jig rods in a sort of traditional, preparative ritual—until early one cold, still dawn, when some robe-clad soul sipping from a steaming mug at a cottage kitchen table will gaze through a frost-glazed pane and discern the silhouette of a zealous ice angler appearing against the rising, molten-metal sun.

I've often seen hard-cores taking grave chances to create this scene, often appearing on fresh ice wearing insulated, waterproof clothing while pushing inflatable boats, canoes or jon boats along in front of them—just in case. I've even seen anglers wearing chest waders and belly boats as they saunter out, inch by inch, onto a thin coating of shore ice. Of course, this is going to extremes, yet I can relate to their feelings of urgency. After all, first-ice often produces the most consistent, productive fishing of the season, and bluegill action is often extraordinary.

Exactly why this tremendous first-ice bonanza occurs has been debated by ice anglers for years, yet there may be several explanations for this phenomenon. In part, perhaps, it's because early season ice fishing offers numerous advantages over late season open water fishing. You don't have to worry about icy launches, frozen gas lines and tillers, dead batteries, or cold fall winds making boat control difficult. More importantly, the first-ice period is characterized by the fact few people actively fish through late fall and struggle against such conditions—so by first-ice, most lakes haven't been bombarded by excessive fishing pressure for an extended period of time, and aquatic life has ample opportunity to move into their preferred and easily accessible shallow water areas.

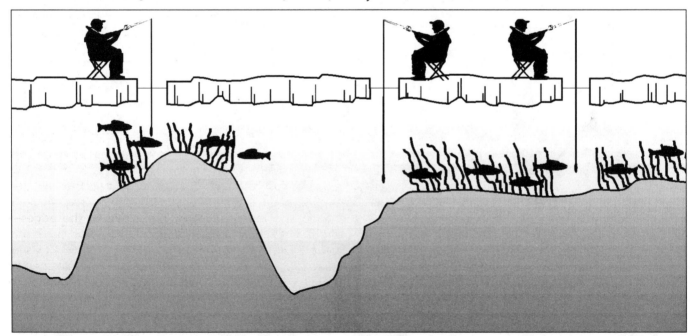

During early ice, pockets and holes amid vegetation in shallow bays, on flats and shallow-topped structures are often hot spots for sunfish and bluegill activity.

**Small, classic first-ice areas must be fished early. After other anglers arrive, such areas are easily fished out.**

Just after ice-up, "stability" returns to the lake environment. Fall turnover is complete, and fierce winter winds stop lashing the surface and stirring up the water. As this stability returns, bluegills begin schooling in tight concentrations in the cover, oxygen and forage-rich shallows. This makes them readily accessible, because key patterns inevitably revolve around easy-to-identify areas supporting a plentiful food source.

As the ice continues forming, calming wave swept waters and increasing sunlight penetration, forage species such as plankton and zooplankton begin assembling in shallow bays and are subsequently followed by baitfish, and eventually, sunfish and bluegills. Over time, these concentrations build significantly—all while the ice thickens, making these fish particularly vulnerable to first-ice anglers. Furthermore, because these fish have been eating heartily without being disturbed much, they not only become concentrated, but fat, feisty, and less wary—and this creates fabulous fishing opportunities for anxious early season ice anglers.

Shallow, weedy flats such as vegetated canals, sloughs, coves, bays, main lake flats, the tops of sunken islands, shallow shoreline points or bars all produce well. For best results, look for holes and edges within and along the weeds to attract and hold the most bluegills. If you can't locate such a spot, create your own by dropping a dipsy depthfinder down the hole and sifting it through the vegetation below. Not only will this alert you to the presence of weeds, but also stir up food items that often attract bluegills.

After the short-lived rush, these classic shallow-water first-ice areas offering food and cover will continue producing fish—just bear in mind not all areas are cre-

ated equal. Smaller bays and structures are likely to draw smaller numbers of bluegills, and consequently, be fished out by early season pressure more quickly than larger, more structurally diverse bays and structures offering additional secondary cover. Larger areas offer more opportunity for the fish to spread out, and specific places within these large areas will likely produce better than others, thus, consistent first-ice catches from these locations depend on the angler's ability to become adept at

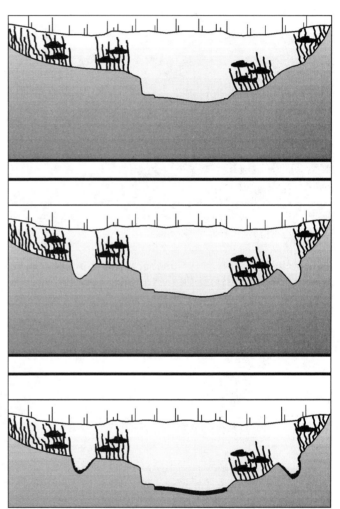

**Search for "spots on the spots." During first ice, you might catch a bluegill every 20 minutes from pockets amid shallow vegetation, but move to the edges—which are the focal points for feeding—and catch one every 15 minutes. (Top). Find pockets offering a weed line and a depth change, and you'll increase your catch to one every ten minutes (Middle). If this depth change also features a bottom content change, you might catch one every five minutes (Bottom). Have the weed line intersect a depth change, bottom content transition and mix of both density and type of vegetation, and you might catch a fish every couple of minutes.**

To catch fish like this, use a mobile approach to search for areas most likely to draw quality fish. Often, such areas offer the largest abundance and diversity of forage.

determining specific areas within these large bays that draw concentrations of fish.

Edges are a primary illustration. The edges of pockets or holes in the weeds, weed lines, changes in depth or bottom content, variations in water temperature near underwater springs and current, or changes in vegetation density or type are all primary examples. When available, creeks and channels connected to structurally diverse coves or bays are also excellent first-ice hot spots, as these areas all act as "structures on the structure" that attract and concentrate bluegills.

Why such areas? Simple! Changes in environment often coincide with changes in the diversity of species present—and this certainly applies to forage. A variety of minnow species, insect larvae, phytoplankton, zooplankton and crustaceans relate to different habitats, thus, areas where environments overlap usually offer the largest abundance and diversity of forage—in other words, produce a virtual smorgasbord for sunfish and bluegills.

First-ice, you can also generalize and assume the most productive of these areas will be relatively shallow, where fresh, green vegetation, cover and food all coexist. However, close proximity to deeper water becomes increasingly important during pronounced weather changes, or more importantly, as the season progresses.

In fact, it's likely they'll move in and out of the shallows periodically as the season progresses. To locate schools of winter sunfish/bluegills consistently, you must be prepared to systematically fish these areas to properly identify where most bluegills are concentrated for the time

When you catch a quality fish, note the situation and conditions you're fishing. Given similar conditions, fishing similar areas in other parts of the lake often results in successful catches.

Say you find a large shoreline point adjoining a classic first-ice bay. You might start out fishing shallow pencil reeds and cabbage near shore in the bay, or pockets and their edges throughout the bay, then begin working over the flat on top of the adjacent point and along its edges and tip, sampling each area carefully in an attempt to maximize your catch. Meticulously evaluate each structure, possible migration routes and holding areas. Is there a large shallow feeding shelf with deep water nearby? Is cover present, and if so, what type? Are there any secondary edges, points, turns or holding areas present that might be especially productive? If so, how are the fish positioned on them? Be sure to make mental notes of what you find, and fish each feature thoroughly. After you've worked the area, review a lake map in an attempt to find similar areas, fish them, and compare notes. Patterns will be revealed.

Generally, you'll find gradual, cover-laden primary contours and breaks are the most productive first-ice

**If you've been catching bluegills shallow and there's a severe weather change, search carefully for suspended bluegills holding in nearby deeper water.**

you're fishing. The bluegills may be in shallow weeds one evening, and with significant weather changes overnight, may trigger a daily movement along a migration route into heavier cover or deeper water, so always be sure to utilize a mobile approach following any major weather change, checking for unusual or specific features drawing fish. And remember, if you can pinpoint the reason bluegills are holding in a particular area, they'll likely be in similar spots on other parts of the lake, and your catch rate will probably increase with each similar location you try.

Sure, there are times you will catch loads of fish from a single location, but often consistent winter catches are the result of taking a few bluegills from scattered, smaller schools—so you'll want to implement a mobile approach. You might try focusing your efforts on top of the shallow food shelf, the adjoining drop-off and base of the drop along the identified migration route, always being sure to systematically work each segment of the structure thoroughly.

**As shallow water vegetation dies off, oxygen concentrations in the shallows drop and bluegills move deeper.**

holding areas, but steep ones can be good, too, depending on the lake and the prevailing conditions—so be sure to fish both shallow and deep and try various times of the day or evening. If there's a severe weather change, search carefully for deeper or suspended bluegills holding off these weed lines as well.

Simply put, if you combine fishing smarter and more efficiently with a mobile approach, you'll catch more fish.

## Mid-Winter

Just the thought of sitting on a cold, windy, snow-blown lake struggling to ice a few fussy mid-winter bluegills is enough to convince many anglers to give up their efforts and turn their attention to sport shows, football, or cleaning their tackle boxes.

But not me. Beneath that foot or two of creaking ice and deep drifts of snow, in the dark, calm depths below, hand-sized bluegills are waiting to be caught. Sure, I'll be the first to admit mid-winter sunfish and bluegills can be difficult to locate and catch—but by using special methodology, it's not as difficult as you might think.

As the season wears on, thickening ice and deep snow filter out sunlight, shallow water cover begins dying off and the process of decay begins overtaking photosynthesis, creating an oxygen deficit. To further complicate matters, diverse shallow water forage bases become dramatically reduced. Insects go into hibernation or die off, as do tiny crustaceans. Inch-long fry have long since outgrown their usefulness to most panfish, and minnow stocks have been depleted to the point of minimal usage. These factors, often combined with heavy

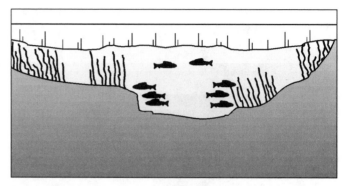

**Just remember, the term "deep" is relative. On deep lakes, mid-winter bluegills may move down long migration routes into water 20 or 30 feet deep. In smaller ponds and lakes, these movements may simply consist of short shifts into deeper pockets or holes only several feet deep.**

fishing pressure and overharvest, force sunfish and bluegills to respond to their changing environment.

Because this environmental change causes severe stress for shallow, cover-loving species such as sunfish, they may hold in place and become semi-dormant—typical behavior for green, redear and longear sunfish—or move with the bluegills, behavior more typical of the more commonly caught pumpkinseed. Given this knowledge, from this point forward we'll simply refer to winter sunfish/bluegill patterns as "bluegill" patterns, simply because pumpkinseed will closely follow the same patterns as bluegills. Other sunfish now become largely incidental catches.

With shallow water vegetation dying off, oxygen concentrations in the shallows drop, and any remaining

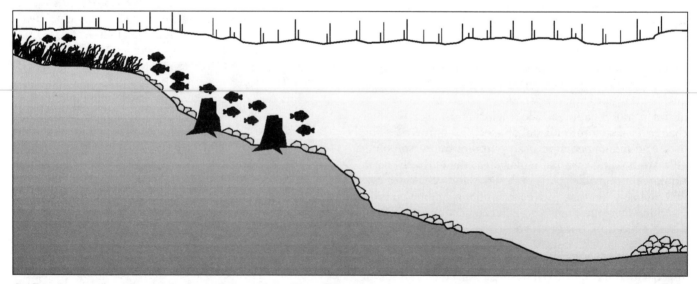

**As first ice wanes into mid-winter, most bluegills will progressively move into more stable, deeper water, either by sliding down a migration route adjoining a structural feature, or on shallower lakes, dropping deeper into pockets or holes. Such areas offering bottom content changes and cover in the form of vegetation, wood or broken rock are the best producers.**

Mid-winter bluegills tend to concentrate around prominent "edges," specific areas where two distinctly different conditions meet. These might be weed lines, depth changes or bottom content transitions.

forage, now lacking sufficient cover and oxygen counts, move deeper. Bluegills merely follow the line of healthy green vegetation, forage and increased oxygen counts deeper—so should you.

Provided adequate oxygen exists in the depths, mid-winter bluegills often seek the deepest water available. Note I did not say the deepest water in the lake—but the deepest water available. This might be a beaver run toward a lodge in a shallow bay, a pocket within a shallow flat, a dredged channel in a bay or a secondary channel in a cove or creek arm—but rest assured, the fish will move. This is particularly common behavior with larger bluegills. While their smaller counterparts tend to lag quietly behind in shallower water, they still show a progressive movement toward the depths.

Not every deep hole is productive, so search them carefully. The best holes usually offer access to shallow water, and lead to deep water drop-offs and offer some type of food-attracting cover such as a vegetated drop-off, flooded timber or bottom-content change. Edges such as these adjoining deep-water cover are often especially good, as they provide food, shelter and something

for bluegills to relate to, plus easy access to deep water. Search for such spots carefully with your electronics.

Deep-water cover often concentrates invertebrates, minnows and plankton, too—all of which provide forage for bluegills—so most deep water fish usually remain near the bottom. However, don't forget about suspended fish. On some lakes, oxygen counts may drop near the bottom, pushing bluegills upward. And zooplankton, a primary food source of mid-winter bluegills, are mobile creatures, moving up and down the water column daily. Big 'gills feeding on plankton may simply follow this food source and drift high above deep-water cover. Don't ignore them.

Just remember, while bluegills gradually begin migrating toward progressively deeper water, "deep" is relative. Deep water in some smaller ponds and lakes might be 10 feet, while in other waters deep may be 20 or 30 feet. This often scares many ice anglers, because they feel this transition makes bluegills difficult to find, but don't give up. Rather, knowing the change is coming, begin preparing. Remember that as the season progresses bluegills move toward deeper holes within bays or flats, and eventually onto nearby drop-offs and adjoining mid-depth hard bottom flats, bays, points, bars, and reefs featuring combinations of weed growth, cover and forage just outside shallower, first-ice hot spots. Simply adjust and follow the fish.

This might sound difficult, but like first-ice bluegills of the shallows, you'll notice deeper mid-winter 'gills tend to concentrate tightly around prominent "edges"— specific places where two distinctly different areas or conditions meet, such as weed lines or distinct bottom or depth changes. These deep-water edges are especially productive if two or more such characteristics overlap in the same location. For instance, if a sudden drop-off featuring a bottom content change coincides with an area where weed growth is present to the break then abruptly ends, you've likely encountered a highly productive mid-winter bluegill spot.

Remember the importance of forage. You might find what appears to be a perfect combination of cover and structural features—but if no forage is present, it's unlikely substantial concentrations of active bluegills will be, either. However, if a dominant forage base is available, these areas may not only attract fish, but may provide numerous clues regarding the depth you'll catch the most fish as well. For example, because winter bluegills depend on phytoplankton or zooplankton as a primary food source on many lakes and phytoplankton need light to survive, they're often suspended. Thus, in lakes where bluegills are dependent on plankton, they're likely to suspend above primary structural features and edges.

Such factors partly explain why mid-season bluegills often show such a strong affinity toward suspending. Bluegills may still feed on bottom, but usually end up

**Once oxygen levels are depleted both shallow and deep, bluegills may have no choice but to suspend over deep water.**

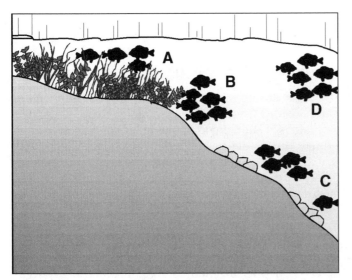

Often during mid-winter, you'll find yourself fishing shoreline breaks along deep, vegetated extensions of submerged points, shoals or bars which act as primary migration routes toward deeper water. Given ideal conditions, mid-winter sunfish and bluegills may move into the shallows (A), although most of their time will be spent along weed lines (B), secondary breaks (C), or suspended over deep water (D).

suspending most of the time because that's where the food is. In addition, just as oxygen deficits occur in the shallows, oxygen depletion may also occur in the depths. This is especially true of shallow, eutrophic waters without adequate flow from feeder streams or springs that replenish diminished oxygen levels. Once oxygen levels are depleted both shallow and deep, bluegills may have no choice but to suspend.

Many anglers cringe when they hear this, because they feel extra work is required to locate these stressed, suspended fish—especially on big water. However, if you can determine which structures have been supporting the greatest concentrations of forage and, more importantly, where the most active fish are holding in relation to them and the times they're most active, you can continue catching these fish because they typically suspend near these features—and they're easily located using sonar.

Sonar can be used to decipher depth, structure, bottom content, vegetation, plankton, your lure—and suspended bluegills. Look closely enough and you may even be able to determine specific types of vegetation they're relating to. Broadleaf cabbage or coontail, for example, stand thick and high, while sandgrass and chara are thin and grow close to bottom.

If you become adept at this fascinating sport and begin focusing your efforts in more specific areas, you'll find yourself increasingly fishing pockets or prominent edges of this thick cover within and along the most productive structures. And by doing so, you can stay on bluegills and enjoy productive angling right through the mid-winter period.

You'll have to experiment to see precisely where the most active fish are positioned. Active bluegills spend most of the winter trying to regulate their body comfort by moving up and down along most migration routes, in a constant effort to find environmental stability near a viable food source—and it's up to you to determine where these conditions will concur while you're on the ice. But do so, and mid-winter bluegills won't be a mystery anymore.

By the way, once you find productive migration routes and deep holes providing adequate cover, food and oxygen, be sure to mark them. Chances are they'll produce successful trips for many years to come, because big 'gills

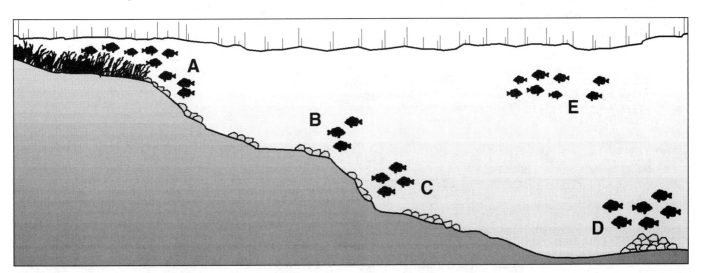

Although some smaller straggler bluegills may remain shallow during mid-winter (A), most hold along secondary breaklines (B,C) on migration routes, or suspend over deep water (E). Some mid-winter bluegills, particularly larger individuals, also hold on deep, main lake structures such as rock piles (D).

frequently use the same deep holes winter after winter. Identify these locations, and your catch rates will soar.

## Fishing the Breaklines

Often during mid-winter, you'll find yourself fishing more distinct shoreline breaks along deep, vegetated extensions of submerged points, shoals or bars that act as primary migration routes toward main-lake deep-water structures. Migration routes featuring gradually tapering points and irregular, cover-laden edges are generally most productive.

As throughout much of the winter, look for these conditions in combination with other secondary transition areas. For example, cover-laden edges where bottom content changes from soft to hard, or a change in vegetation type, depth, current or temperature all draw concentrations of forage, and thus, bluegills. Often, bluegills hold or suspend along such breaklines near the edge of the flat, yet I've often found the largest bluegills holding slightly deeper than active schools of smaller fish. Don't forget larger bluegills lack the strong schooling instinct of their smaller counterparts, and may scatter away from primary and secondary breaks, perhaps even moving onto adjoining main lake structures or suspending over deep, open water. Use sonar to locate them.

## Late Winter

As mid-winter progresses toward late winter, bluegills tend to move even deeper—then reverse movement and begin staging near drop-offs adjacent to spring

Often during mid-winter, you'll find yourself fishing more distinct shoreline breaks along deep, vegetated extensions of submerged points, shoals or bars that act as primary migration routes toward main-lake deep-water structures. Routes featuring gradually tapering points and irregular cover-laden edges are generally most productive. (Courtesy Reef Runner Lures)

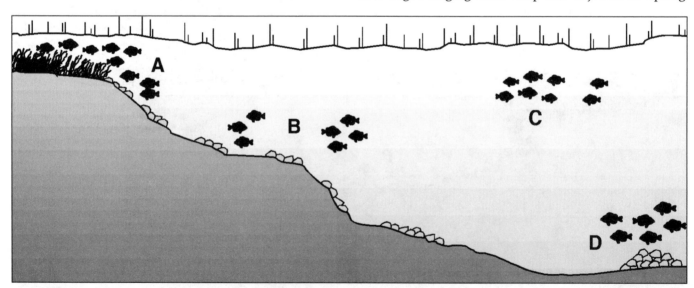

By late ice, scattered sunfish and bluegill still holding in mid-winter areas such as secondary breaks (B), suspended over deep water (C) or holding on deep water structures such as rock piles (D) make movements back toward the shallows, primarily shallow spawning bays (A). As these scattered fish accumulate, large concentrations of easily accessible, active fish are available, creating the classic "late ice" bite.

clouds of suspended plankton—or depending on the lake and oxygen counts, may also drop to bottom, feeding on worms, insect larvae or tiny minnows.

When targeting specifically where to fish, consider the influence of low oxygen levels, daily weather changes and light levels on daily movements. Bluegills may make early morning and late-afternoon feeding forays along the tops of points and humps, shallow breaks and food shelves when conditions warrant, then move down associated breaklines or away from the structure and suspend high over open water during the day. You should, too. With bluegills on most lakes, such movements often occur daily as they follow a pattern of going deeper during midday, then rising during twilight and evening hours to feed, and if you don't move with them, your results will be somewhat less than exceptional.

Just prior to ice-out, bluegills move even closer to main lake flats and spawning grounds, following primary breaklines—but unless suspended, seldom stray far from breakline cover. Gradually sloping extensions of deep lake points and bars are always good, but those featuring weeds, brush or timber adjacent to shallow spawning flats are generally the best.

Doing your homework prior to hitting the ice usually pays of. By simply checking a lake map, you'll be

**Bluegills may make early morning and late afternoon feeding forays along the tops of points and humps, shallow breaks and food shelves when conditions warrant, then move down associated breaklines or away from the structure and suspend high over open water during the day. (Courtesy Custom Jigs and Spins)**

spawning areas before eventually moving back into shallow spawning flats.

Begin by focusing your efforts along the base of primary breaks—or, when necessary, on secondary flats—targeting those adjacent to spring spawning areas. Although large schools typically don't hold on secondary flats, if these areas are substantial in terms of providing suitable cover and forage, they might concentrate migrating bluegills moving in from the depths.

Late-winter bluegills may even move onto adjacent secondary breaklines in search of forage, where they're likely to suspend. Still, always closely check various depths for active fish during the late-winter period. Schools of bluegills often suspend while feeding on

**Areas featuring bottom content and cover changes concentrate a larger diversity of forage in relatively small, hard-to-find locations many anglers overlook.**

**Large bluegills seldom school, are extremely wary and less competitive for food, and furthermore, tend to move under the ice more than most ice anglers realize. (Courtesy Reef Runner Lures)**

able to locate several potentially productive structural features adjacent to secondary breaklines, where deep breakline bottom irregularities and secondary cover appear to provide shelter and form possible breakline migration routes between deep, main lake features and shallow spawning areas.

Holding points along these migration routes may also prove productive. Such areas along the route featuring combinations of secondary structure, cover, forage and bottom content changes can prove to be extremely productive late ice hot spots. In addition, specific microstructures such as humps, holes, points and turns along these routes may concentrate late ice bluegills, creating even more productive patterns. I've found the largest bluegills are often attracted to these unique holding areas because their characteristic bottom content and cover changes concentrate such a large diversity of forage in relatively small, hard-to-find areas most anglers miss.

Locating late winter breakline bluegills can be one of the toughest challenges in ice angling—and even if you're able to find these fish, there's still no guarantee you'll be able to catch them. However, you can greatly improve your odds by regularly changing tactics, moving to new locations and exploring different depths. If you remain persistent as you search, fishing systematically and putting in extra effort along primary and secondary breaklines constituting migration routes, things often turn your way. By pinpointing the right structures providing a wide choice of depth, forage and cover options for your quarry, you'll pattern the bluegills and maximize your catch.

## Ice Out

Just before ice-out, bluegills generally begin moving toward and begin staging just outside spring spawning

**As bluegills grow, their forage preferences shift from insects to shallow water plankton to deep water plankton, small minnows, crustaceans, snails and other invertebrates that often utilize specific habitats—another little something trophy bluegill anglers can use as a tool to pattern their quarry.**

areas on primary breaklines. As they concentrate, the ice and snow pack melts above their heads, increasing sunlight penetration, increasing plankton counts and bluegill activity—hence the classic, shallow-water late-ice bite.

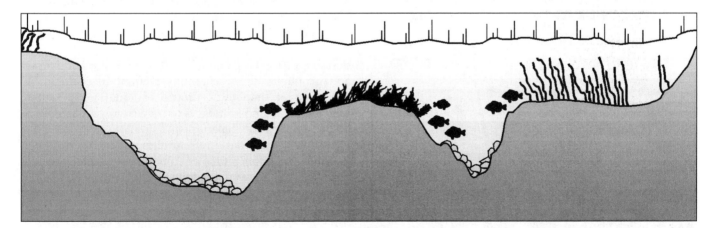

**Large bluegills have a strong affinity for edges, such as where deep water meets shallow water along the edge of a bar, shoal or sunken island—especially if vegetation, wood or broken rock is available. Areas also offering a bottom content transition from hard to soft increase the potential by adding more "edge" effect.**

But again I emphasize: every lake is different and subject to a unique variety of conditions, so the patterns we're covering here are generalities that must be adapted to the water you're fishing and the exact conditions at hand—and the only way to accomplish this consistently is through experimentation.

## "Bull" Bluegill Patterns

"Bull" bluegills are trophy fish, those measuring 10 inches or longer, or boasting weights of 1 pound or more. The search for "bulls" begins with lake type. True trophy bluegill lakes are either small and seldom fished, or expansive and feature just the right combination of depth and amounts of cover and forage for producing large fish.

Smaller, fertile bodies of water typically support few large predators such as pike and walleye, which keep bluegill populations in check. As a result, smaller lakes often sustain higher panfish populations, creating more tiny mouths to feed—in turn creating a somewhat limited food supply, and consequently, a stunted bluegill population.

In addition, the characteristically fertile waters of these small, shallow lakes often feature a murky coloration and thick weed growth, providing cover and making it even more difficult for these already high populations to be accessed by a limited number of predators, allowing more bluegills to survive and promoting further stunting.

However, large bodies of water typically offer relatively clear waters, perhaps showing a slight green tint. These lakes support an abundance of tiny life forms called plankton that support scores of tiny baitfish, and typically feature only moderate weed growth—which in turn supports the best potential for growing trophy bluegills. Larger bluegills are more rare, seldom school, are extremely wary and less competitive for food, and tend to move more under the ice than most anglers realize. In fact, a variety of variables may compel them to change

**Many bluegills have been iced using standard jigglesticks with linewinders and jig pole combos—and they will continue to be caught this way for many years to come. (Courtesy Northland Fishing Tackle)**

locations, and fishing strategies must be adjusted accordingly. Learn these variables and their associated patterns, and you'll catch more trophy bluegills.

Like their smaller counterparts, larger bluegill develop location patterns strongly associated to vegetation. It's just that sparse to moderate growths of deeper aquatic plants in loose groups offer more ecologically sound cover than thick groves of aquatic vegetation, which permit small bluegills to hide from predators and ruin the ecological "balance" of a small lake.

In turn, true "bulls" often follow distinctly different patterns than their smaller counterparts. While weed growth on shallow flats almost always attracts smaller bluegills throughout the winter, "bull" bluegills tend to relate to moderately vegetated mid-depth flats and deeper, main lake structures—in fact, I've often found the biggest 'gills relating to weed growth located in moderate to large size mid-depth, hard-bottom flats and bays or on larger, deeper, hard-bottom bars and rock piles.

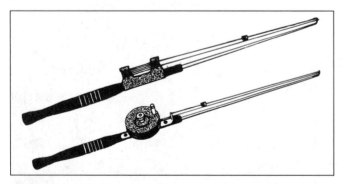

**Many sunfish and bluegills have been caught on standard jigglesticks and jig poles, and used in the right location, such equipment will continue to catch fish—economically, mind you—for many years to come.**

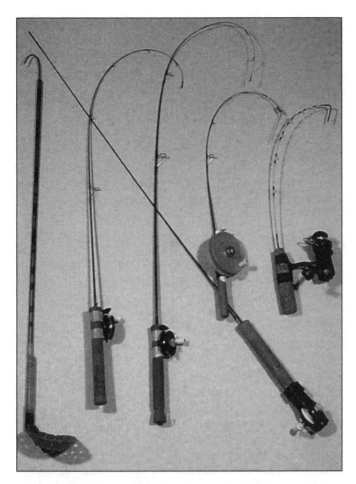

**More and more anglers are discovering the advantages of using lightweight, sensitive ultralight and micro rods featuring sturdy butt sections and fast action tips.**

Bigger bluegills also show a stronger affinity to use edges, such as where deep water meets shallow water along the edge of a bar—especially if weed growth, timber or brush is available. Areas where distinct weed growth meets an open area or where bottom content changes—sand to muck or gravel to rock, especially when weeds are present—are trophy locations.

Edges are secondary to forage, and this becomes even more significant as bluegills grow to trophy status, because the diets of large bluegills are distinctly different from the diets of small ones. As bluegills grow, their forage preferences shift from insects and shallow water plankton to deep water plankton, small minnows, crustaceans, snails and other invertebrates that utilize specific habitats—something trophy bluegill anglers can use as a tool to pattern their quarry.

For example, deep water plankton don't follow the same patterns as shallow water plankton—and this knowledge provides numerous clues regarding where you'll catch the largest 'gills most consistently on mid-lake structures. Deep water phytoplankton largely float freely

with the currents and need light to survive, so they're often found suspended near the surface. The same is true of some types of zooplankton, such as copepods, while other planktonic species—for example, Daphnia—tend to relate more to mid-depth ranges. Recognizing and understanding the fish's primary forage provides clues regarding where most bluegills will hold—and in this case, the situation explains why deep water, trophy winter bluegills often exhibit the affinity to suspend.

The precise depth plankton suspend is influenced by several factors, including ice thickness, snow cover and light intensity. Zooplankton such as Daphnia often migrate, rising when it's dark and descending when it's light. So while main lake structural elements will often hold large concentrations of plankton, trophy bluegills usually move around on these structures horizontally and vertically in response to planktonic movements, demanding angler mobility and versatility for consistent success.

## Effective Winter Bluegill Strategies

Because bluegills are known to inspect lures and baits closely, the best way to hook them is to use sensitive rods, light lines, and small baits.

**Most standard ultralight rods feature a fluorescent colored tip for added visibility—in my opinion, bright orange is most visible.**

Larger bluegills are occasionally taken on tip-downs and balance tip-ups placed strategically along deep weed lines and deep, mid-lake structures. These should be rigged with long, light leaders tipped with tiny treble hooks and minnows or grubs, but such catches are rare. Of all panfishes, bluegills are one of the most suited to jigging.

## Jigging Sunfish and Bluegills

To start with, you need balanced equipment. Many bluegills have been iced using standard jigglesticks with linewinders, and jig pole combos—and they will continue to be caught this way. The systems are simple—all you do is use a dipsy depthfinder or plummet to find your depth, set your bobber or float to the desired depth, remove the depthfinder, bait your hook or teardrop lure, and start fishing. In addition to being effective and simple, these outfits are also relatively inexpensive.

However, more and more ice anglers are discovering the advantages of using lightweight, sensitive ultralight and micro rods from one to four feet long featuring sturdy butt sections and fast action tips. HT's Polar Gold Ultralight and Ice Blue Ultralights are excellent examples.

These rods feature fast-action tips that are so sensitive no float or spring bobber is necessary. The rod tip easily registers bites by itself—the same way a spring bobber would—except this spring bobber is built right into the rod. This design drastically reduces the number of bluegills you'll miss because you'll see and feel every hit. In addition, ultralight action rods expand the amount of sport and fun by letting bluegills fight to their maximum capacity, yet still hook and fight fish with precision control.

Most standard ultralight rods feature a fluorescent colored tip for added visibility—orange is best. This pro-

When fishing relatively shallow water, small plastic ice reels come in handy for storing line—plus offer a drag system in the event you hook a large fish.

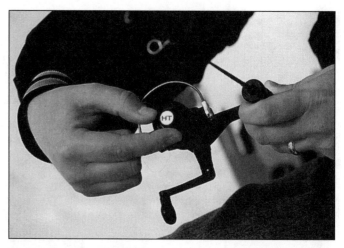

In deep water, ultralight spinning reels with a smooth drag and easy-turning bail roller work well for managing light lines.

vides good contrast against a dark colored hole, making the slightest bump from a fish seen easily as it can be felt, enabling the angler to sharpen hook setting reactions. Some even come with glow tips, for unsurpassed visibility for twilight or evening fishing.

Another advantage to a fast action rod is it allows you to use light line without the greater risk of breakage. The "give" in the tip absorbs the shock of the hookset and transfers it to the lure smoothly without placing too much force on the line. Of course, the ideal rod taper varies greatly. When fishing deep water, a longer blank with a short, sensitive tip that tapers quickly into solid backbone is important for solid hook sets and control. In shallow water, the fast tip can continue further down the blank.

Ice rods of these lengths should have at least three guides—better yet, four, five, six or more—in addition to the tip-top. This helps evenly distribute tension between the line and rod. Poorly placed or too few guides result in too much tension on the line and lost sensitivity, things you can't afford with ounce-rated lines.

Reels? When fishing relatively shallow water, small plastic ice reels will do the trick. In deeper water, ultralight spinning reels work better, provided the drag is smooth and the bail roller turns easily—sticky drags and poor quality bail rollers spell disaster for ultralight lines. Besides, just try hand-over-handing 30 feet of light line. If you can do it consistently without tangling it around your boots you're more dexterous than me.

This brings us to line. I feel the lighter, the better. Why? First, water below the ice has less algae and floating material within it than in summer, so water clarity is much higher. Low visibility lines reduce the chance of spooking fussy jumbos under these conditions. Secondly, light lines help balance your tackle. There are a number of 1, 2, 3 and 4 pound test lines on the market today that

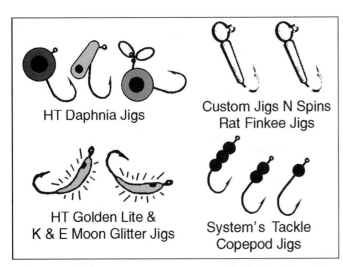

**Bluegills feed heavily on plankton during winter, particularly zooplankton such as Daphnia and copepods. Matching your lure size, shape, color and action to the size, shape and movements of this prey can dramatically increase your winter catch rates. The lures illustrated here are all excellent imitators.**

provide the ultimate in balance and sensitivity when fishing super-sensitive ultralights.

Sound too light? Don't worry! These light monofilaments are much stronger than you might first expect, and when blended into an ultralight system provide the ultimate in ultralight balance, heightened sensitivity and superior lure action. When spooled on a high-quality reel, these light lines offer few, if any, breakage problems under normal conditions.

If you've never fished ultralight mono, you'll be surprised how much better lure action is with thinner diameter lines. Don't believe me? Then try this: tie two tiny ice lures (preferably of the same brand to generate a "standard") onto a strand of six, four, two, one and 3/4 pound line. Begin working the lures just under the ice, and jig with various hops and twitches, watching how each movement transfers to the lures and carefully noting how each wiggle causes the lures to react. You'll see how lighter line allows the bait to appear more loose and natural, dramatically improving the action and sensitivity of tiny teardrops.

To further convince yourself, continue this testing process using a stiff ice rod and super sensitive ultralight ice rod. Since "soft action" rods perfectly balance the use of light line and lures—increasing sensitivity and lure action—you'll be surprised by the striking difference between the presentation control and lure action presented by the light rod and stiff rod. Obviously, these characteristics are critically important to an effective presentation, because big bluegills often study a bait carefully before striking, and anything that looks unnatural is likely to be rejected.

Ultralight ice rods provide another critical dimension by counteracting the shock of hooksets and hard fighting fish that might otherwise snap ultralight lines. This is just a small aspect of properly balanced ice tackle—but something critically important when fishing ultralight systems, particularly in deep water. Just remember to re-tie your knots frequently, check for abrasion after every fish, and use only high break-strength knots such as improved clinch, "Trilene style" knots, snell knots, nail knots or loop knots. Personally, I favor loop knots, which are easy to tie and allow your lure to swing naturally.

Line color is another important issue. I prefer gray or green, both of which are easy to work with on the ice, but tend to become less visible underwater. Clear would be the next option, followed by blue and the bright yellow. The argument for using brighter blue and yellow lines is the enhanced ability to see slight line movements indicating light bites; the disadvantage is increased visibility to fish. If bluegills are striking light and you wish to use brighter lines, I recommend tying a long, less visible length of monofilament or fly tippet to the brighter line, thus gaining the advantage of both.

## Choosing the Right Lures

To top off this high tech ultralight system, you'll also need to choose the right lures. I searched a long time to find lures that had the appearance of small copepods and cladocerans, the tiny organisms bluegills rely on as primary forage during the food scarce frozen water period. Because bluegills often prefer a particular member of these organisms called Daphnia, I collected several from

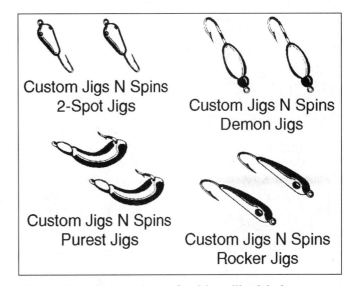

**When choosing ice lures for bluegills, it's important to select tiny, precisely balanced flies and jigs. Custom Jigs and Spins offers several excellent models.**

I generally use Rat Finkees when 'gills are fussy or inactive, because they can be worked with ultra-slow, gentle lift-drop movements. (Courtesy Custom Jigs and Spins)

my lake and after examining them under a microscope, identified and began to study their appearance and movements.

Once memorized, I started searching through several retail stores and bait shops looking for good Daphnia imitations, and managed to find a few. The first is simply called the "Daphnia." They come in several models, and all are shaped like a Daphnia. Some are painted, some offer prism tape finishes—the flash appeals to the fish's sight. One model also features fins on a tiny split ring, which have a tendency to click against the lure body when jigged, attracting bluegills through sound. The Daphnia with fins also allows you to tie to the split ring, so the lure moves freely and naturally.

Another good Daphnia imitation is the Moon Glow, made by K&E Tackle of Hastings, Michigan. The phosphorescent paint attracts fish during low-light periods when big bluegills are most active, and in stained or dark colored waters where fish have difficulty seeing. The lure's counterparts, K&E's Moon Glitter, Lindy's Glow Glitters and HT's Golden Lites, perform well in clear water and on bright days by producing an irresistible flash that attracts 'gills. Each of these baits also features short, relatively heavy bodies for their small size, providing a better sense of "feel"—just be sure to tie these jigs with a loop knot. They don't come with a split ring, and won't jiggle freely if tied with a standard knot.

Copepods are another primary winter forage for bluegill, and again, I was able to find a good likeness under the same name. Made by System Tackle, "Copepods" are basically a hook with one, two or three small round beads soldered to the hook and brightly colored—highly effective.

As for lure specifics, it's important to choose tiny, precisely balanced ice flies and jigs. Custom Jigs and Spins offers a number of premium ultralight ice jigs, including the 2-Spot, Demon, Purest and Rocker—favorites of many—and their #12 Rat Finkees are undoubtedly among the finest and most productive ultralight bluegill jigs ever produced. I generally use Rat Finkees when the 'gills are fussy or inactive, because they can be worked with ultra-slow, gentle lift-drop movements, and their lightweight design is easier for fussy fish to suck in. In fact, the Rat Finkee is one of my all time favorite jigs for bluegill.

Rockers are vertically oriented baits with a long, thin body on a long-shanked aberdeen hook. The unique profile and action works great for active gills. An alternative jigging style with this type of bait is the "rolling" technique. Take your line between your fingers and gently roll it, causing the lure to spin rapidly in place. Often,

If you know bluegills are present but they're being fussy, use ultralight tackle and move your lure gently with sporadic, short twitches, gradually working the bait up and down a fraction of an inch at a time. I usually have multiple rods rigged with various lures and ready to fish, so changing baits can be accomplished with a minimum of retying.

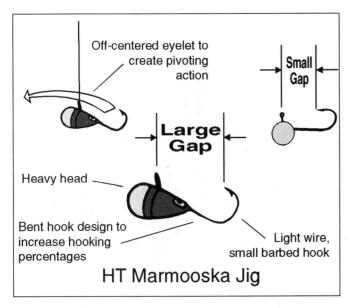

HT Marmooska Jig

Off-centered eyelet to create pivoting action

Small Gap

Large Gap

Heavy head

Bent hook design to increase hooking percentages

Light wire, small barbed hook

**The European Marmooska Jig, introduced to the North American market by HT Enterprises, is one of the most effective bluegill jigs available because of its heavy head, light-wire, small barbed hook, bent hook design and off centered eyelet that creates a pivoting action that turns the hook toward biting fish.**

this method works better than traditional jigging methods when bluegills are fussy.

Two important hints to keep in mind while ultralight jigging: First, be mobile. Try different holes placed strategically along migration routes, and fish your lure at various strata within each hole. Secondly, regardless of the lure you're fishing, pause frequently. Most hits occur while the lure is settling. If you know bluegills are there and only being fussy, move your lure gently and softly in sporadic, short twitches, gradually working the bait up and down a fraction of an inch at a time.

When bluegills really get fussy, the European Marmooska jig has impressed me most. These little gems have been the secret of European ice pros for many years—but have just been introduced to the United States in recent years. The concept behind their effectiveness is really quite simple: Marmooskas are a light-wire, small-barbed jig with a precisely balanced, relatively heavy head. The heavy head creates better "feel" with today's ultralight ice rods, making the subtle hits of finicky bluegills easier to detect.

Secondly, the small-barbed, light-wire hook creates unsurpassed hooking percentages—in fact, the tiny, ultra-sharp small-barbed hook is the main reason for the incredible effectiveness of this lure. Large barbed jigs simply impede solid hook sets, especially with ultralight tackle, and the cause of more lost fish than most ice anglers would care to admit. However, the small-barbed

Marmooska design means less "zap" is needed to obtain a solid hook set—an important point when you consider how little power is available in most fast-tipped ultralight ice rods.

Small-barbed hooks also help in another respect. Remember, bluegills generally inspect baits and lures closely, ignoring anything of the wrong size, shape, color or action. Occasionally, something simple as squishing the end of the maggot or grub with an oversized, unsharpened hook kills your bait—greatly reducing the chance of tempting big 'gills, particularly in clear water. With a sharp, light-wire hook/tiny-barbed lure, however, you can easily nip a maggot just through the skin, thereby keeping the bait active and increasing your catch.

By the way, both the Marmooska and the Rat Finkee—two of my all time favorite bluegill ice lures—are horizontal baits, and since I've found most big bluegills hit while "jigging down" rather than up, this feature enhances effective hook-setting percentages by exposing the hook sideways. Another advantage of these two lures is the head design. The head on the Rat Finkee is tiny, while the Marmooska's is "off center" from the shank. These two small details provide a greater gap between the tiny hook point and the line for better hooking, and this makes a tremendous difference in hooking percentages.

Incidentally, I've also had good luck threading a colored or phosphorescent bead on the line just above these lures. As the lure is jigged, the bead slides up and down the line, attracting the notoriously curious bluegill. This is something different than most anglers are doing in their presentation, and more often than not, means the difference between a mediocre and super catch. With the addition of the bead, your bait will also show up better on electronics.

**Ice ants and ice flies are highly productive winter bluegill jigs. The added hackle causes them to drop slowly, a distinct advantage when fishing fussy or light-biting winter 'gills.**

Ice ants and ice flies are two other highly productive winter bluegill lures. These lures feature rubber legs, marabou or bucktail style hackle, respectively. The added legs and hair cause the lures to fall more slowly, a distinct advantage when fishing fussy sunfish or bluegills. Otherwise, traditional teardrops and their variations also produce well.

## Working Ultralight Ice Jigs

The type of action imparted to a tiny bait should make the lure appear natural. To accomplish this, I've found jiggling the bait upward for 10 to 15 seconds—then jiggling it back down and allowing the lure to rest is generally most effective. Most strikes will come as you jig down, and be noticeable by the simple absence of lure weight. Just be sure to work this way at various strata from bottom to right up under the ice. Bluegills are accustomed to feeding on plankton, which drift up and down continuously, and they may hit at virtually any depth.

Bluegills can hit awfully light, so for best results establish a well-rehearsed, repetitious jigging rhythm—and if anything breaks that confirmed stride, set-up. You'll be surprised how often you'll hook fish. Although most hits will occur when the lure is motionless, watch your line carefully. Big 'gills occasionally hit while the lure is moving, and if your line suddenly goes

**Big 'gills occasionally hit while the lure is moving, so if your line suddenly goes slack or tightens unexpectedly as you're jigging, set the hook immediately.**

slack or tightens slightly as you're jigging, set the hook immediately.

Adapt your tactics to the situation at hand. Use those electronics! How are the fish suspended? Above, just off

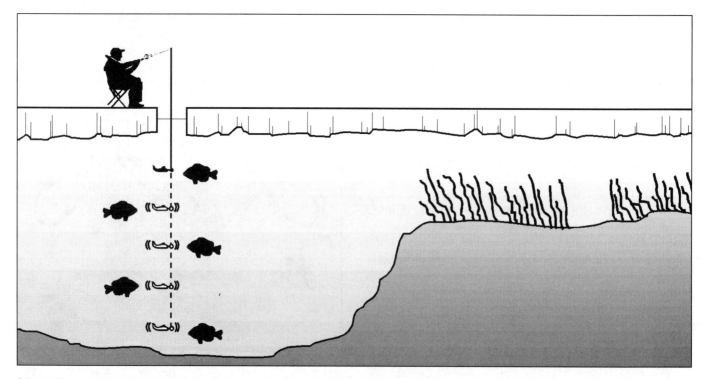

**Bluegills are accustomed to feeding on plankton, which drift up and down continuously and may hold at virtually any depth. For best results, use electronics to pinpoint them, then try fishing different depths above and below the fish, trying to intercept the best "strike zone."**

**Twitching your jig downward with short, 1/16-inch movements best imitates Daphnia, and is highly effective for winter bluegills.**

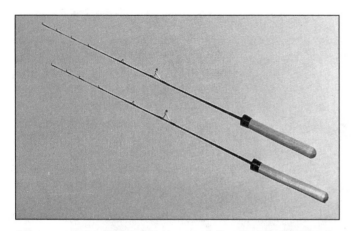

Micro rods include select, specialized tapered blanks of varying lengths that gradually scale down from a thin tenth of an inch to no more than the wispy diameter of an angel hair spaghetti noodle at the tip.

bottom, or right next to forage? Are they reacting slowly, spooking, or aggressively pouncing on your offering? Do they want the bait moved fast or slow? The answers to these questions will help you determine the most productive depth and best lure style, size, color and action.

To accurately mimic planktonic movements with the lure you choose, lower your bait to the fish, pause briefly, then begin jigging upward with slight, steady, well-rehearsed jigging rhythms, moving the lure in tiny 1/16 to 1/8-inch increments. Then pause and repeat the motion downward, always watching your electronics for the response of the fish and carefully watching your rod tip for any interruptions in your established jigging rhythm. And remember, if anything changes or feels different, set the hook.

Because Daphnia usually move upward vertically with erratic twitches, pause briefly, then drift downward repetitiously, occasionally twitching and rolling while pausing. To accurately mimic a Daphnia's movements, slowly lower your jig 12 to 15 inches above the marked fish, then begin twitching your jig in short, 1/16-inch movements as you continue down. Active fish will often come up for the bait. If the fish don't respond, continue working the bait down under the guidance of a semi-taut line. Should the line suddenly go slack or the lure not drop according to your established rate, set the hook—this means a fish has inhaled your lure.

However, if there's no response, work your lure until it's just below the fish. Pause briefly, then begin repeating the procedure, but this time jig upward, through and away from the fish until you're approximately two feet above them. Again, at any indication of a strike, set the hook.

If this doesn't work, drop the lure past the fish, pause just above bottom, then drop the bait straight down. Often they'll follow the lure down and "scoop" it off bottom. However, never repeat these steps more than 10 or 15 minutes. If you don't get into some active 'gills in this amount of time, you're better off trying another hole. Always be mobile, and don't stay in one place if the fish aren't cooperating. I've seen too many folks get hung up trying to trigger inactive fish simply because a school appears on their electronics—and waste far too much time playing games when they could be catching fish in another area.

In summary, ultralight bluegill fishing is a highly involved, fascinating sport comprised of a variety of location and presentation challenges. Learn to better understand and meet these challenges, and you'll often be able to enjoy the thrill of catching bluegills throughout the winter.

## Micro Methodology: A New Level of Sport

Ordinarily, a six-inch bluegill wouldn't be considered much more than a nuisance. But when fishing micro, a six-inch bluegill is a trophy. That's the nice thing about micro tackle. You can fish that stunted population of panfish at the local lake or little pond down the road, and still feel the enjoyment, excitement and challenge of the sport.

At the same time, reducing the size of your equipment can increase the effectiveness of this sport many times over, because micro tackle helps even the most particular ice fishing purest detect the gentle nip of a bull bluegill, faint peck of a jumbo perch or subtle bump of a slab crappie softly sucking in these tiny baits—strikes most ice anglers using heavier tackle never even realize.

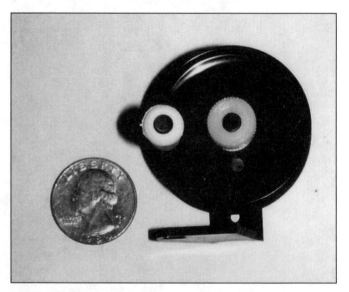

Small, lightweight, plastic ultralight ice reels such as these function primarily as line storage devices for shallow water fishing applications, and balance extremely well with micro rods.

For the ultimate in "micro-balance," choose your rod and reel, then spool with a thin diameter line to create balance in your tackle. Ultimately, you'll feel more hits and catch more fish because of it.

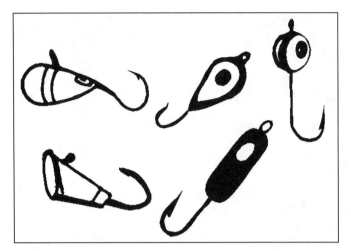

**When using microlight rods, reels and lines, you'll need to balance the system with microlight lures. Many micro ice lures weigh less than 1/100 of an ounce.**

Not that other tackle won't work. Given the right situation, heavier tackle is helpful, even necessary. However, along with other micro proponents, I've learned that using micro tackle is more fun—and often more effective—than heavy, standard, or even ultralight gear.

As you might imagine, micro fishing systems include a variety of specialized equipment, tackle and techniques, beginning with the proper rod. Micro rod designs include select, specialized tapered blanks of varying lengths that gradually scale down from a thin tenth of an inch to no more than the wispy diameter of an angel hair spaghetti noodle at the tip. This design offers more sensitivity and give toward the tip—important for sensing minuscule bites, and reducing the stress placed on light lines when setting the hook or compensating for strong runs from a hard-fighting fish. At the same time, these designs provide the leverage and firm butt strength needed to control jigging motions, set the hook or, when necessary, place pressure on fighting fish.

Other micro rod characteristics include extremely light, fine wire, super-sensitive tip-top guides, along with numerous, tiny, single-foot hand wrapped lightweight wire guides. Larger, heavier, or double-footed guides actually weight these already lightweight, limber rods down so substantially they reduce them to no more than a whippy, "wet noodle" action that offers little presentation control or hook-setting power. Good micro rods also feature thin, strike transmitting handles that keep your hand closer to the blank, creating the ultimate design in ultra-micro sensitivity.

Several manufacturers have developed micro systems specifically designed for ice fishing. Like their longer counterparts designed for open water fishing, these short, thin, wispy rods must be properly balanced to provide the maximum advantage. Most true micro ice

rods are meant to be teamed with miniature reels, super lightweight lines testing only a fraction of a pound, and lures weighing 1/200 of an ounce—or less!

To properly balance your micro system, you'll want to team your micro rod with a lightweight, small diameter micro-style ice reel. These range from lightweight, plastic reels that function primarily as line storage devices to premium, ultra smooth spinning reels with reliable drag systems. When fishing shallow for small to average-sized panfish, plastic ice reel designs are the ultimate in lightweight micro-balanced reels, as they're used primarily as line storage devices and weigh practically nothing, but still feature adjustable drag tension should you hook a larger fish.

When fishing trophies or exploring deeper water with micro-thin lines, a spinning reel featuring a higher retrieve ratio, smooth bail roller and a high-quality, multi-setting drag is mandatory. After all, use of one-pound test or less lines demand smooth, dependable drag systems. Properly set drags are always a primary concern, and settings must be carefully matched to the rated strengths of these super light micro lines. By taking the extra time to properly set your drag you can dramatically lessen the chance of broken lines when you hook into an unexpectedly large or strong fish.

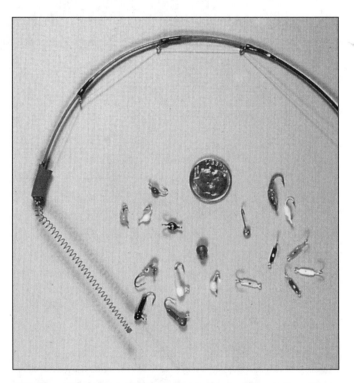

**When using microlight rods, reels and lines the diameter of a human hair, it only makes sense you'll need to balance the system by fishing baits weighing 1/32 ounce or less—much less, in fact, as many "micro" lures weigh less than 1/100 of an ounce!**

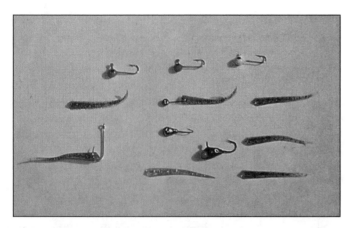

**To help attract finicky bluegills, try tipping your jigs with short, thin strips of soft plastic shaved from various colored plastic worms—the thinner the better.**

Almost all of today's miniature micro reels weigh in at six ounces or less, many are less than five. Most feature a smooth and steady drag—something previously difficult to come by in smaller reels, as the small drag washer friction surfaces in micro reels often made it difficult to get consistent, even pressure applied to the spool. Recently developed spinning models, however, feature drags that perform much like larger, high performance spinning reels.

Be sure to check your drag carefully before you begin fishing, because drag washers sometimes "take a set" when not in use, causing normally smooth drags to stick. Since this can be a real problem, I recommend loosening your drag tension at the end of each day, and resetting it at the beginning of every outing. Not only will this help your micro reel's drag stay smoother and last longer—but will also keep you honest in carefully checking your drag settings each trip out.

Several newly developed micro reels also feature easy to grasp front drag dials—something easy to appreciate when wearing mitts or gloves—and lower, 4.3:1 gear ratios—which means even if the angler makes a mistake and cranks fast, excessive pressure isn't placed on the line by retrieving footage too quickly. And with the addition of quality, multi-drag front drag settings, ball bearing drives, and solid brass pinion gear reversible retrieves, most brand name micro reels feel and perform like high-quality, precision-machined engineering designs.

Other points to watch for are signs of guide wear, smooth bail roller function and properly spooled line. Check to make sure your bail roller springs snap shut firmly, bail rollers rotate smoothly, and reel gears are properly lubricated for cold weather use.

For the ultimate in "micro-balance," spool your favorite model with a small diameter nylon sewing thread, or one of today's high strength, low-diameter monofilaments rated at one pound test or less—just be sure to use smooth, even diameter, limp lines with little memory—or try thin, premium fly tippets. It seems awfully light, I know, but just think back to how impressed you were when your new ultralight ice rod and reel combos rigged with four- and two-pound line revolutionized your fishing of yesterday. I guarantee you'll be just as amazed at the improved control and how many more strikes you'll get using lines testing one, 3/4, even 1/2 pound or less!

Such lines allow you to lower your presentation faster, offer better micro lure sensitivity and control. Just be sure to change lines often, as they can be dramatically weakened by almost invisible abrasion while in use, and with such fine lines, there's no margin for error. When using microlight rods, reels, and lines the diameter of a human hair, it only makes sense you'll need to balance the system by fishing 1/32 ounce baits and less—much less, in fact—as many "micro" lures weigh less than 1/100 of an ounce!

## Micro Lures

Many micro lures are homemade, although some commercially produced models are available. High quality, #14, 16, 18, 20, 22 or smaller straight-eye dry fly hooks such as Mustad's Accu-Points, or those produced by Tiemco or Orvis teamed with a precisely placed ultralight, fly fishing style shot make excellent micro ice hooks—as do #16-20 Micro Trebles. Use only ultra-sharp quality hooks, as you won't be able to set the hook aggressively with this downsized tackle, and while hooks may be the cheapest and seemingly insig-

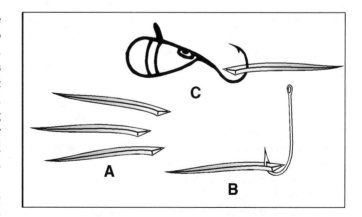

**Tipping small hooks (B) or ice jigs (C) with short, thin strips of soft plastic (A) adds a shimmying action that often drives bluegills into a feeding mode. Be sure the plastic is positioned horizontally for maximum effectiveness.**

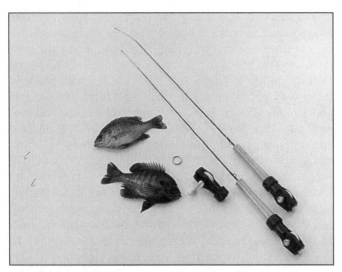

**Still-fish systems were designed by refined ice anglers looking for an "edge" with fussy winter panfish. The main advantage is because the line runs through the blank, the wind has minimum effect on your line and presentation.**

vertical designs produce a slight bobbing motion, while long, thin bodies create a slightly different rocking action. Several specialized micro jigs also exist. Examples include System Tackle's Fat Boys, a vertical design that features flat tops to accentuate visibility on electronics, and HT's #16 Marmooskas and #14 Marmooska Jewels, horizontal micro jigs that actually pivot and turn the hook toward biting fish. At the same time, ironically, many tiny, lightweight micro jigs like Tiny Tears, Micro Flies, Custom Jigs and Spins Rat Finkees offer almost no inherent action at all—only that which is imparted by the user. Actions of tiny micro baits vary with even the slightest differences in design, and it's often these subtle variations that given can make a tremendous difference in productivity. Be sure to experiment.

As for lure color, carry both sides of the color spectrum, plus intermediate colors like subtle chartreuses, whites, golds and glow-in-the-darks. Also try tipping your jigs with short, thin strips of soft plastic shaved from various colored plastic worms—the thinner the better. The added attraction offered by these shimmying, colored strips drives panfish crazy, and helps slow the fall of these lightweight micro jigs, allowing opportunity for hundreds of new and effective presentation options.

Otherwise, darker colored jig heads tend to produce especially well, because they best imitate the plankton and insects panfish feed upon. Since color contrast is always a prime consideration, I'm always sure to carry a generous supply of various colored short twister tails and plastic strips in a rainbow of colors—dull and bright alike—plus metal flake and firetail patterns. Remember to keep them small; in my tackle box, an inch-long plastic is tops.

If you've enjoyed ultralight in the past, you'll be pleased to know that going micro is even more fun and

nificant part of these systems, they perform a vital link in micro system performance.

As when fishing any ice lure, I recommend tying your micro lures with loop knots for maximum action and the highest percentage hooking capabilities. Always tie your knots carefully, patiently tightening each down slowly and smoothly only after wetting the line to prevent line damage.

Commercially made micro lures are also available, in sizes ranging from 12 to 18, and weights of 1/128 ounce to 1/256 ounce. The biggest problem with these tiny baits is consistent hooksets. For best results, tie them using a loop knot, bend the hook shanks out forty degrees, turn the hook point up five degrees to help improve hooking percentages with these tiny, light wire hooks, and tip them with only a single, tiny grub or maggot. The addition of a split shot hinders a lure's action, but it helps get lightweight baits down, especially when fishing deeper water.

Also note the importance of lure style and shape. I'm always surprised by the number of anglers who carry boxes full of various colors, sizes and styles of spinnerbaits, crankbaits and plastics during the open water season and apply each given different situations, but who go ice fishing with just a couple of small ice jigs during the "hard water" season. What a mistake. Like summer, winter fish have distinct preferences for specific sizes and styles of winter lures and jigs given various situations and conditions—and the greater your knowledge and versatility, the greater the chance you'll consistently catch fish.

Vertical, convex, concave and bent-spoon shapes offer the most action and flash. Slightly bent-bodied

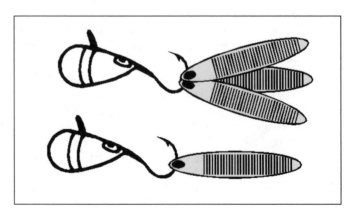

**When baiting your jigs with grubs, barely nip the hook through the bait's tail. This practice keeps the grubs alive longer and allows the bait to wiggle enticingly.**

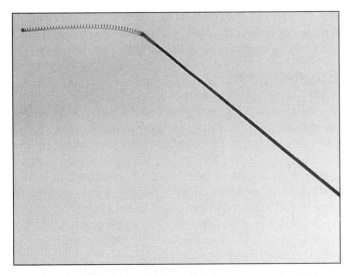

**Spring bobbers for still-fish systems come in various designs, including rubber tubes, lengths of various diameter wires fitted with grommets to accommodate your line—or the most popular still-fish strike indicators, coiled spring bobbers.**

effective. As you may already know, there are times you'll go without a single bite using heavier tackle, compared to near limit catches using ultralight—and the difference between ultralight and micro can be equally significant.

So if you want to get more sport from small fish or increase your odds of fooling those evasive trophy bluegills—go micro! You'll soon find using micro-sized rods, reels, lines, lures and tactics will add a whole new level of pleasure to catching fish through the ice—big and small alike.

## Still-Fish Systems

Still-fish systems were designed by refined ice anglers looking for an "edge" with fussy winter panfish. And now, with the benefits of ultralight and micro tackle becoming increasingly apparent, anglers are continuing to experiment with lighter, improved finesse tackle, and variations of this equipment have resulted in modern still-fish systems.

Briefly, still-fish rods feature specially tapered tubular fiberglass or hollow graphite blanks—shorter models for use inside shanties, longer for outside. Graphite is most sensitive and performs better when panfish are biting lightly. Fiberglass, being stiffer, provides more control when fighting larger panfish. Although some anglers prefer fast tapering tips, most still-fish blanks are relatively stiff and feature parabolic bends. I realize this seems to contradict modern rules of ultralight and micro panfish strategies, but overall, I'd rate still-fish

systems more sensitive than most ultralight or micro ice systems. Here's why.

Precisely balanced still-fish reels are attached to the blank, actually becoming part of the rod. Designed primarily as line storage units, they don't feature a drag system, although the best models include a knurled knob that allows improved control. If the handle is left in the free position, drag can be created by simply applying pressure to the spool with your thumb. This knob also allows spool removal, so you can interchange it with spares offering alternative line tests. Still, the precise balance of this system adds to its incredible level of sensitivity.

To further increase sensitivity, most still-fish anglers prefer 2 lb. monofilament, although I've seen folks using everything from ultra-thin sewing threads to fly tippets. This seems very light, but you'll be amazed by the unsurpassed limpness, sensitivity, balance, control and lure action these dainty lines provide when fishing tiny micro baits on a stillfish system. As for line color, I prefer clear, light green or smoke gray, as they practically disappear in even the clearest water, but fluorescent, hi-vis lines are more visible when watching for strikes. If bright line bothers you, compromise, and tie a low-vis leader to the bright line backing.

Rigging still-fish systems involves spooling the reel, threading your line through its front, into and through the hollow rod blank, then out through a plastic or metal tiptop sleeve and finally, a highly sensitive spring bobber. Given a choice, go with metal sleeved tips. They provide the perfect base for supporting springs and the ultimate combination of micro strike detection capabil-

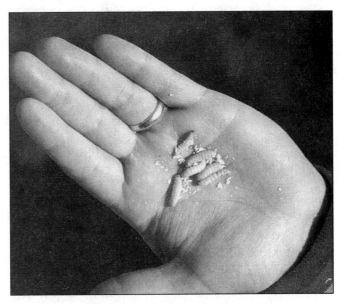

**Many bluegill experts fish waxworms, claiming they outperform all other baits by large margins.**

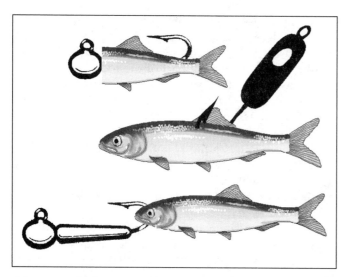

**Often, switching between different baits such as waxworms, spikes, poppers, mousees, wigglers and even tiny minnows will help you catch more bluegills. With any bait, experiment with different tipping methods. Here, three methods of tipping with a minnow are shown.**

ity. And with the line running through the blank, it's not subjected to wind movement, offering an unparalleled level of sensitivity from reel to spring bobber.

Still-fish spring bobbers come in various designs, including rubber tubes, lengths of various diameter wires fitted with grommets to accommodate your line—or the most popular still-fish strike indicators, coiled spring bobbers. These are available in several lengths, allowing varied spring tension. Shorter lengths are stiffer and complement heavier baits, while longer models are "softer" and function better with ultralight and tiny micro jigs. Since springs are typically attached to the rod with shrink tubing, they can also be extended from the rod tip—increasing their length and sensitivity in gradual increments—or retracted, stiffening the action. And because they're made from various wire gauges and diameters, you can widen the range of sensitivity even further.

Most folks use commercially produced coiled springs like HT's SSB super-sensitive spring bobbers. Others make their own using ball point pen springs or tapered, light, soft-wire springs from butane lighters. Either way, you'll find the sensitivity of still-fish systems unmatched, because while relatively stiff, parabolic blanks provide strength for precise presentation control, solid hook sets and better fish-fighting leverage, these spring systems allow subtle strike detection capabilities with a wide range of sensitivity adjustment. This, combined with the fact your line is threaded through the blank and follows its bend perfectly and is

not affected by poorly placed guides or the ill effects of a stiff winter wind, causes many to argue you won't find a more sensitive shallow water bluegill system.

## Bluegill Baits

After choosing your system—be it ultralight, micro or stillfish—select a lure, tie it on with a loop knot to provide the most naturally moving presentation, and prepare to bait up. Be sure to use only lively, wiggly grubs or maggots to help attract fish—and barely nip the hook through the tail. This practice keeps them alive longer and allows them to wiggle enticingly.

Many bluegill experts fish waxworms, claiming they outperform all other baits by large margins. The two leading advantages of fishing waxies are availability and the fact that you can squeeze them to "milk" their internal fluids, thus releasing a scent that attracts bluegills. I've had excellent success flattening a fat waxie over an ice jig, then forming the squished worm into a concave shape. When jigged this way, the waxworm emits natural juices that attract 'gills and adds an enticing fluttering action to the lure bluegills simply can't resist.

Don't ignore spikes, mousies (crane fly larvae, sometimes called rat-tailed maggots), wigglers (large mayfly larvae), freshwater shrimp, poppers, maggots, crawfish tail strips or small minnows. Often these baits perform just as well or better than waxies—depending on the lake you're fishing, how far the winter has progressed and the amount of fishing pressure. On highly pressured lakes, for example, switching to a "different" bait such as a spike, popper or wiggler may significantly outperform a waxie, just as changing lure size, color or style can make a difference. And using small minnows will typically increase your catch of larger bluegills.

It may not appear practical to carry several different varieties of live bait, yet most serious winter bluegill anglers wouldn't consider going ice fishing with only one lure type—and they typically don't go with only one form of live bait, either. I usually carry several types of live bait in a convenient pocket, and experiment with each. Often, one will outproduce the others. Some anglers are taking this to extremes and are also experimenting with "exotic" baits such as Johnson's Crappie Candy, Wisconsin Pharmacal's Ultimate Baits, Berkley's Power Baits and Uncle Josh Ice Flecks—tiny, multi-colored pieces of pork rind—and are having a great deal of success. Plastics—small, short, thin strips of plastic cut from a plastic worm, grub or twist tail and tipped horizontal on a small jig or hook are also popular offerings in some areas.

Not surprisingly, a handful of bluegill experts are experimenting with scents, too, and while the debate

Once a bluegill is caught, note the precise depth you caught the fish, then try jigging slightly higher on your next drop. If you're onto a school of 'gills, skimming fish from the top down helps keep the action going longer, as opposed to dropping your lure in the center of the school and possibly spooking them after catching only a couple of fish.

**Some bluegill anglers are experimenting with "exotic" lure tippers such as Berkley's Power Baits.**

about scents continues to go back and forth, I'm staying neutral. I haven't found a positive increase in my catches when experimenting with them—but haven't noticed a decrease, either. Nonetheless, I have a hunch that each of these baits and scents has their time and place.

## More About Jigging Winter Bluegills

Since winter bluegills can be intensely fussy, be sure to pay special attention to the details of your presentation, particularly lure action. Because panfish are primarily plankton and insect feeders, they're not accustomed to fast-moving aggressive motions. Rather, a relatively slow, steady jigging speed is best for feeling the light bites of winter 'gills. Often, just a steady, light shaking motion interspersed with occasional pauses seems to work best. Finally, concentrate. By focusing carefully on your rod, line or light-bite indicator and always watching for a strike, you'll be surprised by the dramatic increase in your catches.

The recent introduction of ultralight, micro and stillfish ice jigging methodology have been the most revolutionary concepts in the world of bluegill ice fishing since electronics. When combined with electronics, these systems are the answer to most problems caused by larger, light-biting bluegills. Electronics allow you to efficiently find active schools and the depth they're holding—and once there, these systems allow you to catch even the fussiest winter bluegills.

Your total jigging approach must include many considerations. During the winter, reduced metabolic activity makes bluegills respond differently in winter than during warmwater periods. Lure selection must be based on several criteria: size, shape, color, line classification, fish aggressiveness, and jigging speed. These variables all play critical roles in winter bluegill jigging success.

As a rule of thumb, use the lightest lure possible to fish effectively. In other words, use a jig that will get down to the depth the fish are holding and still allow you to feel it. Accurate depth control can really make the difference between no fish and a limit, so before fishing see how many inches of line your reel picks up per turn of the handle. This trick will make it possible for you to return to the depth the fish are at continually.

Also, keep in mind that tiny micro baits are meant to imitate microscopic food items such as zooplankton, so you'll also want your jigging method to closely mimic the actual movements of these critters. To best imitate Daphnia, for example—which are most active and available to winter bluegills during twilight hours—try a slight 1/16 to 1/8-inch vertical motion with a bulbous, slightly bent-bodied jig during low light periods. During the day, switch to a thinner, more erratic moving, spoon shaped rocker style ice jig fished with a more aggressive jigging action interspersed with long hops. This better imitates copepods, a more aggressive type of zooplankton that are more active during daylight hours, and the primary winter forage of panfish in many waters during the day.

Once a fish is caught, note the productive lure size, style, color, rigging method and jigging action—and precise depth you caught the fish—then try jigging slightly higher on your next drop. If you're onto a school of 'gills, skimming fish from the top down helps keep the action going longer, as opposed to dropping your lure in the center of the school and scattering or spooking them after catching only a couple of fish.

Regardless, if the bite stops, try moving to fringe areas around the productive hole. Often the school simply moves down or away slightly and can be relocated. Work each hole quietly, cautiously, and methodically. You'll often take additional fish.

Don't be afraid to use bottom as a key for triggering bluegills. Drop your lure to bottom with a gradual drop, jiggling the bait along the way as you jig down. Work the bait right on the bottom, too—fussy winter bluegills will frequently take the bait right off bottom. Should the school spook, experiment with ultra-micro, tiny lure styles and sizes in a variety of colors, coupled with various combinations of tiny bait tippers, methods of hooking and ultra slow jigging actions. Given such situations, often making just a slight presentation change can make a dramatic difference in your results.

## Timing

Although bluegills may bite anytime throughout the day depending on the waters you're fishing and the local weather conditions, I've typically done best during low-

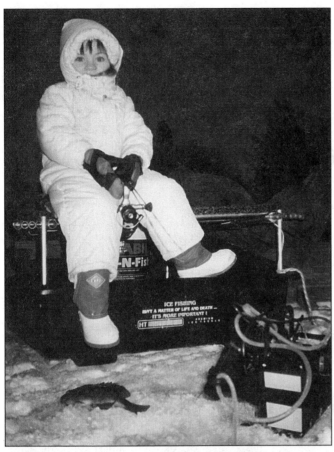

**Often, the last hour before dark provides the best bluegill fishing action of the day—a great time to take the kids out.**

some memorable times, a relaxing experience, and ultimately, the reward of a hefty plate of hot, crispy fillets.

Of course, this is only a glimpse into the intriguing "under-ice" world—a world that holds thousands of secrets to more successful winter bluegill fishing. However, my point is not to cover all the details, but rather to emphasize the importance of experimentation and make you aware how a basic understanding of various location concepts combined with knowledge and versatility can help you ice more winter sunfish and bluegills using specialized winter tackle and techniques.

And with all this put together in just the right combination, you'll be ready to experience the ultimate in winter bluegill catching efficiency.

light periods. For this reason—even in deep water where fish aren't as spooky—it often pays to drill your holes during the afternoon, then return to them about an hour before dark. This way, you can fish the evening bite without creating excessive disturbance.

If you're among the select few that can choose what days you can fish, pay close attention to the weather. If a storm is moving in, be on the ice. I've found the biggest fish often turn on just before major winter fronts and storms. I have no reason for this, but found it true. Likewise, I've found bluegill fishing better during a light snowfall.

## Summary

In this day and age, it seems many ice anglers spend most of their time dreaming of and pursuing trophy pike, bass, walleyes and lake trout on big water. But this winter, before another season slips by, promise to take yourself to a nearby backwater, pond, lake or reservoir in search of bluegills. Plan to take along someone new to the sport, a child—or perhaps the entire family. You'll likely enjoy

# Chapter 5

# *Understanding Yellow Perch During Winter*

Guided by my GPS, I aim my four-wheeler toward a distant waypoint. Icy, frigid air stings my face and hands as I glide across the lake, leaving a trail of loose, blowing snow swirling in the stiff, piercing breeze behind me. Yet a warmth of confident anticipation wards off the early morning chill. After all, I've done my homework and come prepared.

I soon arrive at my destination, where I stop, reach for my flasher and begin outlining the details of a large shoreline point. I start by searching the sharp-breaking side of the feature for fish. Nothing. I walk around to the other end, where a gradually sloping finger projects into deeper water. The screen lights up.

Bullseye.

Anxiously I drill a hole, bait up, and lower my jig toward two wide marks suspended about two feet off bottom. A fish rushes my bait, and as the mark converges around the lure, my rod dips and I set the hook into a respectable 11-inch yellow perch. I'm able to continue following the school throughout the morning with similar results—and while doing so, periodically glance up to spot-check distant anglers. Some are sporadically hooking fish, yet I'm surprised how few are actually implementing a systematic approach to improve their consistency. After all, a skillful, mobile system combining an understanding of the yellow perch's basic habits and behavior—along with the use of lake maps and electronics—makes it possible to effectively determine productive patterns and maximize winter catches.

Yellow perch are a cool-water species and, during active daytime feeding periods when they move shallower and become more aggressive, a strongly schooling species. They're adaptable to a variety of environments, although they prefer backwaters and lakes boasting modest amounts of vegetation and nutrients. Diet is varied, but includes plankton, insect larvae, crustaceans, freshwater shrimp, fish eggs and minnows—mostly plankton and insect larvae with smaller perch and shifting toward minnows as they grow larger.

The key to quality perch catches is learning primary winter location patterns.

## Primary Winter Locations Patterns: The Search for Yellow Perch

Location is the most complicated part of winter yellow perch fishing, because perch have an incredible ability to adapt to a variety of environments and conditions. Jumbos are especially difficult, because they vary widely in their location patterns. Some may relate to rock, others

**Location is arguably the most complicated part of winter yellow perch fishing, because yellow perch have an incredible ability to adapt to a wide variety of environments and conditions.**

A skillful, mobile system combining an understanding of the yellow perch's basic habits and behavior with the use of lake maps and electronics makes it possible to effectively determine productive patterns and maximize winter catches.

to sand, some to muck, a few to weeds—all while part of the population is deep and the rest shallow.

Why so many options? The exact location perch utilize is governed mainly by the availability of food, which can be found in any one of these areas—on reefs, points, weed lines, or even structureless flats for that matter—depending on the lake type. Structurally, this means perch could be in the backs of shallow, vegetated bays and coves, shallow reefs, shoreline points or rip-rap, turns or breaks on well-defined weedlines, deep breaks, mid-depth and main lake structures or mud flats—and a whole host of other areas that attract and support baitfish and zooplankton.

To further complicate matters, perch are nomadic, and the only recourse ice anglers have is to move—and keep moving—until an active school is found. Thus, you must plan your movements strategically and, given the lake, time and conditions you're fishing, carefully choose the highest percentage structural features on a good lake map, locate them using electronics, then go hole hopping to further eliminate unproductive water.

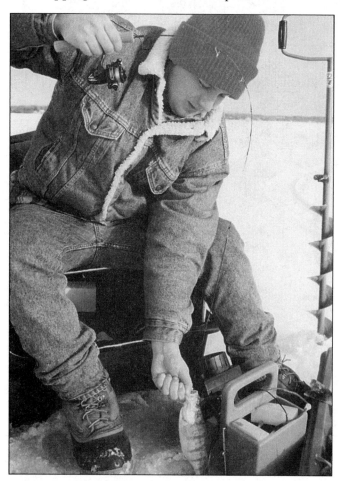

Yellow perch often school by size. If you're not satisfied with the size you catch, move in search of another school.

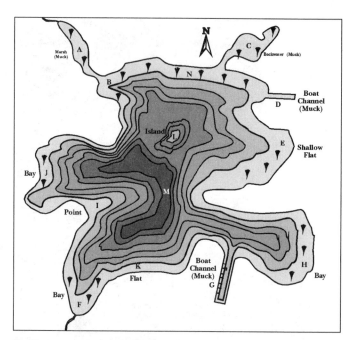

Yellow perch make distinct movements through the winter. Shallow, vegetated areas such as marshes (A), backwaters (C), boat channels (D,G), shallow flats (B,E,H,K,J) are good first and late ice areas. As mid-winter approaches the bases of drop-offs adjoining such areas or main lake structures such as points (I), or islands (L) may be productive. Eventually, most perch scatter across deep, mid-lake flats (M). Late winter, perch return to the vegetated shallows to spawn, particularly those featuring current flow such as inlets (F).

Don't get me wrong. If you simply want to catch a few perch, numerous general winter perch patterns exist, making it relatively easy to access and catch a few small to average-sized perch almost anytime on waters supporting a strong, stable population. Yet this often throws many winter perch anglers out of kilter, because once they catch a fish or two, they keep fishing the same holes, awaiting jumbos. This methodology may work fine for consistent catches of average sized perch, but this is not the case for jumbos. Perch usually school by size, and catching a small perch while searching for jumbos means you must move.

So with the understanding that small, average and eating size perch aren't difficult to find and catch, this chapter will be geared toward fishing jumbos. My reasoning? Big perch are more fun to catch and, being more selective with regard to their feeding habits, high-percentage location patterns can be more readily identified. Like larger predators, jumbo perch try to optimize their feeding efforts to obtain a meal. This means one-pound jumbos aren't going to cruise all day along a shallow, vegetated flat like smaller perch. Instead, they're attracted to locations meeting specific requirements—

During first ice, most schooled, active Great Lakes yellow perch congregate in shallow connecting waters and along hard bottom shoals and reefs in less than 15 feet of water.

## The Great Lakes Challenge

Because of their expansive flats, Great Lakes bays are perhaps the most complex environments that perch inhabit. To complicate matters, ice conditions and snow cover play major roles in Great Lakes perch fishing success, because they dictate accessibility. Heavy snowfall, deteriorating ice, or cracked and heaving ice conditions sometimes make it difficult for anglers to move about and reach hot spots. However, if the bays freeze early and snowfalls aren't heavy, access should be good, and the season's Great Lakes perch catches will reflect good accessibility.

Because of the large, expansive flats typical of most Great Lakes bays, not to mention the oftentimes large amount of structure (Lake St. Clair in Michigan is enough to boggle the mind) Great Lakes perch must be dealt with as a separate entity.

During first ice, I've found most schooled, active Great Lakes perch congregate on hard-bottom shoals

namely thick concentrations of preferred forage. Once found, they will remain in these areas unless their food supply diminishes or conditions change dramatically.

Of course, finding concentrations of forage is not always an easy task. The process requires preparation. With this in mind, consider the concept of selective targeting—meaning fishing specific high percentage jumbo perch locations, at the right times, with the right equipment on particular lake types.

In river backwaters, perch relate mostly to shallow vegetation. Provided suitable cover, food and oxygen remain available, they'll stay there throughout the winter. Otherwise, gradual movement, especially of larger fish, into deeper water and toward the main channel will occur.

On lakes, flowages and reservoirs, first ice finds perch in the backs of vegetated bays and coves and off shallow shoreline points and shoals. Mid-winter will see a movement toward deep water, beginning with schools forming along breaklines near the base of drop-offs, then gradually scattering onto mid-lake flats, or on flowages and reservoirs, cover-laden flats lining the main river channel.

Yellow perch are quite active during the first ice period, and nice catches such as this are possible.

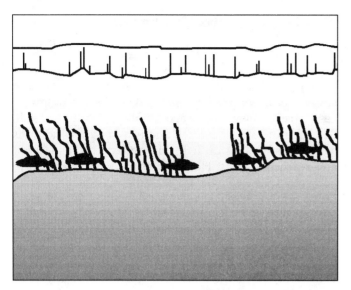

**Perch are very active during the short-lived first-ice period. Expect shallow, sparse to moderately vegetated channels, bays, coves and flats to produce most consistently. Perch are likely to hold on the bottom directly within the weeds, or along the edges of pockets and openings.**

and reefs in less than 15 feet of water that attract and concentrate reliable sources of prey. Find such areas, and you'll be off to a good start. Perch may also hold in shallow, vegetated connecting waters and shallow rocky shorelines and reefs.

During mid-winter, Great Lakes perch gradually move into deeper water, generally from 20 to 30 feet, where they gather along breaklines near the base of fairly sharp drop-offs and breaks. Often you'll find them on edges where hard bottom drop-offs meet soft bottom flats. These spots may harbor food sources not readily available on hard-bottom shoals, such as amphipods, copepods and cladocerans—and may even support several species of small minnows, the preferred prey of many Great Lakes perch.

Ice fishing for Great Lakes perch peaks just before ice-out, when perch tend to concentrate on shallow flats and rock piles adjacent to spawning areas. Hard-bottom shoals and bars with sparse weed growth usually produce best. You often find late-ice perch activity near spawning areas throughout the entire winter. Hard-bottom flats and shoreline points in less than 15 feet of water and covered with sparse vegetation almost always provide a source of food for perch; if forage is present the perch usually are, too. Where available, some perch will also move back into shallow, vegetated connecting waters and flats, preparing for the spawn.

Daily movements depend on the dominant weather conditions and the predominant food source the perch

are utilizing, but mid-morning to mid afternoon hours generally offer the best Great Lakes perch action throughout the winter. Schools often feed heavily as a group throughout the daylight hours. Keep in mind, however, perch tend to school by age and size. If you're catching a lot of small to mid-size fish, don't hesitate to try another area. Large or small, these schools break up as the light falls, and feeding wanes.

Regardless of which area you plan to fish, to be consistent you must be willing to move. The best Great Lakes perch fishing usually occurs between the 25-45 foot depth range, but this varies greatly. One day you may have to drive five or six miles out and fish more than 40 feet of water to find fish, and the next day they'll be a mile or more away in 20 feet of water.

For best results, keep moving until you find active schools. Great Lakes perch—like all perch—are extremely mobile, and movements may change day to day, even hour to hour, so take these hints to heart, then check things out with your sonar. Using this approach will save a lot of wasted time and put you on active fish faster.

Now, let's look at general yellow perch seasonal patterns for river backwaters, lakes, flowages and reservoirs.

## First Ice

Perch are very active during the short-lived first ice period, and understanding some general location principles, they aren't difficult to find. Expect shallow, sparse to moderately vegetated backwaters, bays, coves, flats, points and bars to produce most consistently, as these productive littoral areas harbor vast amounts of cover and support diverse varieties of forage, which in turn attract perch. On many lakes, provided suitable oxygen,

**As shallow water forage dwindles, the base of nearby drop-offs and breaks provide especially attractive habitat for schools of yellow perch, as these areas tend to harbor good quantities of varied forage.**

cover and forage are available and competing species don't stir up trouble, small perch will remain in such areas all winter.

As the season wears on and shallow water cover and food sources become depleted, however, most schools shift location and begin moving slightly deeper, usually congregating near the base of primary, secondary, and main lake drop-offs outside these shallows. On flowages and reservoirs, these movements may lead to secondary channel areas lining high percentage first-ice locations. The shallows will still draw perch if a source of forage is present and competition isn't intense, but the base of the breaks near the intersections of major structural elements and main lake flats provide especially attractive invitations for larger schools, as they tend to sustain a virtual smorgasbord of insect larvae, tubificid worms and minnows.

Note such movements are similar to the first ice patterns demonstrated by bluegills, but different in that bluegills will tend to hold at the top or along the sides of the break—a slightly different ecological niche.

## Mid-Winter

As the first ice period slides into mid-winter, perch begin roaming deep mid-lake flats, often scattering as they hunt for new sources of forage. Unfortunately, since

As first ice slips away, some perch may remain shallow, but most drop down and hold along drop-offs adjoining shallow water holding areas. The base of these drop-offs where they meet the main lake flat are the highest percentage locations, especially if a transition change from hard to soft bottom occurs.

During the mid-winter period, perch begin roaming deep mid-lake flats, often scattering in search of forage. Consistent catches are often dependent on a mobile approach to cover water and locate active schools.

**Mid-winter, most perch spread out over expansive, soft bottom, mid-lake flats. The edges of mid lake structures such as rock piles or rises offering bottom content changes can be highly productive—if they're available. If not, you'll need to utilize a mobile approach using sonar to locate schools of actively feeding perch wandering expansive, featureless, soft bottom flats.**

these schools are typically scattered, consistent catches may seem impossible. Even seasoned veterans using electronics get frustrated this time of year, because these loose roaming schools often appear to be holding smack dab in the midst of structurally bland, featureless flats and seem almost impossible to pattern.

Yet to knowledgeable, observant ice anglers, these areas usually prove to harbor subtle perch-attracting features, including obscure changes in structure, depth or bottom content that support diverse varieties of cover and forage—and thus, draw significant numbers of active perch. Hard spots to pinpoint? Sometimes.

However, if you combine an awareness of such factors with a versatile, highly mobile approach and the proper use of lake maps and electronics, you'll find that locating everything from the rather obvious structural features that attract first-ice perch right down to the most subtle perch holding areas of mid-winter may not prove quite as complex as they first sound.

Start by considering the lake type you're fishing and reviewing lake maps before the ice forms. This way you can predetermine areas that will likely produce through mid-winter well in advance of the ice fishing season. To accomplish this efficiently, I recommend using a boat and today's sophisticated electronics. GPS technology allows you to save these potential hot spots—then repeatedly return to them simply by recording the coordinates for your high-percentage locations—and sonar provides the

opportunity to pinpoint everything from the tiniest to largest structural features.

After the ice forms, use your GPS to quickly and accurately transport you and your gear to your predetermined waypoints, and your sonar to pinpoint fish. Not all productive locations can be saved as waypoints—particularly those often ambiguous mid-winter flat locations—so you'll always have to do some "manual" searching with sonar. But most of the time, previously plotted waypoints will help save time and allow you to find and pattern perch more quickly.

Even during tough mid-winter periods, perch often relate to flats adjacent to the areas frequented during first-ice or, later in the season, areas adjoining spawning flats. This means you can still mark these locations as waypoints, then move around, utilizing the sonar advantage to determine precisely where active schools are holding along the adjacent flats, breaklines or breaks.

**Deeper, more structurally diverse lakes and reservoirs may feature flats offering subtle deep water structural elements such as points, humps, rock piles or main river channels that draw forage, in turn attracting schools of active yellow perch.**

**Incorporating a mobile approach with the use of electronics often will result in fabulous catches in mid-winter, a time when many anglers not using such techniques strike-out.**

Don't make the mistake of finding an active school and enjoying some fast action, then as the school moves and action slows, relax, thinking they'll come back. Rather, try to pinpoint the direction of movement and move with them.

If you understand the basic nature of the perch, active mid-season schools can be tracked fairly predictably. Recall that early in the season, shallow, vegetated bays, bars and shoals are good producers—and provided a reliable food source is available, these structures often hold fish throughout mid-winter as well. In particular, I've found hard-bottom shoals supporting weed growth in three to 15 feet of water produce fairly constant mid-winter results, and you can bet anglers fishing such areas are usually catching at least some perch—at times, lots of them. This also means these structures are quite well-known and receive extensive fishing pressure, so as the season wears on, the productivity of these areas often slacks off. In fact, perch may virtually disappear from these areas by mid-January.

In addition to fishing pressure depleting or spooking perch from these more obvious structures, shallow food sources often become slim in these areas, forcing the majority of the perch to move off these shoals and migrate toward deep water flats. Rather than continuing to pursue stragglers on these early season hot spots, use your sonar to begin probing the base of primary and secondary drop-offs and their adjacent deep lake flats, concentrating your efforts at the point where these drop-offs smooth into deep

lake mud flats. These transition areas provide an abundance of soft bottom prey items such as insect larvae, and hard bottom forage such as crustaceans, which often draw large schools of mid-winter perch.

If this doesn't pan out, move onto the soft-bottom deep water flats. Often, these areas support large crops of bloodworms—especially in nutrient rich eutrophic lakes. Early in the season, these tiny worms bury themselves deep within bottom muck, concealed from predators. When oxygen counts start becoming low in mid-winter, however, these worms anchor to the bottom substrate and extend their rear appendages above bottom to create greater surface area for obtaining dissolved oxygen.

In turn, bloodworms become vulnerable prey, and opportunistic perch simply move from their early season positions along shoals and secondary drop-offs and begin cruising deep-water flats in search of food—and they pig out! I've caught mid-winter perch with mud smudged over

While electronics can't reveal the precise direction a school is moving, they will reveal if a school of fish has moved to the side. To determine the direction of movement, note the direction hooked fish swim. Typically, hooked perch will move toward their school.

**Schools typically contain 50-200 yellow perch, and since these schools appear readily on sonar they're relatively easy to find. By following the schools you can accumulate nice catches.**

their noses from poking into the soft bottom muck, and with mouths, throats and bellies stuffed with these tiny worms.

These schools are seldom easy to locate, especially on expansive, big water flats. But deeper, more structurally diverse lakes may feature flats harboring subtle deep water structural elements such as points, humps or rock piles, or on reservoirs and flowages, banks lining the main river channel or submerged man-made features, any of which may draw a diverse variety of forage, and hence, perch.

If these happen to be long, featureless structures extending from productive first ice flats into the main lake basin, perch will likely settle in loosely around the perimeter at the base of the structure and outstanding catches are possible—but to pinpoint where these loosely schooled fish hold, you'll need to be mobile and employ the help of electronics.

Provided you utilize a mobile approach and use the assistance of electronics to locate these structures and loosely gathered perch, you'll generally pick up a couple of fish from each hole—and believe me, by the end of the day this often adds up, and you'll come off the lake the envy of other anglers.

Obviously, sonar is paramount to consistent midwinter perch success, because you'll need to positively identify bottom content, forage and fish. Once you've found what appears to be an active school within a primary area, drill some holes and start fishing. If your synopsis is correct and the perch are active, note the predominant conditions and the depth most bites are occurring—and always stay with the fish as long as possible. Don't make the mistake of finding an active school and enjoying some fast action, then as the school moves and the action slows, sit back thinking they'll come back. Rather, try to pinpoint the direction and move with them. Doing so, you'll note patterns.

This may sound difficult, but using a strategic mobile approach, especially with a group of other knowledgeable anglers, it's actually quite easy to accomplish. Just fan out in several directions from the holes previously drilled over the school. Today's LCGs with "side finding" capabilities are especially helpful, as they allow you to switch your cone angle from nar-

**Some studies have indicated when yellow perch move into deep water not containing sufficient oxygen, they temporarily draw on the oxygen supply from their swim bladders for survival.**

row to wide upon command, permitting you to more easily monitor a school's movements. Electronics won't reveal the specific direction; however, you can determine they've simply moved to the side, and by fanning out in different directions, the school can be relocated.

Otherwise, if an active school begins thinning out on your screen, carefully watch your line after a hooked fish runs—they'll usually run in the direction of the moving school. Now, switch to the wide cone to determine if the school is moving nearby, and begin drilling holes around your present location, starting in the direction indicated by the previously hooked fish. Once you're back on fish, use the narrow cone to work them. Of course, be sure to drill holes in that direction and repeat the process as necessary to stay with the school.

Still, since perch are very adaptive, roam and willing to capitalize on a wide variety of habitats and prey items, understanding mid-season perch patterns can be a relatively complex matter. I've often noted several productive, mid-winter patterns occurring simulta-

**The best way to find, track and follow active schools of mid-winter perch efficiently, accurately and consistently is to review detailed lake maps, and combine this knowledge with a skilled, mobile approach incorporating maximum use of your electronics.**

neously on many good perch waters—and deciphering the best ones can be difficult, because schools will often become tightly concentrated in specific areas, and if you're not in just the right place at precisely the right time, you're out of luck. A good example of this is when perch go deep.

## Deep-Water Perch

Deep water perch are in a class of their own. They're generally trickier to find than shallow schools, yet since they usually don't see as much fishing pressure, they're also more likely to be active.

You may be wondering if such deep flats, especially on nutrient-rich lakes, sustain adequate oxygen levels throughout mid-winter. Truth is, they often don't. Yet provided a food source is readily available, I've seen schools of mid-winter perch migrate onto deep water flats practically devoid of oxygen.

It sounds strange, but some studies have indicated when perch invade deep water not containing sufficient oxygen, they draw on the oxygen supply from their swim bladders for survival. Thus, perch appear quite tolerant of low oxygen levels, and don't seem to be affected much by temporary periods of feeding in low oxygen conditions.

Case in point: In Lake Mendota, near Madison, Wisconsin, mid-winter perch were found to hug bottom fairly closely, often inhabiting the deepest parts of the lake, regardless of oxygen content. Other studies seem to support similar conclusions. For example, on the same water, large schools of mid-winter perch are often found hovering over deep flats, yet Department of Natural Resources nets set simultaneously on the bottom in the deep, almost oxygenless waters below usually caught perch in greater numbers.

It's entirely possible that these suspended and bottom fish are actually the same schools, simply swimming down temporarily to feed, then shifting back up and suspending where adequate oxygen levels exist until they're ready to dive down for another feeding binge.

However, don't get me wrong—this doesn't mean suspended perch won't bite. Not unlike any other species, suspended perch are often there because forage is present—and they may be actively feeding—so if you mark suspended, deep-water fish, be sure to give them a try. The extra effort can pay off.

## The Challenge

All this may sound great—but alas, the picture's not perfect. Although perch converge in specific areas where bloodworms and other food sources are most

**Late ice is the best period for catching numbers of jumbo perch, because they must feed regularly to prepare for the rigors of spawning.**

heavily concentrated, the most challenging aspect of these mid-winter patterns is that perch may settle almost anywhere on the flats where these adequate food supplies exist. So how can the exact locations of active schools be pinpointed?

Easy. You must go where the greatest amount and variety of food exists—and fortunately, this isn't generally too difficult. You just need to read the signs.

In addition to the edges of deep, mid-lake structure, evidence shows that perch, particularly actively feeding ones, are a strongly schooling species. And because schooling is an essentially daytime behavior associated with active feeding behavior in perch, you can look for schools to consistently provide numbers of active, catchable fish. In fact, schools of 50-200 fish are typical, and since these schools appear readily on sonar, they're relatively easy to find.

The challenge of consistently finding schools of perch on the flats involves mobility. You've got to constantly move, searching for schools of active perch using your knowledge of the species—and more importantly, sonar. You know sonar can be used for finding structure—and can be equally valuable on the flats for locating wandering schools.

I could go on, but the point is this: The best way to find, track, and follow active schools of mid-winter perch efficiently, accurately, and consistently is to: Review detailed lake maps; carefully consider the perch's innate habits and behavior; consider the lake you're fishing and how far the season has progressed to determine which areas have the most potential; then, combine this knowledge with a skilled, mobile approach incorporating maximum use of your electron-

ics. As a result, you'll be able to accurately determine productive location patterns—and tremendously increase your odds of success.

## Late Ice

Late ice is the best period for catching numbers of jumbo perch, because they must feed regularly to prepare for the rigors of spawning. Larger females have an especially high physiological need for nutrients to ensure proper egg development, and this combination of concentrated jumbos and high activity levels can result in excellent fishing.

Perch spawn primarily in shallow, sheltered coves, bays, flats or reefs, especially those boasting a firm bottom and moderate weed growth or submerged wood. Cover in the form of weed growth or wood is essential for a successful spawn, because perch drape their eggs over such substrates.

To find late-ice perch, simply look for drop-offs and breaks with migration routes leading between deep-

**Yellow perch spawn primarily in shallow, sheltered coves, bays, flats or reefs, especially those boasting a firm bottom and moderate weed growth or submerged wood. Look for these areas and their associated drop-offs and breaks to hold large, active schools of late-ice perch staging for the spawn.**

**Not just any cover-strewn structure meets the standards of late-ice jumbos. Use your sonar to locate larger features extending from deep to shallow water which provide more room for structural diversity—things such as breaks, inside turns and diverse bottom contents.**

water flats and the adjacent spawning marshes, then search for combinations of secondary structure, cover and forage that are likely to hold active perch, and try intercepting active schools. Nine times out of ten—with special regard to the lake type you're fishing and the local weather conditions—the edges of large, mid-depth shoreline bars and shoals adjacent to the perch's preferred spawning flats will hold fish.

Vegetated areas can be rare during late-ice on some lakes, especially in cold years that produce thick ice and heavy snow cover, which blocks the sunlight that plants require. During such times, jumbos are often tightly schooled in very widely scattered patches of green vegetation near spawning areas. Again, these can be hard to find, but use your electronics. If you can find vegetated structural variations such as well-defined turns or points on edges of primary, main lake structural features—especially those in conjunction with diverse bottom contents that are supporting forage—you'll usually score.

Not just any vegetation-strewn structure meets the stringent standards of late-ice jumbos. Use your sonar to locate larger features extending from deep to shallow water which provide more room for structural diversity—things such as breaks, inside turns and diverse bottom contents—holding areas. These areas draw greater varieties of prey species that, in turn, draw larger concentrations of jumbo perch.

The most productive bars also ordinarily feature bottom contents comprised of rock-rubble or rock and gravel mixed with sand—but not always. I've often noticed schools of active jumbos holding where there's a change in bottom content from sand to rock, hard bottom to soft bottom, or where one weed type changes to another. This is because such areas draw diverse variet-

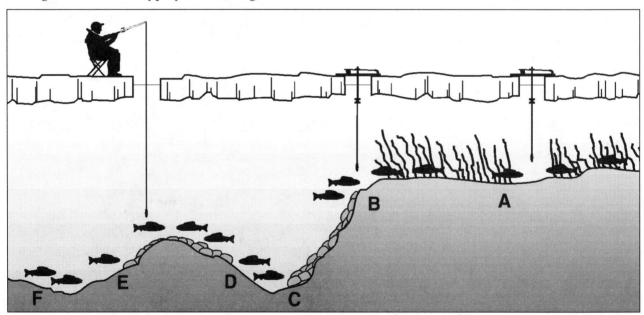

Late ice perch remain scattered across deep, mid-lake flats (F), and the edges of mid-depth and deep mid-lake structures (E,D), but gradually move to the edges of drops adjoining spawning areas (C), onto the edges of spawning flats (B) and eventually into spawning areas (A). For best results, set some tip-ups shallow and along these edges while jigging deep, trying to find the position of an active school.

ies of forage, and perch take advantage of the situation. Springs, which provide oxygen-rich water, can also be productive.

The only major problem with this approach is that perch frequently school by size and age, and you may locate a school of young spawners. If you do—and want to catch jumbos—be prepared to move. Like other times of the winter, late ice perch fishing for jumbos requires mobility.

## Effective Winter Fishing Strategies

Once you're on a large school of heavily concentrated perch, tip-ups or tip-downs can help increase your catch. For best results, use super smooth tripping tip-downs, umbrella style ultralights, or underwater units like HT's Polar or Deluxe Polar II Husky tip-up with a heavy duty, "easy flow" spool, and set them up strategically along migration routes or the base of steep breaks where perch are likely to hold. Rig with long, light monofilament leaders, small hooks and slightly larger than average, 2 to 3-inch panfish minnows. Any way of incorporating added color or flash, such as through the use of spinnerblades or beads, is helpful.

Wind tip-ups, similarly rigged but combining the use of a small, flashy jigging spoon for added attraction, are especially productive on milder days, or when combined with thermal hole covers. Tip the spoon with a small minnow to add natural smell, taste and texture,

and you're off and running. When fishing wide open expanses like Great Lakes bays, thermal style tip-ups like HT's Polar Therm are good bets, as they will keep snow from blowing into your hole and prevent the hole from freezing.

## Jigging

Jigglesticks and jig poles are all you really need to catch perch in shallow water. Simple rigs consisting of a spring bobber or float, splitshot, hook or small to mid-size, brightly colored teardrop or ice spoon tipped with a grub or small minnow have probably accounted for more winter perch than any other system.

However, when perch move deep, longer, slightly stiff "walleye type" ice rod combos rigged with spinning reels are used by many perch anglers, although I prefer medium or medium-light action models like Berkley's Lightning Rods with a smooth, parabolic bend, or better yet, a stiff rod with a sensitive tip section such as HT's Jigging Sticks or Polar Golds. The stiff backbone provides solid hook setting power for larger jumbos or when fishing deep water, and the sensitive tip section provides the opportunity to sense even the lightest of strikes. Many anglers use graphite to increase sensitivity, but for less money, a good fiberglass rod featuring the above design will function well and cost less. A good quality spinning reel and 4-6 lb. test will round out the system.

**Smooth-tripping underwater tip-ups, such as the Polar, set up strategically along migration routes or the base of steep breaks where yellow perch often hold, bring good results and can be used to help identify holding areas along primary migration routes.**

**Wind tip-ups, rigged using small, flashy jigging spoons for added attraction, are especially productive for yellow perch.**

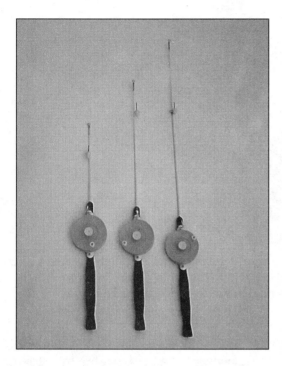

Jigglesticks or simple jig poles with plastic ice reels are really all you need to catch yellow perch in shallow water.

When perch are deep and not striking readily or taking larger, more actively worked lures and baits, I prefer to go ultralight. Aside from the fact that ultralight tackle is more sensitive than standard gear, it's also more fun to fish. I highly recommend premium ice rods such as HT's Polar Ice Brim Rods or Ice Blues, or perhaps a custom designed ice rod. Remember, lighter equipment provides better control, better lure action, and greater sensitivity for detecting the often slight, subtle strikes of light-biting perch.

To properly balance your ultralight rods, combine your favorite model with a small, high-quality ultralight spinning reel featuring a reliable, positive, properly set drag and smooth pickup system. Spool with premium 2 lb. monofilament such as Cabela's Tectan, Berkley Trilene or UltraThin, Stren Easy Cast, or Bagley's Silver Thread. If you're daring, try premium fly tippets such as Dai-Riki, Aeon, or Climax the same way you'd fish for bluegills. Always carry a second outfit rigged with 4 lb. line for situations requiring the use of larger, heavier lures and rigs—which brings us to the next aspect of presentation, lures.

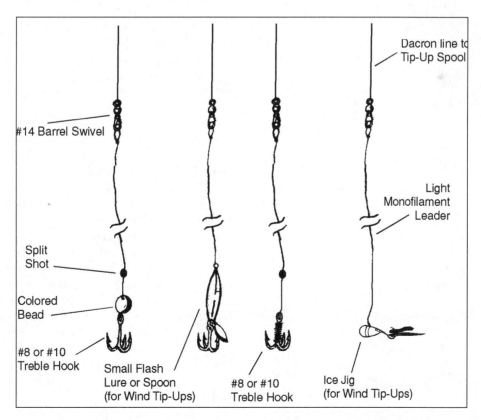

A variety of rigs can be used to catch winter perch. When fishing standard tip-ups, a simple hook or hook and bead rig tipped with a small minnow will work wonders. Below wind tip-ups or tip-downs, rigs tipped with a small jigging lure or spoon and sweetened with a grub or minnow can also be highly effective.

## Lures: Choose What Your Electronics Tell You

The best way to select the right lure is to carefully examine what your electronics are telling you. When you initially mark fish, for example, observe how they're positioned. Are the fish suspended and actively moving, or sparsely concentrated on bottom and sitting relatively still? Is there a food source present? How deep is it? How tightly are the fish grouped and holding in relation to the forage? The answers to such questions provide numerous clues regarding fish activity and help you determine the best lure choice.

For instance, if fishing what appears to be an active school, aggressive jigging approaches with medium action rods, 4-6 lb. test, fast-moving swimming lures like Normark's Jigging Rapalas, Northland's Mini Airplane Jigs or System Tackle's Walleye Flyers or HT's Walleye Ice Jigs will help maximize your catch. Simply lower the bait just above the fish; then, watching it carefully, begin working it. If there's no response, try increasing or decreasing your rate of movement, or dropping the lure into the midst of the school, allowing

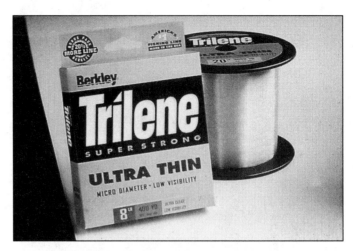

To properly balance an ultralight ice rod and reel combo, spool with a thin diameter, premium monofilament such as Berkley's Ultra Thin.

the fish a moment to react, then start jigging with only slight movements, trying to trigger fish into striking.

Watch closely now. Are the fish spooking easily, ignoring the bait, inquisitive and moving slowly toward it, short striking, or aggressively chasing down the lure? Are they reacting most positively when the bait is moved fast, slow, or moderately? Again, the answers to such questions provide valuable clues toward deciphering the best presentation.

If you try several things without satisfactory results, reel up and begin repeating the procedure with various swimming lure styles, sizes and colors. Do they show any specific preferences? If so, the answers to these questions will provide guidelines helping you narrow down your search for the most productive presentation.

Should the perch turn out to be less active than anticipated, switch to a more efficient presentation. Grab a second rod rigged with 4 lb. line, and try jigging small flash lures tipped with a grub or minnow. Good examples include Custom Jigs and Spins' small Stinger, Bay de Noc's smaller Swedish Pimples, or HT's 1/8 ounce Marmooska Spoons. These small flash baits offer all the flash, attraction, and triggering qualities of their larger counterparts—just in a more compact, shallower water design. However, if the fish won't hit these baits or spook as you work them, switch back to a slightly smaller lure and slower presentation, gradually working your way down until you land on the most efficient combination.

Smaller to mid-size flash lures such as Bay de Noc's Swedish Pimples or Vinglas, Acme Kastmasters, or Bait Rigs Willospoons can also be good, as these lures all get down quickly and provide the flashy attracting power

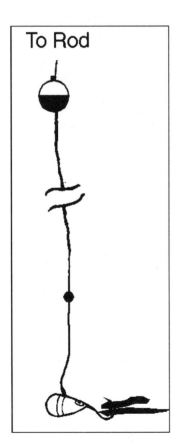

Over the years, a standard bobber rig and live bait tipped ice jig has probably accounted for more winter perch than any other method.

active perch love, but can be worked more subtlely than a larger, more active swimming or flash lure. Again, tip these baits with maggots or a small minnow, then lower the bait to the top of the school. Quickly raise the lure a couple of feet, abruptly drop your rod tip, and being sure to hold your rod still as the lure swims or flutters down, allow the bait to flare and dart from side to side before settling back to its original position.

Next, pause briefly before beginning to gently work the bait, using only a slight jiggling or rocking motion to softly wiggle the hooks at the base of the lure. Perch are normally attracted by the flashy movements, then strike as the lure settles or gently wiggles in place, depending on how active or competitive the school is. Watch the fish's reaction on your electronics. If they're short-striking or somewhat spooky, experiment with little jigging action and longer pauses, and just gingerly shake the hook at the base of the lure. Replacing the existing hook with a beaded hook or jeweled treble can be very helpful in such situations.

No luck? Reel up and try a flash lure/ice jig combo. In this case, a jigging lure or spoon is used as an attractor, and an ultralight ice lure tipped with a grub is tied to the base of the spoon via a short monofilament leader. Here, the flash attracts perch, and the tiny lure and bait gently wiggling in place triggers them. An especially good tactic here includes using hooks of European origin: Painted hooks or "pearls." Both are made of bits of plastic or epoxy, colored brightly and

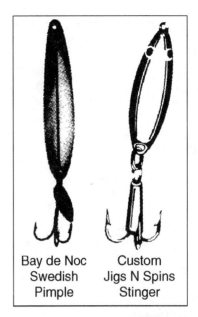

Small flash lures such as Swedish Pimples or Stingers get down quickly and provide the flashy attracting power active perch love, but can be worked more subtlety than larger, more active swimming or flash lures.

adhered to small treble hook, ranging from around size 4 down to 22. These can be used as replacement hooks on swimming minnows and spoons, dropper baits or "stingers" off a jig. Such hooks are available from Bad Dog lures, under the label Jeweled Trebles.

When perch won't respond to flash lures and dropper or stinger lines, many anglers choose leadhead jigs or plain hooks tipped with a small minnow or grub, and they catch fish. If the perch are really fussy, try slow-falling baits such as Bad Dog's Water Fleas and many of K&E's ice flies, all single-hooked vertical lures. Otherwise, try adding a small piece of yarn, plastic or if you wish, Uncle Josh's Ice Flecks or flavor-enhanced soft baits like Berkley's Power Baits to slow the drop rate of your favorite jig. My preferred method is to tie a small tuft of marabou onto a sharp, light wire hooked ultralight jig like a Marmooska, then barely nip two or three spikes or wigglers on the end, allowing them to wriggle seductively. Perch love them.

If the perch are deep and you need to tune down your presentation, you'll be faced with the unique situation of trying to efficiently lower a tiny, slow falling jig into deep water. To tackle the odds, I recommend using HT's Hanger Rigs. These rigs are simply short lengths of metal tubing with swivels attached at each end that act as an in-line weight for getting light jigs deep quickly. One swivel is tied to your terminal line, the other to a light monofilament leader to prevent twist, with the leader shorter in length than the tube itself to prevent tangling. The leader is then tipped with a tiny ultralight ice lure

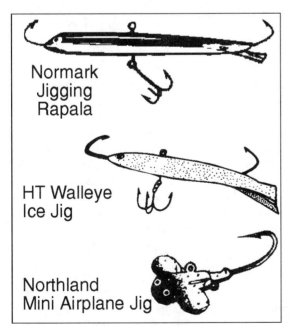

When winter perch are active, swimming minnow and swimming lures such as Jigging Rapalas, Walleye Ice Jigs and Mini Airplane Jigs drop fast, are easy to work quickly and will help maximize your catch.

such as HT's Marmooska, Custom Jigs and Spins Rat Finkee, Bad Dog's Water Fleas or System Tackles' Copepod baited with a spike, mousie or waxworm.

The idea? The tube is used as a means of getting tiny ice lures down quickly, making an ultralight presentation practical in deep water. Allow the weight to "load" your rod, then begin jigging in short, 1/16-inch to 1/8-inch movements. If anything interrupts this rhythm, set the hook.

## The Marmooska Secret

I have to elaborate on one secret to the effectiveness of any winter ultralight perch outing: HT's Marmooska Jig. I first came across these little gems in Sweden dur-

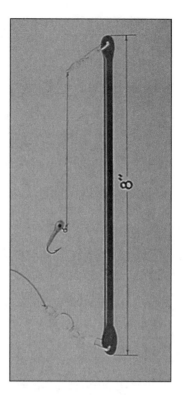

HT's "Hanger Rigs," are short lengths of metal tubing with swivels attached that act as twist- and tangle-free in-line weights for getting smaller ultralight lures into deep water efficiently.

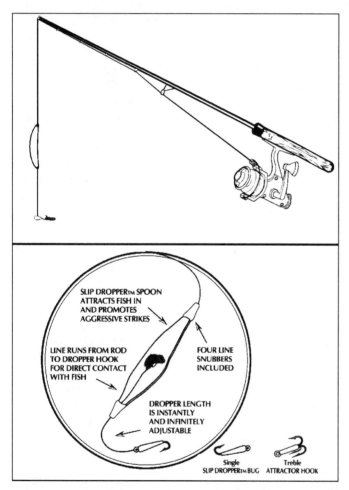

At times, dropper lines are a highly effective means of catching perch. To make one, remove the hook from a flash lure and replace it with a short monofilament leader tied to a hook or small lure tipped with a grub or minnow. The flash of the lure attracts perch, and the baited hook draws the strike. Custom Jigs and Spins "Slip Dropper," shown here, allows you to adjust dropper line length with simple line snubbers—ingenious!

ing the 1991 world ice fishing championship—and found most members of the Swedish, Finnish, Icelandic and Russian teams using them almost exclusively. The reason? They catch perch! Since they're available in sizes 6 through 16, they can be fished by themselves, ultralight, or used as the dropper lure beneath a jigging spoon or hanger rig. Because they're so effective and so versatile, I think they deserve a close review.

Of all the ice lures available today, HT's European Marmooska Jig has impressed me the most for perch fishing. The concept is simple: Marmooskas are a light wire, small-barbed hook with a precisely balanced, relatively heavy head. The heavy head allows constant contact with the bait—hence better "feel"—and the small light-wire hook and tiny barb facilitate better hooking.

In fact, if your hook is sharp, it only takes a tiny nubbin of barb to hook and hold a perch. Best of all, the smaller the barb is, the less "punch" you'll need to pack into your hook set, and one of the most important things to remember when fishing light lines for big perch is to never set the hook with a sharp snap—but rather just a firm, authoritative lift of your rod tip.

Many folks don't believe me when I point this out, but it's true. Large barbs are intended to provide insurance that hooked fish won't get off, but they weren't designed for ultralight ice fishing because they also make solid hook sets with ultralight tackle difficult—especially in deep water—causing missed fish.

The light-wire hook/light barb concept also helps in another respect: Perch often inspect baits and lures closely, ignoring anything of the wrong size, shape, color or action—and something so simple as squishing the end of a maggot or grub with an oversized, unsharpened hook often kills the bait—greatly reducing the chance of tempting jumbo perch, particularly in clear water.

With a properly sharpened, light wire hook, however, you can easily nip two or three maggots barely through the skin, keeping the bait active and increasing your catch. Yes, I know it's hard to believe something so small can make such a big difference, but alas, in the strange world of ultralight ice fishing, such simple, tiny details are often the keys to consistent success.

**One of the most important things to remember when fishing light lines for big perch is to never set the hook with a sharp snap—but rather just a firm, high, authoritative lift of your rod tip.**

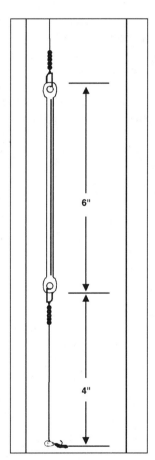

**When perch are deep and you want to fish ultralight lures, HT's perch hanger rig is the answer. A short length of metal tubing acts as an in-line weight. Swivels at each end prevent line twist, and a short monofilament leader from the tube to your jig eliminates the possibility of lure-to-main line tangling. Some anglers paint the tube a bright color to help attract perch.**

6"

4"

One more thing: The Marmooska is a horizontal bait, and since I've found most big jumbos tend to hit while "jigging up" rather than down, this feature enhances effective hook-setting percentages by exposing the hooks sideways. The head is also off center of the shank to provide a greater gap for better hooking, and actually spins the hook toward a biting fish should it strike the lure in an awkward position.

Marmooska Jewels are yet another derivative of the original Marmooska Jig. These little lures are different than anything else you'll see on the market. Besides coming in a variety of unique shapes, they feature no eyelet. A simple modified improved clinch knot or nail knot both work well to rig the lure, which because the knot cannot slide to the side on the eye, will remain in a perfectly horizontal position at all times. They work great with live bait or strips of colored plastic.

For best results with either Marmooska Jig style, establish a well-rehearsed jigging rhythm, and if anything breaks that confirmed stride, set-up. You'll be surprised how often you'll hook a fish.

## Great Lakes Presentations

Since Great Lakes perch live in such a unique environment, let's take a little closer look at presentation.

The first time you drop a lure, you'll be confronted with what can be a rather frustrating problem: the sometimes strong currents of Great Lakes bays. I've even heard some local residents call them "bay tides." The theory behind these currents on one of my favorite Great Lakes bays, Green Bay in Lake Michigan, is that they're actually wind-driven, originating at the southern part of the bay near the mouth of the Fox River. The general current circulation pattern moves along the east side of the bay, then extends around the northern part of the bay before returning down the west shore. This is only a general pattern, however. Wind direction and pressure systems may dramatically alter these patterns from day to day. Regardless of what causes these currents or the direction they're moving, they pose numerous challenges for the ice angler.

As a whole, Great Lakes perch usually remain within two feet of bottom, and if your bait isn't presented within this area, your catching percentage will drop dramatically. And all too often—if you're not careful—the strong currents will sweep your bait out of this productive zone.

This is why the preferred presentation of most Great Lakes bay ice anglers is the perch rig, a heavy bell sinker/three-way swivel type rig, tied with a light mono leader and a small hook. These rigs are popular because they make it easy to keep your bait on bottom. Most anglers bait these rigs with shiner minnows, spikes, or

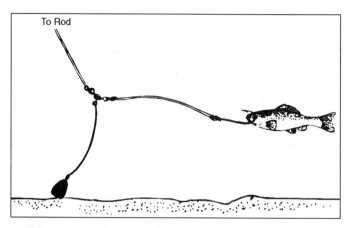

**When fishing Great Lakes bays, heavy perch rigs are used to drop presentations deep, then hold them in position on the bottom, despite the sometimes strong upwelling currents.**

wigglers. Such rigs can be fished on either a light or medium-light action ice rod spinning combo, or a smooth, easy-tripping underwater tip-up such as the Polar, Polar II Husky, or Icemaster.

However, don't be a "one method Joe" and forget to experiment with other presentations just because of the limiting factors caused by the current. I've had success

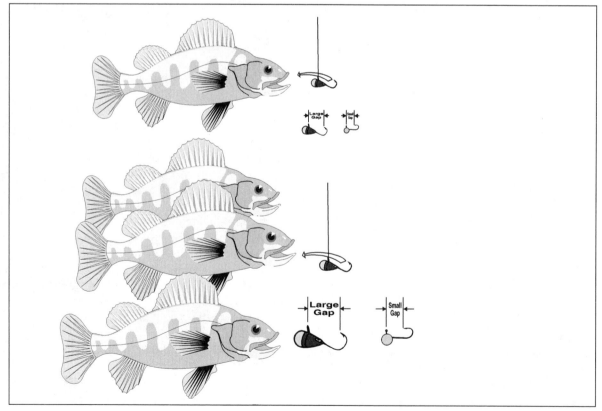

**The pivoting action of HT's Marmooska Jig has proven to be an asset when fishing finicky perch in deep water.**

**By combining productive bodies of water supporting strong, healthy jumbo perch populations with knowledge, preparation, determination, skill, mobility, versatility and use of lake maps and today's electronics, you'll be able to assemble various pieces of even the most complex winter location patterns.**

working #5-7 Jigging Rapalas tipped with crappie minnows or grubs, HT's new "Hanger Rigs" tipped with ultralight jigs and a maggot—and more recently, found weighted blade baits such as Reef Runner's Cicada tipped with a minnow head highly effective, as they add flash and vibration to attract more fish.

One of my favorite Great Lakes perch rigs is a small leadhead jig worked in conjunction with a flash lure like the Swedish Pimple or flash lure/dropper rig such as Custom Jigs and Spins Slip Dropper. The leadhead jig, tipped with a tiny "crappie" minnow or several waxworms, should be tied to a leader extending down from the flash lure. These droppers should be kept relatively short, however, to avoid tangling. Many veteran perch anglers keep two rods in the water at all times— one rigged with a heavy lure tipped with live bait and one rigged as a still-set perch rig set with a minnow.

## Fishing Schools of Perch

Once you've pinpointed an active school and determined the primary lure pattern for the day, be sure not to fish directly in the midst of the school, bringing struggling fish right up through the rest of the fish. This seems to scatter and alert other individuals to danger. Instead, immediately drop your line back down, and work the bait just above or at the top of the school. This will allow you to maximize the number of perch taken from each school by minimizing the spooking factor.

If a crowd develops around the school, fish the perimeter of the major activity. While crowds and activ-

Few anglers will refuse a plate of fresh-fried yellow perch fillets from fish of this size, which provide pure delight for the taste buds.

ity don't always spook perch, I've noticed that jumbos often repel to the outside edges of the center of activity.

And if action wanes, move. After all, if the fish won't hit after this kind of versatility, you're better off to move on in search of a more active school. Never waste too much time trying to make inactive fish bite. Instead, review your map and search for other potential areas to repeat the process. Given time, you'll likely locate another active school.

## Timing

In terms of timing, late morning and early afternoon are best, with the heaviest feeding occurring during mid-afternoon. Studies have shown that perch eat about 7 percent of their body weight daily throughout mid-winter, with most of their primary feeding activity taking place between 10 a.m. and 2 p.m., although in

One of my favorite Great Lakes perch rigs is a small hook or jighead worked in conjunction with a flash lure. Shown here is Custom Jigs and Spins "Slip Dropper," a self-contained dropper rig that allows adjustment of the dropper leader length without re-tying. (Courtesy Custom Jigs and Spins)

some situations, you'll have flurries of activity throughout the day as schools of active perch move through.

This knowledge makes the winter perch picture start to become more clear, because anytime you combine a good perch lake with a knowledge of their preferred location patterns, forage availability, top presentations and primary activity times, you're closing in on functional patterns.

## Winter Perch Recap

That's the system. By combining productive bodies of water supporting strong, healthy jumbo perch populations with knowledge, preparation, determination, skill, mobility, versatility and use of lake maps and today's electronics, you'll be able to assemble various pieces of even the most complex location patterns. In the process, you'll discover exactly where, when, how—and perhaps even why—perch are relating to certain structural elements and following specific patterns.

Even more importantly, you'll be able to determine and monitor their activity levels and, in turn, be able to modify, refine and perfect your presentation according to the activity levels and responses of jumbo perch, all to the envy of your friends—and pure pleasure of your taste buds.

**If a crowd develops around an active school, try fishing the perimeter of the activity. Jumbos will often repel to the outside edges of the center of activity.**

# Chapter 6

# *Understanding Crappies During Winter*

*T*he bright, golden setting sun gleams off the glistening ice, casting long, gray shadows across the frozen expanse before me. My heart beats anxiously. Several crappies already flop in the pail beside me, and we haven't even reached prime twilight crappie time.

I raise my rods to lift the floats from the water, skim a thin layer of ice from my holes, then return the rod stands to the ice. After all, the crappies have been biting well for the last half hour, and I'm anticipating another bite.

No sooner do the sponge bobbers settle when one is suddenly pulled under the surface with such force the bobber makes a popping noise. It hovers just under the surface for a moment, then begins disappearing slowly down the hole. I grab the jig rod, set the hook and feel heavy resistance that doubles my rod over. Crappie number twelve.

Slab crappie are probably one of the most rewarding of all winter panfish. Often, they're challenging to find in numbers—and there's something especially thrilling about setting the hook and feeling the solid, stout resistance of a big slab pulling downward. But for many ice anglers, consistent catches of slabs seldom come easy.

**Often winter "slab" crappies are challenging to find in numbers—but once you locate them, there's something especially thrilling about setting the hook and feeling the solid, stout resistance of a big crappie pulling downward.**

**A mobile approach using electronics and the right equipment can yield outstanding winter crappie catches.**

**Crappies are subject to strong population cycles and inter and intra-species competition for forage, causing them to follow some unique winter location patterns.**

Sure, catching crappies from an abundant, stunted population isn't difficult. But truly large winter crappies—those 14-inch-plus trophies—aren't always easy to find consistently, because crappies adapt well to an extensive range of environments. This wide variety of adaptations often results in a diverse array of complex, almost confusing sets of unique patterns.

While these vary depending on a number of factors including lake type, primary forage base and how far the winter season has progressed, crappies are also often subject to strong population cycles and inter- and intraspecies competition for forage, causing them to follow some unique winter location patterns. To further complicate matters, crappies are very light sensitive and will often bite only during particular times.

## Two Crappie Species

Two prominent types of crappies are present within the North American ice fishing belt—white crappies and black crappies. White crappies are traditionally a southern fish, with the mid-North American ice fishing belt

comprising the northern fringe of their range. However, while white crappies prefer slightly warmer, more turbid water than black crappies, environmental changes—increasing turbidity from development in watersheds, and increasing water temperatures from agricultural run-off and industrial discharges—along with stocking, have spread their distribution farther north.

Largely a pelagic or open water species, white crappies prefer waters featuring sparse vegetation. Their diet consists primarily of suspended zooplankton, insects, fish eggs and small minnows. While not usually traveling in the larger packs characteristic of black crappies, white crappies display schooling tendencies, and feed mostly during early morning and late afternoon twilight periods. Early evening and night bites aren't unusual. Although willing biters, their tendency to prefer warm waters makes their winter bites light, and with reduced activity, their fight is not particularly strong.

Black crappies, which inhabit river backwaters, ponds, lakes, flowages and reservoirs, are more conducive to winter fishing. Black crappies prefer clear, quiet, slightly turbid waters featuring moderate to heavy vegetation, but remain more active in deeper, cooler waters than white crappies. Feeding habits and diet are very similar to the white crappie; both species favor suspended zooplankton, insect larvae and small minnows, with most feeding activity occurring at dusk or dawn.

Black crappies, as pelagic, midwater feeders, are a more strongly schooling species than white crappies, and often travel in schools of two dozen or more fish under the ice. At times, evening shallow water movements are common, with limited feeding taking place over deep water during the day. Because they are more active in colder water temperatures, the sporting quality of black crappies is regarded as much better than white crappies.

Both white and black crappies have large eyes and are quite light sensitive. Their populations are often cyclic. Given the right conditions, good numbers of large fish may be found in many environments. Less-than-deal conditions may lead to dramatically lower population densities, or large numbers of smaller, stunted fish.

The food value of both white and black crappies is good, although white crappie from turbid waters may require an overnight soaking in cold saltwater prior to preparation.

## Primary Winter Location Patterns

Consistently locating winter crappies begins with choosing the proper lakes—those supporting good crappie populations. This may sound obvious, but I still find many winter crappie anglers fishing waters with excellent reputations, but during a "low ebb" in the crappie cycle. Or worse yet, they focus their efforts on second rate or poor crappie waters. Rather, contact a local fish biologist, guide, or other reliable source that will be up front with you regarding the current status of the crappie population in your target waters. More often than not, these sources know what lakes are "on," and can provide up-to-date information including structural "hot spots," primary forage types, favored lake patterns, and ice conditions.

Winter crappies are most known for their nomadic, roaming, open-water tendencies—and while winter patterns are similar, movements vary slightly depending on the lake type, weather and water conditions. Let's review contrasting lake type tendencies, then discuss specifics.

In river backwaters, crappies typically hold in shallow sloughs offering cover in the form of green vegetation or wood near a spring or slight current flow. Crappies remain in these areas unless the cover, forage or oxygen supplies wane, in which case they'll move closer to the current, or back into main river eddies adjoining the backwaters. Daily, twilight and evening movements between the adjacent backwaters and main channel may occur.

In natural ponds and lakes, crappies hold in shallow cover first ice, then move deep and hold near deep weed lines or flats, deep structural features such as points, rock piles and reefs, or they may suspend over deep water. If warm-water discharges or springs offer warmer temperatures than the surrounding water, crappies may be drawn to them. Late ice, crappies stage just outside shallow spawning bays, flats and structures. Again, daily twilight and evening move-

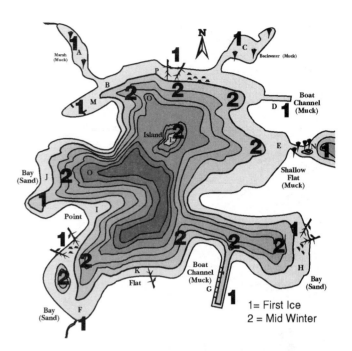

Crappies make distinct movements through the winter. During first ice, shallow, vegetated bays (M), marshes (A), backwaters (C), boat channels (D,G), and shallow flats (B,E,H,K,J) are good first and late ice areas. As mid-winter approaches many schools suspend within pockets and holes in the shallows, and along drop-offs adjoining such areas or main lake structures such as points (I) or islands (L). On smaller lakes, most mid-winter crappies spread out and suspend over deep, open water holes and flats, but near breaks into the shallows (O). Late winter, crappies return to vegetated or wood-strewn shallows to spawn, particularly areas featuring current flow such as inlets (F).

ments between shallow feeding shelves and the depths may occur.

In flowages and reservoirs, crappies hold in shallow, vegetated coves and cover-laden flats and shorelines during early ice, then move toward or into the main river channel, deep sections of creek channels, sharp breaking shorelines, deep shoreline points and deep coves on the main lake during mid-winter. They often move back toward the main lake and main river channel and forming tight schools in main lake areas running 20, 30, 40, 50 or more feet deep—although shallower schools are typically more likely to bite. Stands of deep, flooded timber and brush piles can also be good mid-winter crappie locations. Late ice, movements toward shallow spawning coves and flats will occur.

Although crappie populations are very limited in Great Lakes bays, they'll usually follow patterns similar

**Stands of deep, flooded timber and brush piles can be good mid-winter crappie locations in flowages and reservoirs.**

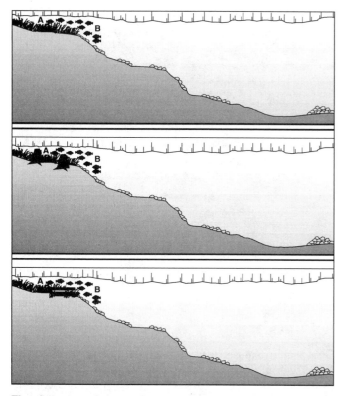

First ice, crappies are drawn to cover-laden shallows (A) and their edges (B). Bays offering vegetation (Top) are good, those offering a combination of vegetation and wood (Middle) are better, and those offering vegetation, wood and fish cribs (Bottom) are even better yet.

to those found in large reservoirs, holding in shallow cover early and late in the season, and suspending out from such areas over deep water during mid-winter.

## First Ice

Remember, "first ice" is a relative term. By my definition, "first ice" consists of a relatively short period right after ice safe enough for walking forms, before much snow settles atop the pack and much fishing pressure occurs.

This first-ice foray occurs at various times on different lake types. Within a region, "first ice" might occur on isolated river backwaters, small ponds and smaller, shallower natural lakes several days before larger, deeper natural lakes, and several weeks before very deep lakes, flowages or reservoirs. Fish each of these lake types in sequential order, and you can stay on hot "first ice" action for several weeks. Such travels can result in tremendous catches, as first ice and good crappie fishing have always been synonymous—and for good reason, as crappies tend to concentrate in easy to identify, easily accessible forage-rich areas and bite readily during this period. Ice anglers should make every effort to capitalize on this situation.

Just as safe ice develops, small boat channels and marina harbors featuring permanent dock pylons and supports provide crappies with fabulous shelter and forage options. Smaller, shallower coves and bays offering submerged wood, stumps, green vegetation, fish cribs or other forms of cover are also productive for the same reasons.

During first-ice, small boat channels and marina harbors featuring green vegetation and permanent dock pylons or supports provide crappies with fabulous shelter and forage options.

Once you learn to use sonar to track, find and follow active schools of winter crappies as they move across shallow bays, flats and shoals, you'll become more proficient at patterning first-ice crappies and learn to create more consistent first-ice catches.

A week or two later, as shallow water forage is eaten down and spooky crappies are chased out by increased activity and noise on the ice, deeper holes amid these flats, vegetated weed lines near the top of a drop-off, larger or mid-depth bays, feeding shoals and flats featuring secondary cover and convenient deep water access become centers of action. Bays fed by small creeks or streams seem to have enhanced fish attracting capabilities—just be careful, as currents retard ice development and can be a hazard.

Crappies are both ambush and open water feeders. They often use their dark camouflaged bodies to sneak up on their prey, undetected through the cover of brush or weeds. But they also school in large open water areas adjoining shallow feeding flats, then simply dart out, undetected from the dark depths, to feed on plankton or baitfish.

For some beginning anglers, this combination plus the crappies tendencies to follow wandering, open-water packs of forage can make consistent first-ice crappie catches a tremendous challenge. Consequently, it's important to use sonar for locating high-percentage hotspots on primary structures holding active crappies.

Winter crappies can be spooky at times, yet if you use your electronics and utilize a quiet approach to follow these wary schools, they're often very catchable.

**As winter progresses, crappies move into deeper water. Twilight and evening periods often offer the best action.**

Don't spend too much time working any one area. If you're not able to mark fish or convince those marks on your electronics to strike consistently, move.

Once you learn how to use sonar to track, find and follow active schools as they move across shallow bays, flats, shoals, structures or open water areas, you'll become more proficient at patterning crappies and learn to create more consistent catches. Use electronics to find the best spots, forage, and largest concentrations of fish, then drill a series of holes on the structure, carefully cover the best areas and prepare to fish, always utilizing a mobile approach.

However, keep in mind crappies are a spooky species, and there's one rule about ice fishing for crappie that is paramount: Minimize activity and noise. First-ice crappies can be highly spooky, and increased movements and noise from people walking or drilling can make them restless. Should this happen, crappies will either move out over adjacent open water areas, or cease feeding. Yet if you use your electronics and utilize a quiet, solitary approach to follow these wary schools, they're often very catchable.

In the event a noisy crowd moves in and hopelessly scatters the school, don't forget about these fish. Often, during quiet periods after most anglers have left, these fish will move back in, regroup and offer excellent fishing. First ice crappies often concentrate in easily accessible shallows and bite readily at night. However, this blitz usually doesn't last long. By morning, when activity on the ice increases, crappies spook and again, move deeper or suspend over deeper water. In most situations this movement is simply to a nearby, deeper hole or adjacent drop off, and you should be able to follow the fish there using electronics and continue catching crappies while others don't.

To be consistently successful, anglers must realize the full impact of these factors. Many ice anglers fish for crappies in the same areas with the same methods all winter—with little if any modification.

Mistake.

Crappies in most environments dramatically change their habits and behavior throughout the season—meaning location and presentation patterns change with them. By compensating for these changes, you can increase your consistency with this roaming, often fickle species.

After a week or two, when the initial "first ice" blitz has slowed in shallow, easy to locate hot spots, many folks give up until the late ice flurry. Too bad. Progressive first ice patterns are actually quite simple to decipher...and often continue further into the season than most folks realize.

## Mid-Winter Crappies

As the season progresses, many anglers are still focusing their efforts in the shallows—but typically, crappies are already beginning to move deeper. I speculate that increased activity on the ice—and possibility of underwater currents—instigate these movements.

Increased activity spooks fish, that's obvious. What many folks don't realize is that with the coldest water now at the surface, warmer layers of water begin accumulating along the bottom in the shallows. Being more dense than the cold water above, this warm water may start moving toward deeper portions of the lake. It has been speculated that this movement may result in faint underwater currents that slowly flow from the shallows into deeper water. This makes sense, because such currents would carry suspended plankton deeper, and no doubt baitfish and crappies would follow.

As the icepack thickens and warmer water settles out, current flows cease, and, with sunlight penetration reduced, shallow weeds begin dying off. This decomposition process uses dissolved oxygen and releases hydrogen sulfide and other gases into the now stagnant environment. Because of rising levels of noxious gases, less available cover, lower oxygen counts, over-predation from concentrated schools of panfish plus intense competition from larger gamefish for decreasing numbers of baitfish, crappies vacate the shallows and concentrate on primary dropoffs adjacent to productive first ice bays and flats. The only exception is when shallow, first-ice holding areas are fed by freshwater flow from an inlet or spring.

Without an inflow, the action generally starts slowing in the shallows. Now, look for significant drop-offs adjoining the most productive first ice bays or flats to draw crappies. Try fishing near flats at the top of these breaks, near bottom along the drop, the base of the break, and along outside weed lines and adjacent open-water areas in case the crappies suspend. Sure, these are transition crappies, but they're active, and large schools of active fish may hold in any of the above locations.

However, all breaks are not created equal. The best breaks feature a good combination of cover along the entire break, from the bay or flat right down to the base dropping into deep water. Breaks fed by feeder creeks or springs bring additional "warm water" and can be especially productive, because stronger underwater currents are formed. Also look for nearby mid-depth structures such as rocky bars, shoals or sunken islands near such breaks. Among the most consistent mid-winter crappie-producing structures are rocky saddle areas between islands and deep shoreline points. While weeds are often sparse in such areas, they still hold fish because minnows can relate to the rocks as a secondary form of cover. If sunlight reaches along these deeper contours permitting weed growth, you'll have an especially good spot, because the vegetation draws plankton, minnows, and crappies.

On typical breaks and structures, most active crappies hold on top of the structure, especially during twilight or cloudy days. Neutral and inactive fish relate to the sides or suspend out from them, particularly during mid-day or under bright conditions—which brings up another point.

As the ice thickens and snow cover builds, sunlight penetration is reduced, causing shallow weeds to die off, reducing cover and dissolved oxygen concentrations. In response, crappies gradually begin moving deeper on a more permanent basis. Some crappies may hold shallow or make regular feeding forays into the shallows, provided fishing pressure drops off and oxygen, weed growth and forage are sufficient to attract them. But generally by mid-season, most crappies show an affinity for deeper water, and either hold deep or suspend over deep water.

On structurally diverse lakes where cover, oxygen and forage are available in the depths, the edges of prominent, main lake structural elements such as bars, points and sunken islands are most productive. Long, main lake points featuring projections and turns leading from deep water toward the shallows are especially good. These structures act as migration routes, and the projections and turns act as holding points offering cover and forage, drawing concentrations of crappies. Open water adjacent to these features may also hold suspended, active fish. They'll usually suspend anywhere from a foot off bottom to halfway down, relating to plankton or baitfish. Either way, locate them using sonar.

Crappies in featureless, "dishpan-style" lakes or in large bays off expansive lakes are likely to suspend over the deepest available water in the main lake or bay. Although they may roam somewhat from day to day, crappies in this situation rarely make dramatic locational movements, as the combination of cold water and lowered oxygen concentrations slow their metabolism, reducing the distance they'll likely travel. Once you find fish, they'll probably remain in that same general area throughout the mid-winter period, a time that may last several weeks.

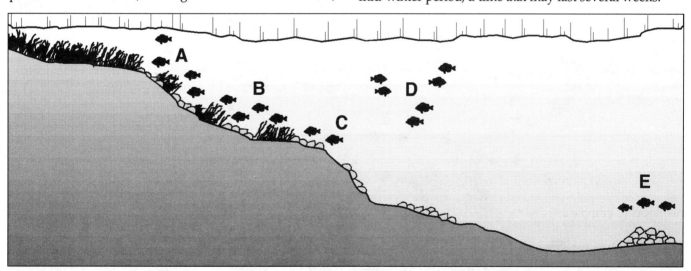

**Mid winter, most crappies drop out of the shallows (A) and hold along breaks adjoining productive first ice areas (B,C). Cover and bottom content changes often constitute primary holding areas along migration routes. Some crappies may also suspend over deep, open water areas (D), especially on smaller, shallower lakes. On larger lakes offering mid-lake structure such as rock piles or sunken islands (E), crappies may also relate to these features.**

## Late Ice

As the season progresses toward ice-out, crappies begin moving along migration routes connecting deep water and shallower spawning grounds. Using electronics and a mobile approach, look for likely migration routes, always watching closely for schools of migrating crappies. Long shoreline bars, shoals and points extending into the main lake basin that offer secondary structure and cover are especially good late ice locations.

You may have to search, intensely at times, to find late winter crappies, because they often roam the main lake area at the deepest tips of migration routes, following pelagic clouds of plankton and schools of baitfish—and these schools may break up and become scattered. Mobility, use of electronics and versatility become the keys to consistent success.

As ice-out approaches, schools begin moving shallow along their migration routes, staging near the outskirts of spring spawning areas, and hence, regrouping. As the meltdown begins and fresh water begins flowing back into the lake through opening pressure cracks, old fishing holes and springs, these crappies gradually move shallower and again become active. Be cautious of the ice, but if you can get out there, you'll experience some of the best action since first ice.

## Timing

Weather and time of day can effect crappie activity levels, simply because crappies are very light sensitive. This may not come as a surprise to many veteran crappie anglers, but for those not familiar with the crappie, understanding this may be the difference between catching a limit and catching nothing.

Long, main lake points featuring projections and turns leading from deep water toward the shallows act as migration routes, and often draw concentrations of crappies.

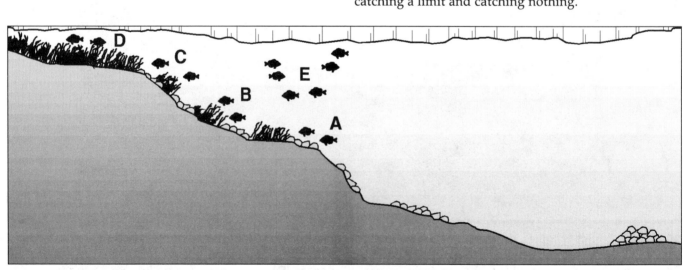

Late ice, crappies gradually move along established migration routes toward the shallows (D), where they begin staging along cover-laden drop-offs and breaks (A,B,C) or suspend off primary and secondary breaks (E). When conditions are suitable, crappies may periodically move shallow to feed (D).

**If I had to choose my favorite times to fish winter crappies, I'd choose the three hours in the morning starting one hour before sunup, and the late afternoon/early evening two hours before and after sundown.**

**Late ice, as the meltdown begins and fresh water begins flowing back into the lake through opening pressure cracks, old fishing holes and springs, crappies gradually move shallower and become quite active.**

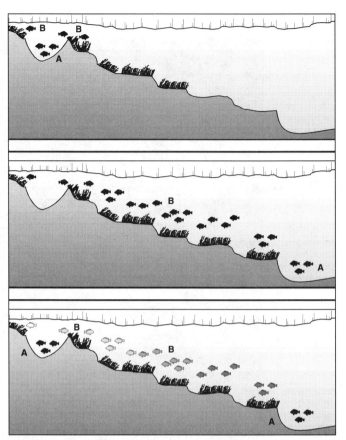

**Movements along migration routes occur daily, and the routes can be long and complex, or small and simple. Daily movements on a small, shallow lake (Top) might be within a shallow pocket amid vegetation. Given suitable conditions, crappies move up and feed (B). Under lesser conditions, they'll move deeper (A). On a larger, deeper lake (Middle) offering more complex structure, optimum conditions may cause crappies to move shallow and feed (B), but a severe cold front may send them scurrying deep (A). Both types of movements can occur at the same time, in the same area (Bottom). During ideal conditions, the fish will be shallow and active (white fish); during poor conditions, they'll be deep and hard to catch (black fish). Otherwise, you'll find crappies somewhere in-between (gray fish).**

Since crappie are more sensitive to light than most other panfish, water clarity has a major impact on primary crappie locations and activity levels. In clear water environments, for example, crappies spend most of their time in deep water, particularly during daylight hours. The best "bite" on these lakes is on cloudy days or during twilight periods. If you're a night person, ultra-clear lakes often offer excellent night fishing opportunities.

In dark water, light doesn't penetrate very deep, and the reduced light penetration allows crappies to move comfortably into shallow water to feed. Remember, heavy snow cover also reduces light penetration—which in effect can turn even clear water lakes into "dark water" lakes, changing the crappies' behavior. Under these conditions, crappies may bite well throughout the day.

If I had to choose my favorite times to fish winter crappies, I'd choose times between the first hour before sunup and the first two hours of the morning, and again two hours before sundown until a couple of hours after dark. These times are probably best because crappies have a vision advantage over their prey during twilight periods and after dark—once their eyes have had a chance to adjust to the reduced light.

I've often noticed there's a slow activity period the first 30 minutes after dark. I've heard this may be because the fish's eyes are readjusting to the changing light conditions—somewhat akin to having someone shoot our picture with a bright flash in darkness, or stepping from a well lit room into a dark one. Just as our eyes need time to adjust because the change in intensity makes seeing difficult, a crappie's eyes need time to adjust, and as they do,

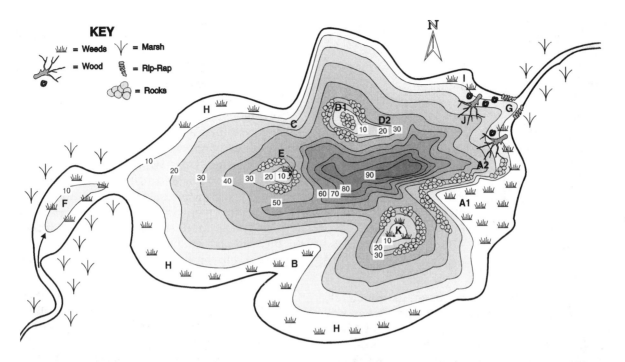

You'll have various structures to choose from when selecting where to fish winter crappies. First ice, areas F and A2 would be good bets. Look for the edges of secondary structures lining the deepest available water and establish the migration routes and holding areas. Mid-winter, mid-lake structures such as K, E, and D1 and D2 are high-percentage locations. Try the northeast side of K first because it adjoins the deepest water in the area and another major structural feature (A1)—the deep slot between K and A1 is a classic winter crappie holding area. Secondarily, bar D2 would demand time. Late ice, return to hole F, outlet G and areas A2 and J—classic cover combinations adjoining a spawning area.

feeding slows. For lack of any other logical explanation, I assume such a theory may be valid.

## Daily Movements

Always consider daily movements when trying to pattern winter crappies. As with any species, daily movements and activity levels are extremely important facets of location patterns, and in the case of crappies, are largely dictated by weather and light.

In clear water environments during bright or unstable weather conditions, expect most daytime activity to occur on flats featuring the thickest cover. There, active fish feed in pockets or edges within and along heavier batches of cover, or hold in deep water areas where the most intense light is filtered out. Also expect fishing to be sporadic, because these fish will likely be loosely schooled and somewhat inactive. In ultra-clear water environments, crappies often react to bright sunlight by moving deeper or tighter to cover and becoming less active—but given cloudy or low-light conditions, may be downright aggressive.

**Standard stick, underwater and thermal tip-us rigged with light monofilament leaders, small, well-sharpened light-wire hooks and small minnows placed strategically over a school of active crappies will take numbers of fish.**

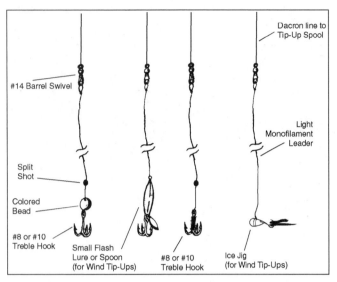

**#14 Barrel Swivel**

**Split Shot**

**Colored Bead**

**#8 or #10 Treble Hook**

**Small Flash Lure or Spoon (for Wind Tip-Ups)**

**#8 or #10 Treble Hook**

**Ice Jig (for Wind Tip-Ups)**

**Dacron line to Tip-Up Spool**

**Light Monofilament Leader**

**Tip-ups and tip-downs can be used to effectively catch winter crappie. Simple hook and sinker rigs tipped with a small minnow are usually best, but small flash lures or ice jigs set beneath tip-downs, wind or balance tip-ups can also be highly effective.**

In dark water, however, bright sunlight may generate a greater amount of plankton activity, kicking off the food chain and making crappies quite active throughout the day. During twilight and evening periods when crappies likely cannot see well, fishing is seldom productive.

If you're serious about making the most of your crappie fishing this winter, carefully plan your strategies in advance, consider the time of year and conditions, always be mobile, use electronics and experiment. You'll soon find that your properly applied knowledge and versatility will lead to more consistent winter crappie success.

## Effective Winter Strategies for Crappies

Once you've chosen a lake; considered how far the winter has progressed, the time of day and the light intensity to decipher structures offering the best fish-holding potential; and, hopefully, located active fish, you can begin considering the most effective presentation.

Crappies can be caught with consistency using tip-ups. Standard, underwater and thermal tip-ups rigged with light monofilament leaders, small, well-sharpened light-wire hooks and small minnows placed strategically over a school of crappies will take numbers of fish. Tip-ups also can be set along probable migration routes to help decipher the time and distance of movement, and primary strike zones. Stagger the depths your baits are set to cover water, and be sure the trips are set lightly. The slightest amount of resistance may cause crappies to drop the bait.

Wind tip-ups, tip-downs and ultralight "umbrella" style tip-ups are also highly effective. If you've never fished such units, you might want to give them a try. Such designs are simple. Basically these modified tip-ups feature sturdy frames supporting a single upright that provides a base for a fulcrum-like "rocker arm." On wind tip-ups, the reel spool is mounted atop one end of the rocker arm, while the other end features a thin plastic or metal flap that increases surface area to catch the wind. Line runs from the spool to a hole in the wind flap, so when the wind blows against the wind flap and rocks the arm, the generated movement provides a "jigging" action to your presentation.

This movement is also adjustable, regulated by a tension spring mounted on the upright and extending to the spooled end of rocker arm. When tension is increased, movement is lessened and better controlled, especially when using larger, heavier baits or while fishing in strong winds. When tension is released, movement is increased—a distinct advantage when fishing smaller baits or relatively calm conditions.

The advantage of using such strategies for crappies is that the additional regulated jigging action helps attract their attention, and when they strike, the resistance felt by these light striking fish is minimal because the rocker arm dips and the line simply unwinds effortlessly from the spool. Ultimately, this results in better tip-up catches.

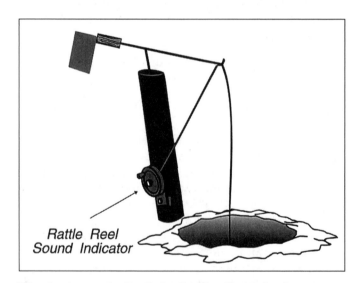

*Rattle Reel Sound Indicator*

**Tip downs and ultralight "umbrella style tip-ups are becoming increasingly popular each year. One advantage of using such units includes additional jigging action designed to enhance the attracting qualities of your presentation. More importantly, however, tip-downs and ultralight umbrella style tip-ups offer minimal resistance to finicky, light-biting winter crappies, thereby enabling anglers incorporating these units to catch more fish.**

Recently, extremely particular winter crappie anglers have taken this concept even further with the 'tip-down" style tip-up concept. Like wind tip-ups, these highly sensitive designs feature a sturdy frame supporting an upright fitted with a rocker arm often made from the lightweight wire from an umbrella stein—hence the name—or in some cases, a lightweight jig pole. Depending on the model, a spool of line is attached to the base of the upright or the rear of the jig pole.

As with a wind tip-up, the fulcrumed rocker arm or jig

**Always spool with fresh, strong thin diameter low memory premium monofilament when ice fishing for slab winter crappies. (Courtesy Berkley Outdoor Technologies Group)**

pole provides an automatic jigging motion, just to a lesser degree. When a fish strikes, the rocker arm or jig pole dips effortlessly, indicating the strike, and as the biting fish moves away with the bait, the free-spooled rattle reel sound indicator or jig pole ice reel smoothly feeds out line. Obviously, since the light-biting fish feels virtually no resistance, crafty anglers using these ultra-sensitive designs often enjoy substantial winter crappie catches at times other anglers catch few or none.

Remember to rig lightly, free spool your reels and set your trips delicately. When a fish strikes, gently set the hook and ice the fish hand over hand in traditional tip-up style, or grab the jig rod and fight the fish jig rod style, depending on the design you're using. Either way, however, always use care when setting the hook and fighting these fish, as crappies have tender mouths and hooks can easily be torn free if you're not careful.

## Jigging

Many crappies are taken each year on jigglesticks and jig poles and, when fishing shallow water, they're really all you'll need. I prefer somewhat longer rods with good bend

**Because of their light-strike sensing capabilities and low resistance to biting fish, tip-downs are a highly effective means of catching finicky winter crappies.**

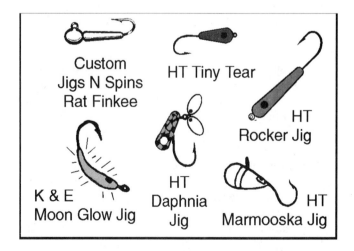

**Small, ultralight and micro jigs such as HT's Marmooskas, Tiny Tears, Daphnias or Rocker Jigs are fabulous crappie baits. Other popular lures include K&E's Moon Glow, and Custom Jigs and Spins Rat Finkee.**

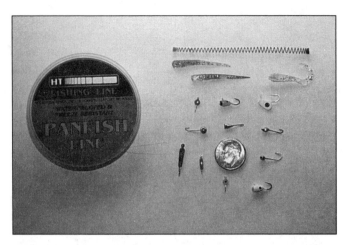

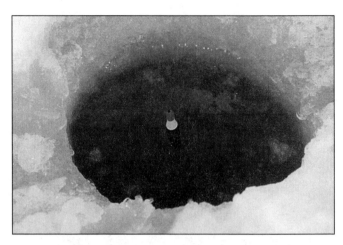

**When crappies are fussy, bites will be quite passive, so lighter, smaller and slower ultralight presentations are often the key to success.**

**Advanced ice crappie float techniques include the addition of a good quality, balsa-style slip float such as Thill Tackle's Center Slider or HT's balsa slip floats.**

at the tip for sensitivity, soft hook sets and fish control, and I also prefer using a spring bobber for improved bite detection.

Be sure your rod features a soft, sensitive tip that tapers to a firm backbone, as found on HT's light action Polar Gold, Icemaster or Blue Polar Lite rods. Sensitive ultralight or micro ice rods such as HT's Ice Blues, Icemaster or Polar Gold micro ice rods with genuine cork or thin wood handles are also good bets for feeling the subtle bites of finicky crappies. Such actions offer maximum sensitivity when the crappies are biting light, allowing you to lift up slightly and watch your rod tip to sense if a finicky fish has sucked in your jig, instead of having to set up hard and risk spooking fish. But remember, these designs offer more in the way of sensitivity than firm fish fighting power, so be prepared to lose some crappies fishing this way. Many anglers prefer to use slightly stiffer rods and the help of a spring bobber to detect bites, allowing both strength and sensitivity.

Once you've compromised on the best rod action, combine this with a smooth, lightweight, ball bearing spinning reel that features smooth, multi-setting drags and smooth-turning bail rollers. Be sure your reel is properly lubricated for cold weather use. Spool with fresh, strong, thin diameter, low memory premium monofilament such as Berkley's Ultrathin, Trilene XL or DuPont's Stren in 2 to 4 lb. test. By doing so, you'll have a system so sensitive that even if you breathe on your rod tip you'll see motion. When crappies are fussy, bites will be quite passive. Seldom will hits feel like a tap or a pull, but rather just a sense of weightlessness, and you'll need a sensitive system to detect these light bites.

As for lures, use lightweight jigs no heavier than 1/16 ounce, as they sink slowly, provide excellent depth control, and closely match the crappies preferred natural for-

age sizes. In most instances, 1/32 and 1/64 ounce horizontals in hook sizes 6, 8, 10 or 12 work best, depending on the situation. Of course, the fussier the fish, the smaller, lighter and slower the presentation should be. Small, ultralight and micro jigs such as HT's Marmooskas or #14 Marmooska Jewels, HT's Tiny Tears, Custom Jigs and Spins' Rat Finkees, Bad Dogs Water Fleas or K&E's Moon Glows also work wonders.

Most anglers also tip their jigs with some form of live bait. Ultralight ice jigs tipped with waxworms, spikes or small minnows seem to produce best, especially around weedy areas where crappies are foraging on water lice and small baitfish. I prefer grubs and maggots to minnows as jig tippers, namely because they're much easier to transport and keep alive, and can be used on a variety of lure sizes, including tiny micro jigs. Waxworms, goldenrod grubs, poppers, mousies, spikes and wigglers are also well-known favorites.

Another less available but regionally popular winter crappie tipper is chena bait. Chena bait consists of strips of seal skin brought in from Alaska. While not always legal and often difficult to find, chena bait is a white, fleshy, neutrally buoyant mass that swells in water, and when used in thin, tiny strips, quivers and closely resembles water lice, the favored forage of winter crappies in many lakes. For best results, fish chena bait strips on small horizontal jigs or ice ant style lures. Black jigs seem to produce best, mainly because the color contrast helps crappies find your lure, but also because the black bodies look like a tiny insect or water bug and the white chena bait resembles water lice.

Minnows are also productive. No doubt, a small 1 to 3-inch minnow such as a shiner or fathead dangled on a tiny jighead below a small bobber has accounted for the majority of the crappies caught through the ice

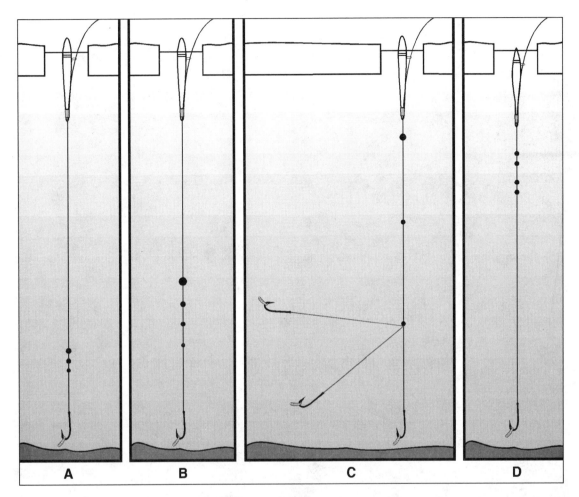

For maximum efficiency, rig a slip float until it's weighted almost neutrally buoyant, which usually means most of the float is underwater. This allows a light biting crappie to strike and swim away without feeling much resistance. Placing several shot together toward the bait will help drop it quickly and hold it in place, even in current (A). Placing several shot of gradually larger to smaller size close to the bait will result in a moderately fast drop (B). Spreading the shot will allow the bait to slowly filter down—a great technique for fussy crappies in still water (C). Placing the shot high will hold the float low, but allow for an extremely slow drop rate of the bait (D).

each season on many waters. The traditional all-around favorite winter crappie rig is probably a 1/2-inch or smaller diameter sponge or styrofoam bobber, a BB-size split shot, and a #6 teardrop or specialty hook, such as a Tru-Turn, tipped with a minnow. The Tru-Turn has improved my hooking percentage tremendously because of its so called "cam action." You may want to try them.

Better yet, try a balsa float. Small styrofoam bobbers work, but tend to ice up and must be cleaned off periodically to minimize resistance to the fish. Sponge floats are a slight improvement, as ice can easily be squeezed off however, in both of the above cases lines cannot be reeled up, but rather must be "hand over handed"—causing problems when fishing light lines or deep water.

Advanced ice crappie float techniques include the addition of a good quality, balsa slip style float such as Thill Tackle's center slider or HT's balsa slip floats. When properly weighted and used on a jigging rod or still line, slip floats enable you to use spinning tackle in shallow or deep water and will help you sense the subtle bites of those big, wary slabs. Remember, big crappies get big by expending the least amount of energy to feed, and being particular, when big fish hit they must not feel anything. Any unusual pressure felt while swimming away with their food will cause them to expel it many times faster than you can react to set the hook.

For maximum efficiency, rig your slip float until it's weighted almost neutrally buoyant, which usually means most of the float body is underwater with only the top of

**Use your electronics to locate active schools, select a beginning presentation and monitor the crappies response to your lure styles, sizes, colors and action, then choose the presentation that generates the best response.**

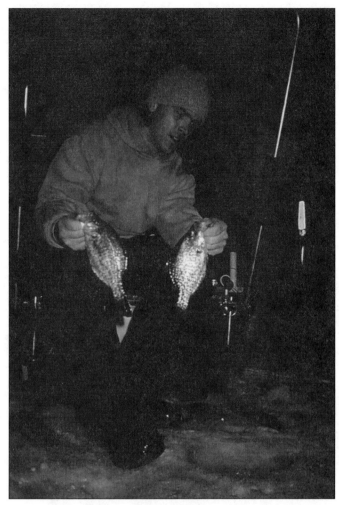

**Since both plankton and baitfish are part of the crappie's winter diet, you must keep both behaviors in mind when fishing them if you want to be consistently successful.**

the stem protruding. This allows a crappie to strike and swim away without feeling any resistance. Just remember, while efficient, such systems must be fished in a shanty on all except the most mild days, because they will freeze up, rendering the system ineffective.

Once you've selected a lure or bait, lower it to the fish, always experimenting with various lure types, styles, sizes and colors, and with a variety of live baits. This is important, because often, crappies will show a distinct preference for a particular style, size, color or combination over another. Also consider jigging action. At times, simply a slight shaking or quivering motion rather than an aggressive up-and-down working of the lure will produce.

After discovering the best bait style, type, size, color and jigging action, work your school from top to bottom. While it's best to catch them above or on top of the school so the rest of the fish aren't disturbed, crap-

pies can be notoriously depth oriented, and you must experiment to find the primary strike zone, and these vary from day to day. Once you've detected what depth the crappie prefer to feed, key in on that level.

Finally, be cautious when setting the hook. If you jerk the line to set-up, you'll miss quite a few, but if you simply lift up and keep pressure on the fish, you'll experience better hooking percentages, because this gives the fish time to get the hook into its mouth and places the hook in a better hooking position. Crappies have a very thin tissue surrounding their mouth, and if you set the hooks with a hard thrust you'll likely tear a hole in this membrane, meaning if the fish gains any slack line, your hook will simply fall out.

If you lift your rod tip sharply to stick the hook point through this membrane and simply allow the resistance of the fish to poke the barb through, you'll ice more crappies.

## Minnows or Plankton

This brings us to the age-old presentation debate of minnows versus plankton.

Correct winter crappie presentations depend on the crappie's primary forage. I've found that plankton-oriented species such as bluegills and sunfish respond primarily to tiny, subtly worked micro-style ice jigs and flies lightly tipped with small grubs, maggots or thin plastic strips, because they best mimic plankton—while baitfish-oriented predators such as pike, walleyes and lake trout seem more receptive to larger, more aggressively worked jigging lures that better imitate minnows.

However, since plankton and baitfish are both part of the crappie's winter diet, you must keep both behaviors in mind. Early in the season, when the crappie's primary forage is comprised of baitfish, spoons and other minnow-imitating lures are the key. But when baitfish numbers drop later in the season, opportunistic crappies respond by switching largely to suspended plankton as a primary forage base. So, even if you're a highly accomplished jigging spoon enthusiast, tiny micro lures tipped with grubs will generally outproduce most flash lures during late-ice.

Basic micro methods are fairly easy to master. Begin with a super-sensitive light-action spinning rod with solid backbone and a thin, sensitive, wispy tip. These designs provide the necessary sensitivity for feeling the barely discernible, half-hearted strikes of late-ice crappies—yet provide the strength to set the hook. HT's Micro Ice Rod Systems combined with a smooth ultralight or micro spinning reel such as HT's MP-1750 series, are perfectly suited for the job.

Spool with premium 3 lb. test such as Berkley's Trilene XL, Ultrathin or Fenwick's Liteline when fishing twilight periods, dark water, or less spooky fish, and one or two pound when fishing smaller lures, clear

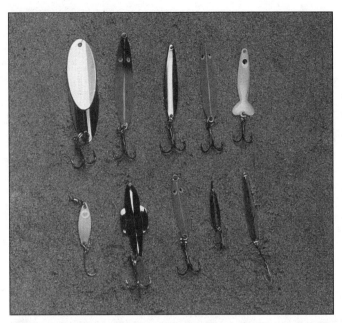

When ultralight plankton imitations don't work efficiently, try switching to a more aggressive jigging approach using smaller size jigging spoons. It's likely the crappies are feeding on minnows, and such lures better represent the larger, flashier movement of baitfish.

water, daylight periods or fussy fish. You'll find lighter lines are less visible and allow better lure action.

Productive jigging actions depend on the time of day. Daphnia, a species of plankton active during twilight periods, make slight wiggling, horizontal movements. Copepods, on the other hand, make sharp, darting vertical motions and are active during midday. Consequently, active, aggressive jigging motions with spoon-shaped micro baits such as HT's #14 Tiny Tears tend to produce better during the day, while more subtle actions produced by tiny horizontals such as Custom Jigs and Spins #12 Rat Finkees or HT's #16 Marmooskas produce better during twilight periods. The addition of live bait to add natural scent, taste and texture to your presentation is extremely beneficial, especially with dramatically slowed micro methods that allow crappies ample time to examine your offering before deciding to strike.

Once you've chosen your weapon, lower your bait to the marked fish. Provided your transducer is level, micro lures register clearly on electronics—as will any crappies that wander within range of the transducer. Lower your bait to their level or slightly above them, and begin jigging, always working above or right at the top of the fish. This allows you to draw hooked fish away from, rather than through the school. Using this trick, you can often take several late-ice crappies from a school before spooking them.

Once they spook, the action you impart depends on the crappie's activity levels and response time, but normally, gentle, 1/16 to 1/8-inch jiggling motions interspersed with occasional pauses seems to produce best, but watch the fish's reaction on your electronics. They'll let you know what they like—and what they don't.

Finally, keep in mind that since crappies have specialized eyes, they have a vision advantage over prey during twilight hours, and feed most heavily during these periods, especially in clear water environments. Still, being dark, lures featuring a touch of phosphorescence will help crappies find your bait, increasing your catch.

## Spoon Feeding Winter Crappies

When plankton imitations don't work efficiently, the switch to more aggressive jigging lures such as smaller size spoons and jigging minnows is often the answer.

I've often taken numerous electronic readings searching for crappies, marked suspended fish, and strongly suspected they're crappies. I usually start by lowering a smaller plankton imitating bait tipped with a grub into the depths, stop and begin subtle jigging motions. If the fish aren't interested, I'll begin experimenting with a variety of jigging actions, then various ultralight and micro-style lures, sizes and colors. If this still doesn't work, I often rely on a winter crappie tactic

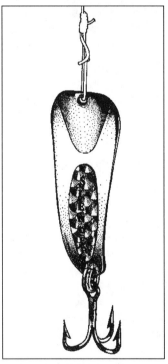

Reef Runner's Slender Spoon is a lightweight, slow-falling flutter spoon available in a wide variety of sizes. It's highly effective for winter crappie holding in shallower depths.

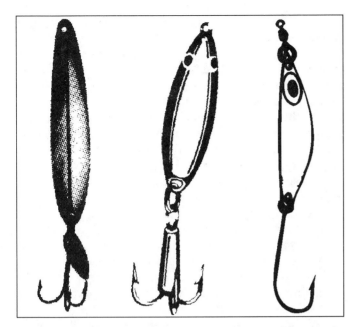

When winter crappies are feeding on minnows in deeper water, small heavy-bodied spoons such as Bay de Noc's Swedish Pimple or Custom Jigs and Spins Stinger work well. For a slower fall, try Bait Rig's Willospoons. All create good representations of wounded minnow, and will be more effective than smaller, plankton imitating lures and baits when crappies are feeding on minnows.

that worked in a similar situation on a northern Wisconsin lake several winters before.

The crappies weren't biting my ultralight plankton presentations, but marking fish on bottom, I decided to try jigging a Swedish Pimple on bottom for walleyes. After icing several hard-fighting walleyes, I began lowering my spoon, and about halfway down, discovered a twist in my line. While pausing to straighten the twist, I was inadvertently working the spoon up and down. Watching my electronics from the corner of my eye, I noticed one of the suspended marks rise for the spoon. Thinking quickly, I wrapped the twist into the spool of my spinning reel and closed the bail, just in time to feel the strike and set the hook into a fourteen inch slab crappie. After landing the fish, I replaced the tangled line with a replacement spool of fresh line, re-rigged, and using small jigging spoons, proceeded to limit out on respectable crappies inside two hours.

Thinking this tactic might work again, I located another school the next day, drilled a hole, tied on and lowered a #2 silver Swedish Pimple and began jigging. To my surprise, a crappie rose immediately and smacked the lure aggressively. I took four fish from my first hole, and moving around the area, wound up taking another 15 from the school in just a little over 45

minutes—then the action slowed. With the sun quickly sinking lower in the sky, I packed up and located a second school, and was able to add a couple of more fish to my pail before darkness settled in and my growling stomach sent me ambling back to shore.

Since that time, I've often used smaller jigging spoons for winter crappie, and often seen fabulous results. What makes jigging spoons so deadly? One reason is they give off a flash, vibration and fluttering action that closely resembles an easily obtained crippled minnow—an easy meal that's hard for crappies to resist, which really isn't so surprising when you consider crappies aren't a typical panfish. Remember, they not only feed on plankton during winter, but baitfish as well.

I've found plankton-oriented fish such as bluegills, sunfish and smelt respond mostly to tiny, subtly worked micro-style jigs tipped with grubs, while baitfish-oriented feeders such as pike, walleyes and lake trout seem more receptive to larger, more aggressively worked jigging lures. However, since both plankton and baitfish are parts of the staple winter diet for crappies everywhere, crappies cross the line between these two categories, and you must keep these habits in mind whenever attempting to choose the proper presentation.

When crappies are plankton oriented, anglers choosing micro jigs and subtle presentations do well. However, on days when their primary forage is comprised of baitfish, micro jigs and grubs can be a zero. I've seen it. That's why dedicated crappie anglers rely heavily on jigging spoons throughout the winter season—although most anglers will agree they experience the most jigging spoon success from first ice through the early portion of the mid-winter period, before baitfish populations are reduced. At this point, opportunistic crappies often respond to this environmental change by switching to plankton as a primary forage base.

So even if you're a highly skilled ultralight or micro jig enthusiast and have enjoyed success with tiny jigs tipped with maggots or grubs, don't forget: There will be days when jigging spoons tipped with minnows often out-produce all other lures...sometimes dramatically.

Just as this spoon strategy dictates primary productive timing, it also dictates primary location patterns. In many waters, you'll find baitfish-feeding crappies relating mostly to mid-depth or deep-water structures such as prominent hard bottom or vegetated humps, rock bars, weed lines with gradually sloping edges, or occasionally, depending on the minnow species they're feeding on, extensive open water pelagic areas adjoining deep weed lines.

Jigging spoons are especially well-suited for fishing such situations because you can cover more water in search of active fish faster and more efficiently with a spoon than with a jig. Furthermore, once you locate a

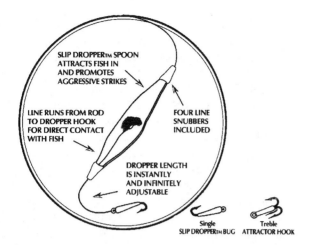

SLIP DROPPER™ SPOON ATTRACTS FISH IN AND PROMOTES AGGRESSIVE STRIKES

LINE RUNS FROM ROD TO DROPPER HOOK FOR DIRECT CONTACT WITH FISH

FOUR LINE SNUBBERS INCLUDED

DROPPER LENGTH IS INSTANTLY AND INFINITELY ADJUSTABLE

Single SLIP DROPPER™ BUG

Treble ATTRACTOR HOOK

**Dropper rigs are also highly effective presentations for winter crappies. The flash of the lure draws the fish's attention, and the trailing hook tipped with a grub or minnow draws the strike. Pictured here is Custom Jigs and Spins' Slip-Dropper, a self-contained dropper rig that allows you to change the length of your dropper without re-tying, using the line snubbers at the top and base of the spoon body.**

school, you can jig spoons on prominent secondary structural features such as tight turns in an irregular weed line with pinpoint accuracy.

Basic jigging spoon methods are fairly easy to master. Begin with a slightly longer than usual, medium-light action spinning rod with a sensitive tip. Longer, sensitive, strong-backboned rods take up slack and provide the necessary leverage and control when jigging, yet provide sensitivity for feeling subtle strikes and increasing hooking percentages. HT's ultralight Polar Gold or Berkley's ultralight Lightning rods combined with a smooth ultralight spinning reel such as those made by HT, Mitchell, Shakespeare, Daiwa, Silstar or others are perfectly suited for the job.

Next, spool up with premium quality 3 lb. test when fishing clear water with smaller spoons, and 4 lb. when fishing larger lures, darker water, twilight periods or less-spooky fish. However, keep in mind lighter line is less visible in clear water or when fishing particular fish with smaller spoons, plus allows more lure action—and I've found line heavier than 4 lb. test really isn't necessary—with the exception of situations where you're fishing over thick vegetation or wood, close to jagged rocks, where the 4 lb. takes the nervous edge off when fighting a heavy crappie. You can also get away with heavier line when fishing fast-falling spoons, depending on their specific weight and sink rate, the depth of the water, wind speed and the presence of currents.

As for specific lures, smaller Bay de Noc Swedish Pimples, HT's 1/8-ounce Marmooska Spoons, Bait Rigs

Walleye Willospoons, Northland Fire-Eye Spoons or Custom Jigs and Spins' Stinger—or "Slip Dropper," the flash lure attractor with adjustable snell and attractor hook all in one—are good bets. Light colors often perform best, probably because they resemble natural forage such as light-colored minnows or plankton. For best results, try tipping these jigs with a thin strip of plastic, small grub, nymph, waxworm or small minnow to add contrast, natural taste, texture and scent to your presentation. A small strip of glow tape such as HT's Nuke Tape, can help attract fish in deep or dark water, or when fishing during twilight or evening periods.

Tie jigging spoons on using a split ring to enhance their action, and attach a small, ball bearing swivel about a foot above the spoon. This helps reduce line twist, especially when fishing deep water—and if you wish, allows you to spool your reel with light line for a faster drop rate and increased sensitivity, and still add heavier leader material near the lure.

By the way, selecting a spoon featuring the proper drop rate for the fishing conditions is the primary key to success. In general, smaller, lighter, flattened bent designs drop the slowest, with larger, heavier, slightly rounded spoons falling the quickest. But there are exceptions. Say, for example, you like the shape and action of a particular heavy spoon but feel the crappies are unable to respond to its fast fall. In such cases, you can switch to a similar size, shape and action spoon made of zinc or another similar, lighter metal that displaces more water and falls more slowly.

When an especially slow fall is needed, try light-weight jigging spoons like Bait Rig's Panfish Willospoon or Reef Runner's Slender Spoon, or dress your spoon by sliding a plastic tube lure over the body to further slow its descent rate. Lures rigged this way also feature a more active and erratic flutter than other spoons, helping attract fish. Because of their light weight and slow fall, you'll likely have to go with lighter line when using spoons of this design. Small spoon-shaped "teardrop" style lures such as HT's Walleye Spoons, Custom Jigs and Spins' Rocker, Striper Special, Purest or Rembrandt may also be a good compromise. In deep water or situations where a quick fall is desired, use heavier, fast sinking models.

As for color, metallic finishes such as gold or silver that give off flash that mimic baitfish are best. My favorite colors include silver or chrome with blue prism in clear water, silver or chrome with chartreuse or gold prism for stained water, and gold or hammered copper and a touch of florescent orange in dark water or low light conditions. Contrasting-colored, painted hooks can also be a helpful fish-attracting addition.

Adding live bait for adding natural scent, taste and texture is usually a good idea—but isn't always necessary when crappies are going for the higher and faster lifts,

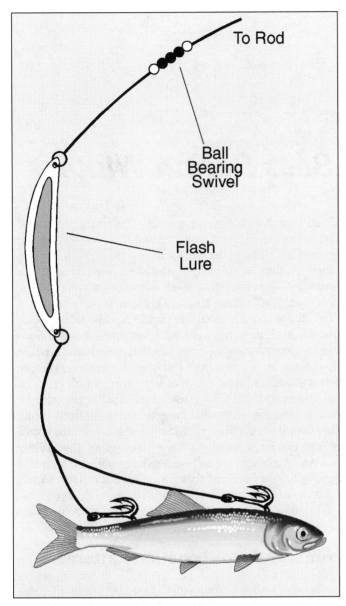

To Rod

Ball
Bearing
Swivel

Flash
Lure

**When crappies are really fussy, go with a long line, light-leadered dropper with a stinger hook tipped inside a small, one-inch shiner. Attaching a ball bearing swivel about 10 inches up the line from your spoon will eliminate the problem of line twist and reduce frustrating tangles.**

such as chemically sharpened or reversed barb designs, are especially good. Normally, tipping the hook with a two inch fathead minnow will help increase the number of strikes. When the crappies are really fussy, go with a long line, light-leadered dropper with a stinger hook tipped with a one inch shiner. It helps!

Once you've chose your weapon, begin lowering the bait to the marked fish. With your sonar's transducer situated level in the hole, the spoon will show up clearly on the display, as will crappies that wander within range of the transducer's signal. Lower your spoon to their level or slightly above them, and begin jigging.

The action you give the spoon depends on the crappie's activity level. When they're sluggish, a slow, methodical jiggling motion interspersed with occasional three to six inch lifts off bottom is adequate. For especially active crappies, I've found lifting the spoon up six to eighteen inches will trigger more strikes. Just remember, no matter how high you lift the spoon, you should allow it to free fall all the way back to the base of your drop. With few exceptions, making consistently natural, loose fluttering motions with the lure after every lift is the bread and butter method for jigging winter crappies with spoons. At times, much slighter movements will be the key.

Finally, very aggressive minnow-feeding crappies may even take swimming minnows and lures. If you're really into them, try a Normark Jigging Rapala or System Tackle's Walleye Flyer. They may work wonders. Regardless, watch the fish's reaction on your electronics. Again, they'll let you know what they like—and perhaps more importantly, what they don't.

As you can see, to be consistently successful with winter crappies, you must be mobile, versatile in the proper use of a variety of lures and presentations, and well-versed in applying the right lures and techniques given the lake type, time of year, structure, forage base and other related factors. By doing so, you can learn to apply total winter crappie patterns, and as a result, improve your winter crappie catches.

since this action triggers more of a reflex strike. On the other hand, live bait is extremely beneficial with slowed, short lift jiggling methods that give sluggish crappies ample time to study your offering before deciding to strike.

When tipping with live bait, some anglers opt for spoons featuring single hooks larger than the standard treble found on most jigging spoons. While some popular spoons come rigged with single hooks, you'll likely have to replace the treble hook yourself. Specialty hooks,

# Chapter 7

# *Understanding White Bass During Winter*

After nearly two hours on the ice searching for evasive schools of white bass, I have yet to land one. In fact, other than a couple of wayward crappies and a perch, I haven't had so much as a strike. I've searched several shoreline points adjacent to deep water, a couple of mid-depth reefs, a large expanse of mid-lake flat area, a vegetated shoreline shoal with baitfish all over it, even some deep, open water. No luck.

I decide to try a rocky, deep mid-lake bar. To my relief, I set up my electronics and mark a large batch of tightly schooled, suspended fish. Quickly, I fire up my trusty power auger, drill a hole and drop a Marmooska Spoon baited with a minnow into the icy depths. Instantly, my rod tip slams down with such power the handle is almost ripped from my hand. I set up, and with the rod doubled over and drag whining, begin fighting what feels like a sailfish toward the surface.

Soon, the wide, silvery body of a plump, sassy white bass flops onto the ice at my feet. I breathe a sigh of exuberance as I remove the hook and toss the fish to the side, then quickly lower the lure again, and within seconds, enjoy a repeat performance.

White bass can be difficult to locate, but since they're a very active species, once a school is found, white bass provide some of winter's fastest fishing. The trick is knowing how—and where—to find them efficiently.

On the ice, white bass are easy to recognize, as their silvery-white bodies are lined with distinctive, black-dotted horizontal stripes along their sides. They're most commonly found in rivers and adjoining river backwaters, large lakes, flowages and reservoirs, but have been stocked successfully in a number of smaller inland waters as well. They are primarily meat-eaters, feeding on open water baitfish such as shiners or shad, but they also feed on microscopic crustaceans, insect larvae and small minnows. Because their winter feeding habits often coincide closely with those of the yellow perch and crappie, mixed bag catches with these species aren't unusual. White bass have a tendency to feed more by scent than sight, however, and while typically most active during daytime hours, good night-bites can occur.

Although white bass are known to relate to shallow structure and suspend just beneath the surface during open-water periods, in winter they tend to hold deeper, either relating to mid-depth and deep water main lake structures or suspending over deep, open water areas. However, don't expect them to remain in one place very long—these schools are quite mobile and probably demonstrate the most frequent and longest sub-ice migrations and movements of any panfish. In addition, white bass can be very cyclic in population densities, so be sure to call ahead and time your fishing efforts wisely.

The yellow bass is a close cousin that is also caught through the ice. Differentiating yellow bass from white bass isn't difficult; the prominent yellow coloration and broken black stripe along their sides gives the yellow bass away. They're usually somewhat smaller than white bass, but fight hard for their size. Their primary winter patterns are very close to the white bass.

Fried or baked, the food value of both white and yellow bass is delicious.

## Primary Winter Location Patterns

When fishing winter white bass, be prepared for a hunt. Location and behavior can vary greatly from lake

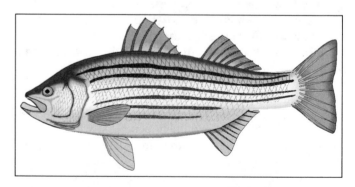

**The characteristic long, dark stripes lining the sides of white bass give this fish its unique appearance. Many anglers argue that white bass are winter's most aggressive and hard-fighting panfish species.**

**White bass are possibly one of winter's scrappiest and hardest-fighting panfish.**

Once the ice, white bass are easy to recognize, as the sides of their silvery-white bodies are lined with distinctive, black-dotted horizontal stripes. (Courtesy Custom Jigs and Spins)

to lake, even location to location, day to day and hour to hour, depending on the lake type, depth, water clarity, available structure, and primary forage base.

In river backwaters and sloughs, white bass usually hold near the mouths and openings of current-laced backwater sloughs leading to the main river channel, but periodic movements into shallow backwater lakes and coves may occur when conditions are right and adequate forage is present. In natural lakes where large populations of white bass exist with little competition, it may seem like they're everywhere—deep and shallow, on bars and humps, along shoals and in open water. This is because white bass roam in search of food, and wherever they find it, they'll stay. In flowages and reservoirs patterns are similar, although deep water next to flats, reefs and deep water surrounding the river channel, especially near the lower end of the lake adjoining the dam, can be particularly productive.

However, while white bass may be concentrated in several large schools, because they must compete with other panfish—in many environments, yellow perch, cisco and crappie—they will typically feed aggressively but tend to scatter. In fact, it's not uncommon to find schools of white bass within the same lake environment following several patterns, using two or more types of structure, even utilizing various ecological niches. Ironically, this means white bass are often hard to track consistently, but once you find them, fishing is usually fast.

This won't sound very scientific, but the easiest way to consistently find wandering winter white bass is by keeping your eyes peeled for crowds of anglers. In waters receiving a lot of intelligent fishing pressure, someone usually finds white bass, and it doesn't take long for the word to spread. Don't be afraid to join in the fun.

Yellow bass are a close cousin of the white bass and are often taken through the ice in some regions of the North American ice fishing belt. Notice the broken stripe along the fish's side, identifying it as a yellow bass.

**White bass are often hard to track consistently, but once you find them, fishing is usually fast.**

If you're fortunate enough to fish a lake with only slight fishing pressure, you'll enjoy the thrill of one of ice fishing's most challenging hunts. Since white bass are typically competitive and aggressive, they forage efficiently in open water, over shallow structures, along the outside of bars and shoals—just about anywhere for that matter. To make matters more intense, white bass aren't particularly structure-oriented, so even when they're in a general area and you catch some, they seldom stay in the same spot long. Yet the situation isn't impossible. Patterns develop as white bass migrate to given areas during certain winter periods.

## First Ice

First ice, high percentage white bass locations are often similar to areas where you'd look for winter crappies or yellow perch. Holes within shallow cover-laden backwaters, flats, bays or coves and inside turns, points, slots or openings close to main channels or main lake basins along primary shoreline drop-offs are usually good first-ice possibilities because they funnel baitfish

into limited areas. Since these spots tend to hold more available forage than open water and prey is easier to ambush, white bass frequently remain in such areas until the available food source thins.

At this point, check current or necked-down areas, confined open water areas adjoining deep weed lines, or mid-lake structural elements such as points, reefs and shoals, all locations where white bass often move in like a swarm of locusts to feed on available baitfish. But again, as the food sources are diminished in these areas, expect the schools to move on.

As first ice wanes, don't ignore adjacent deep water areas, where large schools of white bass may begin to suspend over deep, open water. In river backwaters, white bass will usually move toward the edges of the main river channel, where oxygen is more abundant.

## Mid-Winter

With shallow water forage eaten down and scattered, white bass often begin roaming through deep, open water areas, so you'll have to search the depths for suspended fish. In river backwater systems, this generally means a movement toward, near or into the main river channel. On lakes and reservoirs, open water movements

**First ice, high percentage white bass locations are often similar to areas where you'd look for winter crappies or perch, and mixed bag catches are not unusual.**

On lakes and reservoirs, open water movements are common, although schools of white bass may be gathered by forage-holding elements such as points, reefs, sunken islands or roadbeds extending into the main lake basin.

By late ice, white bass make noticeable movements from deep water toward river, stream and tributary mouths, which they eventually enter to spawn.

are common, where schools are often gathered by forage-holding structural elements such as points, reefs, sunken islands or roadbeds extending into the main lake basin. If these schools move along the structure and find what they're looking for—namely forage—they'll stay.

Once in a particular area, they may even begin roaming the shallow edge of a structure, then move directly along the edge or onto the top, stopping as they encounter cover and food. In some cases where such breaklines or structures stretch long distances, such as a distinct drop-off on a deep, natural lake or main lake channel on a flowage or reservoir, white bass may utilize them as migration routes along or toward the shallows. The frequency and distance of these movements will depend on the conditions, but they'll continue to remain and feed until they've consumed most of the available forage, then move on.

You may also find active, deep water schools of white bass that have encountered baitfish while migrating across expanses of open water between structures. If you do, expect the action to be fast and furious—but only temporary, because these fish are usually on the move. Under normal conditions, you'll catch a couple of fish from these mobile schools, then the action will suddenly stop. This is because these schools are moving in search of forage and chasing wandering schools of baitfish, and they'll usually keep right on moving—eventually right out of the area you're fishing.

Note the time and conditions you encounter these fish. On some lakes, I've noticed white bass will make "rounds"—essentially following open water migration routes between structures. You, too, must play their game. Like the white bass themselves, you must keep

**During first ice, you'll find white bass in shallow cover-laden backwaters (B), flats, bays or coves (C), drop-offs surrounding islands (E), inside turns (D2,D3,D4,D5,D6), points (D), and slots or openings close to the main lake basin near primary shoreline drop-offs (A-1). Necked-down areas adjoining deep weed lines can also be good. Mid-winter, open water movements over deep, mid-lake structures extending from the shallows into deep water such as points (D), bars, shoals and sunken islands (A-2) are productive. Late ice, white bass begin migrating toward river stream and tributary mouths (F), as they prefer currents and running water for spawning.**

moving, and not stop until you mark an active school with your sonar. By doing this repeatedly, you'll eventually develop winter patterns as you note white bass repeatedly using or migrating through particular areas year after year, and as you learn to better understand the timing of these movements on your favorite waters, you'll stand a better chance of catching them consistently.

## Late Ice

By late ice, deep water white bass will begin migrating toward river, stream and tributary mouths, as they prefer the currents and running water of feeder creeks and tributary streams for spawning. In river systems, they will make movements toward sloughs surrounding dams, which may or may not be iced over. On smaller waters where navigable streams aren't available, they'll usually spawn on windswept, hard-bottom lake shores and shoals. In any of these cases, under-ice movements toward these spawning grounds will occur.

**Tip-ups or tip-downs rigged with light monofilament leaders, split shot and #6 hooks tipped with small, active minnows will catch plenty of white bass.**

**On many lakes, both white bass and yellow perch suspend, feeding on plankton and minnows, so mixed bag catches of the two species are not uncommon.**

Carefully review the outlay of these shoals, river mouths or dams on a lake map, and try to locate cover-laden structure leading from the depths toward shallow spawning grounds—probable migration routes. White bass will gradually assemble in deep water adjoining such areas, and usually make a series of "false runs" along these migration routes before moving onto their spawning grounds. Be aware of when these migrations and movements occur, and you'll do well.

## Effective Winter Fishing Strategies

Just as mobility and efficiency are the keys to locating winter white bass, so it is with catching them. After finding a location holding fish, drill several holes, and begin implementing a run-and-gun jigging approach.

As for presentation, white bass really don't demand specialized equipment. Standard, underwater, thermal and wind tip-ups or ultralight tip-downs and balance tip-ups rigged with light monofilament leaders, split shot and #6 hooks tipped with small, active minnows will catch fish. For added attraction, any piece of bright colored yarn, plastic or flashy spinner or spoon bodies added to or above the hook will help increase your number of strikes. Many anglers also clip the minnow's tail fin back slightly to create an irregular swimming motion that drives white bass wild—and makes them easier to catch when attacked.

Small, flashy spoons set below an aggressively jigging wind tip-up are particularly effective. Relatively lightweight, slow-falling flutter spoons such as Reef Runner's Slender Spoons or Bait Rig's Willospoons are good examples. Simply sharpen the hooks and tip them with a small minnow, strip of belly meat or ripple tail pork rind—and let the lure work its magic. In deep water or when fishing at night, a strip of glow tape wrapped around the hook or added to an attractor such as a "flicker" blade above the hook can also be helpful.

## Jigging

Because white bass move often and are so active once found, jigging is a more practical means of fishing them. Standard jigglesticks and jig poles work fine when whites are holding in water less than 15 feet deep. When they move deeper, premium quality medium-light action ice rods such as HT's Polar Golds or Jiggin' Sticks and lightweight spinning reels spooled with 4 to 6 lb. test function especially well.

White bass are often quite aggressive, so swimming minnow style baits like Normark's Jigging Rapala, System Tackle's Walleye Flyer, Northland's Mini Airplane

**Reef Runner's Slender Spoon**      **Bait Rigs Willospoon**

**Lightweight, slow-falling flutter spoons such as these are highly effective presentations for white bass when set beneath wind tip-ups.**

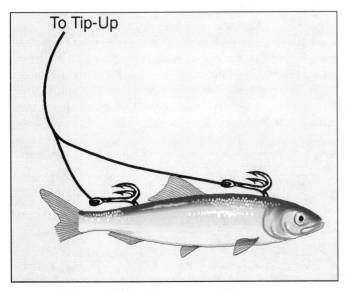

To Tip-Up

**Clipping a minnow's tail fin creates an irregular swimming motion that drives white bass wild—and makes the minnow easier to catch. Also note the position of the hooks with the hook points facing the tail. Like most panfish, white bass usually strike minnows at the head, and this hook position aims the hook points right at the fish making a solid hook-set more easily attained, as opposed to lining up the smooth bends and lessening the likelihood of a solid hook-up.**

Jig or HT's Walleye Ice Jigs work great. Flash lures like Bay de Noc's Swedish Pimple, Reef Runner's Slender Spoons, HT's Marmooska Spoons, Northland Fire-Eye Minnows or Bait Rig's Willospoons are also good bets. These spoons tipped with dropper lines to small ice jigs can produce well, as can a variety of swimming style or rocker style jigs. With any of these baits, a small minnow is generally the best tipper.

When the bite slows, such as after a front or during periods of heavy fishing pressure, smaller teardrops and ice ant-style baits, tipped with either a small minnow or grub and jigged lightly or set beneath a slip bobber, can be productive.

Otherwise, for the added challenge and enjoyment of battling powerful white bass on light tackle, I suggest going ultralight. I prefer ultralights with a little extra backbone, such as Berkley's light action Lightning Ice Rods, or HT's Polar Gold ultralight systems. Combine these with lightweight, premium ultralight spinning reels to help reel fish up from deep water quickly, and you're in business.

As for line, 2 to 3 lb. test works well in most situations—just be sure to check your line frequently for cuts. White bass have razor-sharp gill covers that can nick light lines, causing frustrating break-offs. You can save yourself a lot of trouble by retying often.

Standard jigglesticks and jig poles work well when white bass are holding in water less than 15 feet deep.

## Lures and Techniques

For best results, efficiency is the key to catching winter white bass. After identifying a potentially active school, begin fishing with medium-light action ice rod combos and fast-moving baits such as Normark's smaller size Jigging Rapalas, Northland's Fire Eye Minnows, Bay de Noc's Swedish Pimples, HT's Bohemian Rockers or Ice 'n' Spoons. These lures are all good "search baits" because they work fast, enabling you to cover water and locate schools quickly. Secondly, these highly active, flashy lures readily attract whites.

Since white bass are generally active, you can jig them relatively fast. Recently I've even experienced good success with blade baits such as the Cicada, Cordell Gay Blade and Heddon Sonar. Even Normark's Rattlin' Raps tipped with a dropper line work well for winter whites. Rattlin' Raps work with tight, vibrating actions and rattle chambers, and the combination of fast action, vibration and noise seems to draw white bass—and the dropper coaxes them into striking.

Don't get too hung up wondering what bait to tie on. I've found white bass will strike just about any kind of lure—provided it's similar in size to their food. This is best determined by examining their stomach contents.

Look especially close at the minnows inside—these are great indicators of the bass' preferred forage size.

Once you've chosen a particular bait and rigged up, drill ample holes over the school, and begin working your bait upward slowly through the school. Don't worry about spooking them, feeding activity tends to turn these schools on. If an interested fish appears on your electronics, begin working the bait faster. I've had many whites smash the bait just as the lure starts wiggling aggressively—or just as I pause after such motion.

If this doesn't work, drop your lure while twitching the rod periodically to make the bait look like a wounded minnow. Work from just under the ice to the bottom—whites are liable to strike almost anywhere. This approach works especially well with fast-moving "search" type baits, so use this approach as long as it continues to catch fish.

Occasionally, the action will slow somewhat after several fish. If this happens, switch to a 1/16 to 1/32-ounce jig tipped with a white, yellow, or motor oil colored plastic twister tail and a minnow head. The biggest advantage of small, lightweight jigs is they're extremely versatile: you can work them fast or slow, bump them on bottom for deep running whites, or let them fall slowly through suspended fish. This versatility helps increase hits.

And keep this in mind: If the action gets hot again, you can remove a jig hook from a fish's mouth faster than a treble-hooked spoon or jigging minnow, allowing you to get your line back into the water more quickly, and consequently, catch more fish. When the white bass are really biting, I sometimes flatten the barbs on all my lures with a pliers, enabling me to unhook fish quickly before the school moves. This may not seem like much, but when fishing active schools of white bass, saving a few minutes can add up to several extra fish.

Spoons and swimming-style jigs are all good "search baits" for white bass because they work fast, enabling you to cover water and locate schools quickly.

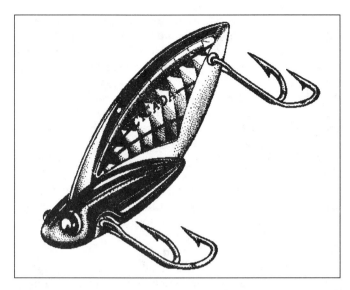

Blade baits like Reef Runner's Cicada generate a distinct vibration when jigged that draws white bass. When active, white bass will strike these lures with a frenzy.

Where legal, some anglers also tie a three way swivel to a second rod, and attach two droppers tipped with lightweight jigs and minnows to the swivel. They allow this rig to sink to the desired depth, and if a fish grabs one jig, they set the hook—but allow the fish to swim back toward the school while keeping the line tight. The commotion tends to attract other fish, which usually strike the trailing jig.

By the way, if you hook a couple of white bass consecutively, pause a few seconds before reeling the fish in, giving your fishing buddy time to lower his or her lure toward your hooked bass from a nearby hole. Because of the fiercely competitive nature of white bass, other bass from the school often swarm a hooked fish, and many times this method will result in a quick strike for your partner.

If your partner hooks a fish, quickly land yours and drop your lure back down while he or she waits. Continue this tactic as long as the school remains in the area and falls for the trick. Incidentally, if you know you're near a school but not marking fish in a particular hole after experiencing action, I've found it's best to try working your bait from the bottom up before leaving, in a last ditch effort to draw them back. White bass may hold directly on bottom or suspend at virtually any

Once you've located fish and chosen a bait, slowly work it upward through the school. If you don't get a strike, begin working the bait upward quickly. I've had many white bass smash the bait just as they sense it's "escaping."

**Where legal (check your local regulations book) some ice anglers tie up a three way swivel to a second "sitter" rod, and attach two droppers tipped with jigs and minnows to the dropper lines. The bottom jig should be slightly heavier to help avoid tangles. Once set, a strike on one jig allows the caught fish to trail the second jig, often drawing a second strike and allowing the angler to enjoy a two-for-one catch, ice fishing style.**

depth just outside your transducer cone, and if you follow through, you might catch an extra fish or two that might otherwise have been missed.

Should a school of white bass be near, they'll usually come over to investigate your bait quickly and generally hit quickly. If not, react by pulling your lure upward away from the fish, or simply working your bait faster, then pausing suddenly. Apparently the white bass' instincts tell them to strike before the bait gets away, as I've often had one smash my bait just as the lure starts wiggling more aggressively—or just as I pause after such motion. If this doesn't work or you miss a strike, quickly drop your lure while twitching the rod gently to give the bait added action on the fall. This closely imitates a wounded minnow, and often triggers additional strikes.

Speaking of minnows, if you're catching whites and the action suddenly goes dead—despite the fact you're still marking fish on your electronics—try the minnow option. In this situation, the fish are spooked, and unless worked precisely, larger, flashier lures will likely turn them off. Plain minnows dangled beneath a slip-float, however, might bring the school back to life—and work great when you're into fish.

However, live bait also takes a long time to rig and limits your ability to cover water. So, if you wish to use minnows, fine—just keep in mind it makes more sense to locate a school with a fast-moving presentation, because jigging makes it a lot easier to move to a new hole. Instead of having to stop to reposition the bobber and hook a fresh minnow after each move, you simply drop the bait to bottom and begin jigging. Consequently, live bait presentations should be reserved for spooked schools.

Never spend excessive amounts of time fishing white bass in any one hole. If the fish are there, you'll either mark them on your electronics—or more likely, they'll strike. If neither happens within 15 minutes, move. Remember where the school was located; you'll probably want to return to the area later. If the school is still there, you may find they've turned on.

One last note: White bass usually school according to size. If you catch several small fish, move. I've often found that it pays to move off and pursue another school of larger fish. Also, should you simply catch one fish and find the action slows quickly, you've likely picked up the last of a school moving through a particular area, or a straggler. Move on and continue searching for an active school.

**While not as efficient as working search lures such as spoons or jigs, plain minnows dangled beneath a slip-float may be just what's needed to bring a school of white bass back to life after it's been spooked.**

If you locate a school of semi-active white bass that for some reason are biting lightly, go to smaller lures and sharpen the hooks carefully, add small live bait tippers and work your baits in a more subtle manner. The practice makes a difference.

## Other White Bass Tips

To increase my efficiency, I like to carry several rods pre-tied with my favorite lures and rigs. This way, I can start by working blade baits or other fast-moving search baits with one rod, and easily switch to a jig, dropper rig, smaller lure or live bait rig—each conveniently set on other rods—efficiently. Besides, if a tangle or break should occur I don't have to stop fishing to re-rig, I only have to reach for a different rod.

Believe me, you'll appreciate this once on the ice—it's unbelievably frustrating when you locate a school, white bass are feeding heavily all around you, and you're not able to fish because your line is fouled up and your cold fingers won't tie a simple knot.

Speaking of fingers, avoid grabbing white bass across the gill plates when handling them. These plates feature needle-sharp spines that can inflict painful wounds if not handled properly. Instead, hold the fish by the lower lip or grip it firmly by the throat or across the back. You'll be glad you did.

Because white bass are readily available to a large number of anglers, bite aggressively and fight hard, it's not surprising the popularity of whites to ice fisherman is growing rapidly and gaining an ardent following of die-hard anglers. And if you enjoy a good fish fry, there's nothing quite like fresh white bass fillets deep-fried in crispy brown batter with lemon and tartar sauce, then sandwiched between thick slices of buttered

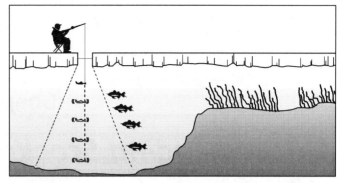

**If you know you're near a school of white bass but not marking fish in a particular hole after experiencing action, try slowly working your bait from the bottom up before leaving the area. White bass may be holding outside your transducer cone, and if you don't follow through, you might overlook a heavy concentration of fish.**

rye bread. This, plus the challenge of finding an active school and knowing white bass are one of winter's most-willing, aggressive biters and hardest fighting fish, is reason enough to keep me on the ice.

So if you're like me and dreaming about getting out and icing a few feisty fish, white bass are an excellent way to scratch your itch.

**When white bass become spooky, plain minnows dangled beneath a float sometimes bring additional strikes. (Courtesy Berkley Outdoor Technologies Group)**

# Chapter 8

# *Understanding Stocked Trout During Winter*

$F$or most panfish anglers, ice fishing offers hopes of catching bull bluegills, jumbo perch, slab crappies, or perhaps a feisty white bass.

But thanks to increased stocking efforts, stocked trout are fast becoming popular targets as well. Agencies and anglers alike are enthusiastic about this opportunity because, given the proper environment, stocked trout grow relatively fast, bite readily, fight hard, offer a colorful option to commonly sought winter panfish species and are often stocked in waters that would otherwise support little if any good winter panfishing.

While some western parts of the United States offer wonderful blends of salmonids, including golden, cutthroat, cutbow and dolly varden trout and Atlantic, kokanee and other strains of salmon, stream trout—namely brookies, browns and rainbows, along with splake, a genetic cross between a male brook trout and a female lake trout that grows fast and offers good trophy potential)—are the most commonly stocked species across North America. While each of these species prefers clear and clean water, low-temperatures, and high oxygen content, each occupies a slightly different ecological niche, and therefore offers unique ice angling opportunities. Diet varies between species according to lake type, season and availability, but consists largely of zooplankton, leeches, snails, clams, crayfish, freshwater shrimp, insect larvae and small minnows.

As for human food value, trout are among the most palatable of panfish and for many ice anglers this is reason enough to spend countless hours on the ice seeking them.

## Choosing the Lake

Begin your search for good trout waters by checking with local fisheries agencies to determine lakes in your area offering good populations of native fish, or, for the scope of this chapter, waters that have been stocked—and when. Recently stocked lakes virtually guarantee you'll catch fish, because freshly stocked trout are typically aggressive...but seldom large.

I prefer to search for lakes featuring stocking programs beginning three to five years prior to my inquiry, and haven't been heavily pressured. You may have to conduct intensive research to find them, but since these gems often hold stronger classes of older, larger fish, they offer exclusive fishing.

Second, check to make sure the trout season on your chosen waters is open during the time you plan to fish. Some trout waters are closed to winter angling. Also check on local regulations regarding size, bag and possession limits, all of which vary greatly from state to state, region to region—even lake to lake.

## Primary Winter Location Patterns

Ordinarily, the key to locating stocked trout involves water temperature. However, unlike the open water season, water temperatures are uniformly cold beneath the ice, so trout are not restricted by temperature zones that force them into limited areas. In response, they move, often far and frequently. Consequently, locating stocked trout is a primary key to consistent winter catches.

As with the other species profiled in this book, electronics and mobility play integral roles in winter trout

**Thanks to increased stocking efforts, stocked trout offer a colorful option to commonly sought winter species.**

**Rainbow trout are the most common stocked trout species.**

strategies. Lake maps for many small stocked trout waters are not available, so sonar combined with a mobile approach are needed to identify potential fish-holding structure, breaks, bottom content, weeds, rocks and their associated available forage selection.

Prior to fishing, identify the features and areas on your map likely to attract trout. Once on the ice, pinpoint these structures using sonar, always moving to determine how the fish are relating to various bottom contents, forms of secondary cover and forage. To maximize your efficiency when preparing these strategic pre-fishing approaches, consider the individual species being sought. Each species fills an ecological niche—which in turn, provides clues for where to catch them.

Brookies are homebodies, generally not moving far and holding shallow, usually near obvious cover such as shallow weeds, rocks, fallen timber docks or piers—especially those influenced by current. Rainbows, although known to suspend in open water, tend to roam along shallow, mid-depth or deep structures regu-

**Brook trout are homebodies, generally not moving far from shallow, obvious cover such as weeds, rocks or timber—especially those influenced by current.**

larly, following specific depth contours and bottom configurations as they move from structure to structure—so when you catch a rainbow, be sure to note the spot and the time. Given similar conditions in the future, they are likely to be in the same areas.

Browns also cruise along deep structures, breaks and over deeper pelagic waters, constantly moving and often suspending, making them difficult to find. But this, combined with the fact they're often wary, helps them grow, sometimes to trophy proportions. Splake demonstrate similar tendencies, but can also be bottom-oriented.

Cutthroat trout are the wonderful native trout of the western United States and Canada. They're easy to identify by the rampant splash of red color below the lower jaw and a prominent spattering of black dots along each flank. Cutthroat are distant cousins of the rainbow and in most mountain lakes follow patterns similar to the rainbow. Expect them to roam along shallow and mid-depth structure and cover throughout most of the winter, although like rainbows they may occasionally suspend over deep water.

**As with any specifically targeted species, electronics and mobility play integral roles in winter stocked trout strategies.**

**Brook trout are homebodies, generally not moving far from shallow, obvious cover such as weeds, rocks or timber—especially those influenced by current.**

Finally comes the last of the western, high country trouts, the Dolly Varden. This species is among the least likely of the trouts to be caught through the ice, and in most regions, aren't considered a popular species because unlike the other trouts, they don't fight as long and dutifully, their food value is among the poorest of all trout species, and their cannibalistic tendencies to diet on smaller trout is unpopular with conservationists and ice fishing purists alike. However, Dolly Varden can get large, which captures the attention of some trophy-seeking ice anglers.

Of course, all trout species demonstrate similarities and differences given their unique environment and sets of conditions, so despite these inclinations, such evaluations are only guidelines. When trying to assemble such generalities into specific patterns, you'll find they vary, depending on lake type, how far winter has progressed, the availability of cover and forage, amount of fishing pressure, time of day and weather. Always attempt to tie these variables together to establish viable winter trout patterns.

Cutbows, as the name suggests, are a hybrid blend of the cutthroat and rainbow, and consequently demonstrate similar location tendencies beneath the ice. I've found them slightly more mobile than purebred cutthroat or rainbows. Be prepared to move often in search of these fish. Just because you find cutbows relating to a particular structure of cover in the morning doesn't mean they'll still be there in the afternoon. Maintain an open mind!

Golden trout are beautifully colored fish and arguably the most brightly colored of trouts. Native of the high Sierra Nevada mountains where the waters are nearly entirely comprised of infertile, high altitude, cold water lakes, goldens seldom get large, with the average fish running less than one pound. They're also somewhat limited geographically throughout the ice fishing belt and even considered somewhat rare by some anglers, so a golden trout taken through the ice is regarded by many as a major milestone of attainment in the ice angler's portfolio of accomplishments.

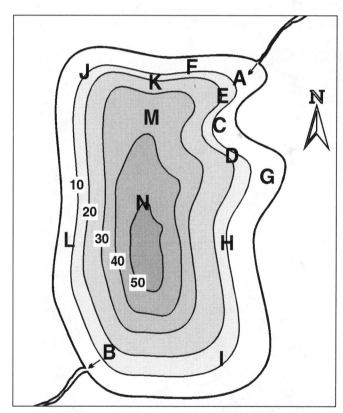

**Most reclamated lakes feature little structure or cover, so trout tend to suspend. However, inlets (A) or outlets (B), if present, can be good. Points (C), turns (D,E), shallow flats (F,G,L) and corners (E,J,I) are more common fish holding areas, and if available and offering cover, will hold trout. More often, expect trout to suspend off drop-offs (K), deep flats (M) or deep, mid-lake holes (N).**

## Stocked Trout Lake Types

Biologists primarily target four lake types for creating winter trout fisheries: "reclaimed lakes," "two story lakes," Great Lakes bays and harbors, and high-country lakes and reservoirs.

Reclaimed lakes are either cold water ponds or small bodies of water too cold or infertile to support balanced warm-water fisheries, or deep, cold, infertile waters such as spring-fed borrow pits or reclamated mine pits that support little else but cold water species.

Most pits don't feature much structure—just sheer, undeveloped sterile rock cliff shorelines and breaks that basically drop straight off into deep water. There isn't much shallow, productive littoral zone, so just about any available cover is sure to hold fish. Gradually tapering drop-offs, breaks, access areas, submerged roads, points, broken rocks or boulders tend to provide something for trout to relate to and will often hold fish. Flooded timber, pilings, and piers near launches, if

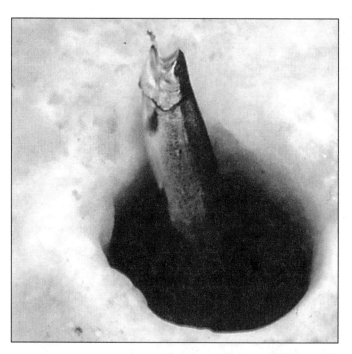

Two-story lakes support both cold and warm water fisheries. The name is derived because these lakes, when summer stratified, are two-tiered—warm water species such as bass use the upper portions of the lake, while cold-water species like trout inhabit the colder depths.

available, are particularly good because these areas often provide the only readily available cover, plus they harbor insects, minnows, green algae and other forage.

However, since most pits feature straight, steep, sharp-breaking drops with little structure, suspension over deep water is common, and these suspended trout almost invariably are on the move. As an accomplished ice angler, it's your job to search for these fish using a mobile, strategic approach.

Fortunately, this isn't always as difficult as it may sound. Most pits simply aren't that large, and because of the clear, excellent water quality of most pits, trout can often be seen approaching and striking baits beneath the ice, even over deep water. Furthermore, most pit trout have a tendency to suspend less than 30 feet below the ice and they're easily spotted by laying flat on the ice and gazing down through the hole—be sure to watch for them.

Two-story lakes and reservoirs support both cold and warm water fisheries. The name is derived because these lakes, when summer stratified, are two-tiered—meaning warm water species such as bass use the warmer, upper portions of the lake, while cold-water species like trout inhabit the colder depths. Recall, however, that a stratification reversal occurs during winter. So while still called "two-story" lakes, the stratification

Since most pits feature such deep, sharp-breaking drops with little structure, fish commonly suspend over deep water.

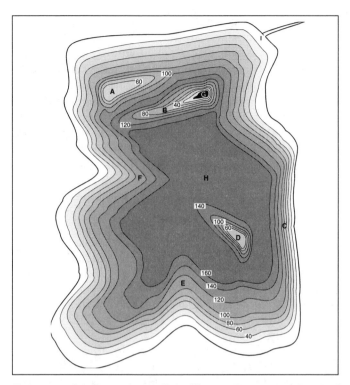

Two story lakes generally offer a diverse variety of trout-attracting cover and structure, and with water temperatures being uniformly cold, features such as points (E,F), sunken islands (A,D), sharp shoreline drops (C) and bars (B) at a variety of depths may hold fish. They may also suspend over deep water (H).

bringing that name is dissolved, so winter trout have more freedom to move. Again, trout simply relate to whatever combination of structure and cover is available, based on the preferred forage and where they're holding, and inter-and intra-species competition. They may also suspend over deep water.

Great Lakes bays and harbors also offer a combination of stocked trout species. While part of a much larger, complex system than either reclaimed or two story lakes, if you simply look at these bays as a lake in themselves and carefully evaluate how stocked trout relate to them, effective patterns can be derived.

Most Great Lakes bays can be divided into three segments: River hole fishing, near-shore shallow bay and harbor fishing, and deep water fishing. In terms of "panfish" by our definition, river holes and shallow water fisheries are mainly comprised of smelt, perch, brook trout, browns and rainbows. Deep water fishing usually means splake, or perhaps rainbows.

Most Great Lakes ice fishing for stocked trout takes place within shoreline bays and harbors, namely because this is where the most forage is available and ice formation is safest. Many good winter Great Lakes stocked trout catches of brookies, browns and rainbows come from less than 25 feet of water, because these fish are actively cruising the shallows in search of food. Mixed-bag catches are not unusual. While not a panfish by our definition, don't be surprised if you catch a trophy in such areas, too—I've taken double digit browns and steelhead in less than five feet of water.

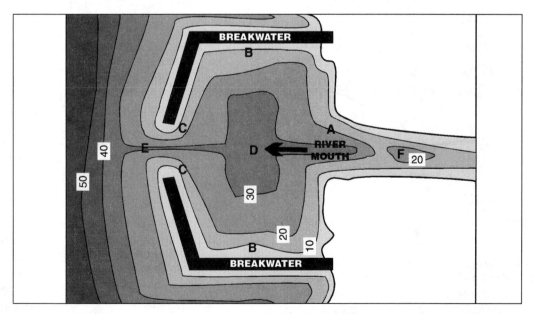

Most Great Lakes ice fishing for stocked trout takes place within small shoreline bays and harbors, because this is where the most forage is available and ice formation is safest. Most fishing will take place near river mouths (A), deep holes (D), flats and breakwater edges (B,C), the deep water slot at the harbor entrance (E) or during spawning runs beneath the ice, in deep river holes (F) adjoining the bay or harbor.

In terms of specific location in these shallows, current is a major factor. When present, current from incoming rivers and feeder streams brings relatively warm water runoff and food, making trout slightly more active. Better yet, wait until some of these species make their annual pilgrimage into the rivers for spawning. Spawning time varies with various species and strains so you'll have to check with local biologists to determine when these runs occur. Carried out properly, many ice anglers intercept these winter "running" fish in Great Lakes harbors adjoining spawning rivers, and in some cases, will even fish rainbows in deeper, frozen river holes and pockets just upstream of the bay or harbor. In fact, depending on forage availability, both trophy steelheads and browns may also move in and out of these areas on a regular basis from late December through ice-out.

Larger Great Lakes bays often feature deep pockets or channels extending from the main lake, lined by breaks extending from the deep water and connecting to mid-depth shoals. Projections along these breaks—particularly in areas where they cut tight to shore or islands—are by far the best structures to focus your efforts, although any adjacent mid-depth or shallow flats, shorelines, backbays or river areas featuring a weedy bottom and holding baitfish may also be produc-

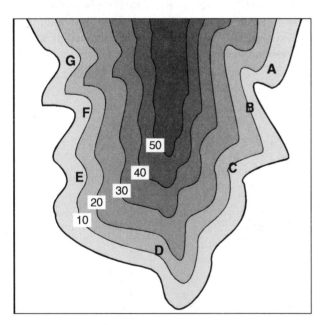

**The bottom configuration of larger Great Lakes bays often consists of deep slots or coves featuring a deep trough or channel extending down the midst of the bay. Most stocked trout hold in shallow littoral zones offering cover, or along points (C,D,E,F,G) and turns (A,B) extending from them toward deep water. Some trout may also suspend over deep water (primarily rainbows and browns) or hold deep (splake).**

tive. Be aware of current and potentially dangerous ice conditions, particularly around mid-bay islands.

The final category of stocked trout lakes includes the high country mountain lakes and reservoirs of western North America. There are few places in the world will you find such picturesque, beautiful, rugged wilderness ice fishing. Often characterized by steep, quick dropping breaks of rocks and boulders, deep, clear cold water and very limited fertility, these lakes will often leave you spellbound with their incredible beauty.

A good portion of these lakes are either glacial lakes, deep basins filled with cold, clear blue mountain runoff and rainwater, deep pockets where cascading whitewater streams pool into ponds and lakes of varying size, or man-made impoundments on such rivers. And in these lakes, along with the standard blend of rainbow, brown and brook trout, you'll find what many consider to be the aristocracy of the stocked trout world: The cutthroat, cutbow and golden trouts, along with the more controversial or even disdained Dolly Varden trout.

These high country lakes vary in altitude from a couple of hundred feet to two or more miles above sea level. As you might imagine, this is one of several factors affecting the species of trout found there and their primary habits and patterns. In Montana, for example, high country lakes could be divided into three types: Man-made impoundments of eastern Montana; natural lakes of the west; and high country alpine lakes. Each have different features and characteristics, and each are fished differently.

Some lower altitude Western lakes and ponds may actually be relatively shallow, dark water fertile environments capable of supporting rich fish life. But many are also used to supply water for cities or irrigation, so through some times of the year water levels may become low, allowing water temperatures to soar, which can harm trout fisheries. In contrast, some high country lakes are so remote, cold and infertile that little forage is available to support fish life, and some don't offer sufficient depth to prevent winter oxygen deprevation and winter kill. These waters are heavily dependent on stocking and often poor choices for ice fishing. Alas, many ice anglers have clambered up steep, icy trails to such lakes, only to find them winter-killed.

Bottom line? Be sure to carefully research your intended fishing destinations before setting out. High country and Western lakes can vary dramatically in stature, and you will save time, and likely catch more fish if you simply take the time to do your homework. I recommend making a list of target lakes, then sharing that list with local Fish and Game Departments personnel, local anglers and guides, bait shops and businesses. They'll help you choose the ones most likely to meet the experience you're seeking.

The author lifts a beautifully colored Western brown trout from the waters of Montana's Lake Hebgen. Note the non-traditional use of ultralight tackle, which adds sport to the tremendous fighting of Western trout.

At this point, inexperienced high country trout anglers might begin feeling confused. With such a variety of waters and thousands of lakes at various altitudes, some large and some small, some deep and some shallow and all offering different forage and species, the beginner might wonder how these fish can be patterned for consistent catches.

The answer? Follow basic patterns based on a law of averages. Since most high country lakes are capable of supporting trout and are stocked, but are also clear and limited in structure and cover, the best "bites" usually occur early and late in the day or during overcast conditions.

On larger impoundments, focus your efforts along the main river channel and its related structures. On smaller or remote, higher elevation lakes, search for shady, overhead cover. Such places often consist of off-shore ledges or steep breaks along these edges, although in smaller lakes, objects so simple as a large fallen boulders or overhanging rocks may offer the same type of protective cover, and offer productive fishing. In addition, rocky ledges, drop-offs and overhead cover also provide habitat for forage, which helps increase the odds of holding fish.

Although lake maps are sometimes available to help locate such features, many smaller, remote lakes have never been mapped, and you'll have to pinpoint this cover yourself, either during the open water season, or by using sonar. If available, the presence of alternative cover such as fallen logs or plant growth can also

**First ice often finds stocked trout holding near shallow water structure and flats. The combination of cold water, cover and forage allow most species to move shallow and feed actively.**

**The author embarking on a journey toward a secluded, high-country mountain trout lake. Snowshoes are often helpful—if not mandatory—for accessing many of these remote waters.**

be helpful, as can current providing inlets, outlets, or underwater springs. Watch for all of the above. They may appear obvious, but remember, few of these lakes receive heavy fishing pressure, so cover many anglers might consider too obvious and tend to overlook may be just the locations holding fish.

One word of warning: While many remote high country Western lakes offer fabulous and easy fishing because they receive only limited fishing pressure, access may be nearly impossible throughout much of the winter. But where it's lawful and there's a will and a way, these frozen lakes offer some of the most breathtaking, rewarding winter fishing available. Try planning your trips early or late in the season. Ice and snow may make many of these lakes difficult to reach during mid-winter. Also bear in mind that while fishing pressure is often nil, most smaller high country glacial lakes offer limited chances for a trophy.

However, the true adventurer searching for winter solace will find ample opportunity for one of the most picturesque and pristine of all ice fishing adventures: the thrill of seeking high country stocked trout.

## First Ice

Regardless of lake type, first ice often finds stocked trout holding near accessible shallow structure or flats close to banks and shorelines. The combination of cold temperatures, cover, forage and lack of disturbance allow most species to move shallow and feed actively.

Vegetated or current-influenced areas such as narrows between lakes, flats near inlets or outlets, gradually sloping points, bars, drop-offs, breaks, ledges and their associated bases are especially productive, because stocked trout can forage on a variety of aquatic insects, minnows and crayfish among the weeds or along rocky bottoms.

Each species will relate to such areas in a slightly different manner: Brookies in shallow cover, cutthroat along shallow and mid-depth flats, rainbows and cutbows along deeper breaks, browns suspended off these breaks, and splake suspended or directly along bottom of these deeper breaks. If there's a lot of activity on the ice or a lack of shallow cover, first-ice trout may spook and respond by suspending off primary drops and breaks, or move into adjacent mid-depth pockets or holes. In either case, use your electronics to locate them.

## Mid-Winter

Toward mid-season, ice anglers must work harder to consistently catch stocked trout. While still active and catchable, stocked trout typically exemplify a progressive movement toward deeper water, often suspend,

**Mid-winter, trout suspension over deep water is common. The best approach is to take numerous sonar readings until you mark fish. When you note them, simply adjust your lure to their level and try to trigger a response.**

and with the exception of brook trout, move frequently. These movements are governed largely by random movements of drifting masses of suspended plankton, wandering schools of baitfish and oxygen differentials—which vary, depending on the lake type.

During first ice, for example, trout in reclaimed lakes move freely, actively feeding wherever adequate forage exists. As the season wears on, temperatures remain cold, but reclaimed lakes may suffer forage depletions in the shallows, and smaller, reclaimed lakes that aren't spring-fed may suffer oxygen depletions that drive oxygen concentrations in the extreme shallows below the trout's preferred levels. Such conditions stress trout, mean less activity and frequently cause fish to suspend over deep water.

Two-story lakes, however, are generally larger and offer greater structural diversity and better oxygen distribution than reclaimed lakes, so trout may remain shallow into the mid-winter period. However, with

**The best winter trout fishing usually occurs during the first couple of weeks of the season.**

**As the season wears into the late-ice period, batches of plankton and schools of minnows scatter, so trout continue to disperse and fishing can become sporadic. Use a mobile approach. If you work enough holes and hook a fish here and there, by day's end you'll have accumulated a respectable catch.**

more location options available, they may also relate to "classic" mid-depth or deep water structural features including reefs, bars, points, humps, turns and flats, especially those supporting secondary cover such as rocks or vegetation. Just where depends on forage preference and availability, and inter-and intra-species competition.

Great Lakes bays demonstrate similar mid-winter patterns, but certain species and strains of stocked trout make spawning runs into rivers beneath the ice. Learn when, and you'll be able to intercept large schools in relatively small areas, leading to fabulous catches.

Mid-winter patterns vary little from early ice on high country lakes. Most trout continue searching for the best combinations of cover and forage. This often means relating to breaks, drop-offs, ledges, and rock or wood providing overhead cover, which may be cover found relatively shallow, or within the deepest available water, depending on the lake. Be ready to move in search of fish.

Obviously, all four lake types are inherently different, and each requires inherently different fishing approaches to create consistent winter success. Such diverse mid-winter patterns help explain why many winter trout anglers have difficulty consistently finding stocked trout during mid-season. However, if you're well-versed using electronics, you'll likely increase your mid-season stocked trout catches considerably, because you'll have the capacity to mark clouds of suspended plankton, baitfish and trout, or fish relating to deep structural features.

The best approach is to take numerous sonar readings, starting with the highest percentage areas, until you mark fish. Should you notice trout moving through above or below your lure, simply adjust to their level. If the fish disappear or won't bite, move.

## Late Ice

As the season wears into the late-ice period, batches of plankton and schools of minnows scatter in all four lake types, so trout continue to disperse and fishing can

**Most stocked trout catches will average 10 to 14 inches, although some larger fish are occasionally taken.**

**Where legal, smooth-tripping tip-ups rigged with long, light monofilament leaders tipped with tiny hooks and a small minnow can offer a highly effective winter stocked trout presentation.**

become highly sporadic. Except on smaller reclamated or alpine lakes where limited oxygen concentrations may force trout to suspend, for best results focus your efforts in deeper areas, always moving in search of active fish. You may catch only a fish or two from any given hole this time of year, but by utilizing a mobile approach, it's possible to accumulate respectable catches by day's end.

This basic pattern will continue producing until last ice, when the meltdown begins and warm runoff from feeder creeks infiltrates the shallows. Now, warming water draws forage, and active trout gather near shoreline cover and drop-offs in the vicinity of these forage-rich flows.

In Great Lakes bays, movements along current-lined breakwaters and into rivers are also common this time of year. Be cautious in these areas—the combination of current, warming temperatures and melting snow may cause ice conditions to deteriorate rapidly.

## Timing

The best winter trout fishing usually occurs the first couple of weeks of the season—generally from mid-December through the first part of January when trout are concentrated near shoreline breaks—and again just prior to ice-out when they're drawn shallow to feed. For some reason, trout seem to feed more selectively during mid-season, and the action often slows. Yet depending on the lake, don't hang up your fishing just because the ice gets thicker. At times, mid-winter can offer tremendous trout action.

On a daily basis, stocked trout may bite all day, especially where they're not heavily fished, but most consistent catches occur during twilight periods. Lakes receiving heavy pressure demand anglers fish early and late in the day, deeper and tighter to structure, along confined open water areas off primary breaks, or in open water pelagic areas. Daily weather conditions also influence primary trout patterns, with mild, slightly overcast, calm days following cold snaps seeming to produce best.

## Effective Winter Fishing Strategies

Because stocked trout fishing often requires fishing in wide-open expanses, staying warm, dry and comfortable is top priority. A highly portable shelter or windbreak such as Winter Fishing System's FishTrap, Frabill's Ranger, HT's Deluxe Polar Shelter, Frabill's Explorer or Ice shuttle are helpful assets for carrying supplies and providing protection from the wind and cold while setting tip-ups and jigging in a mobile approach.

If you're a mobile angler carrying a lot of equipment and fishing reclaimed quarries and pits, the high-sided, plastic bottomed Fishtrap and Ranger are hard to beat. If you're highly mobile or fishing remote high

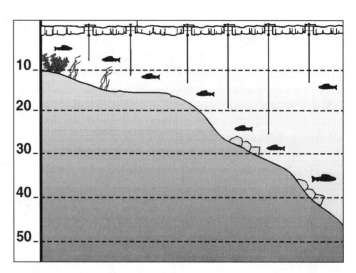

**To place your tip-ups most effectively on a Great Lakes bay, cut numerous holes along the channel to cover water, and set them strategically along its edges, covering a variety of depth ranges from the base to the top of the break. Also stagger a couple tip-ups over the middle of the channel, setting them half-way down in case a school of suspended fish tries slipping by.**

country lakes and want to travel light, try HT's Deluxe one-person Polar Shelter—a one-piece fully enclosed unit that sets up in less than 30 seconds and breaks down even faster. The unit features no loose parts, a tear-resistant floor, two large windows, an opening to accommodate two holes, convenient inside tackle pockets and four shelter anchors, all of which fold into a compact, convenient shoulder strap carrying case—and the entire unit plus anchors and case weigh less than seven pounds!

Once on the ice with primary locations and fish pinpointed, drill a series of holes on and around target areas, set up your shelter, organize, and prepare to fish.

## Tip-Ups

Where legal, smooth-tripping underwater and wind tip-ups such as HT's Polar or Windlass rigged with long, light monofilament leaders tipped with tiny hooks and a small minnow can be effective. Tip-downs and ultralight balance tip-ups rigged similarly but using smaller, lighter hooks and lively grubs can also be good when trout are fussy. Attractors, such as small, flashy spinners or colored beads may also be helpful.

For best results, try setting your bait high, anywhere from just below the ice to approximately 30 feet down, depending where you've been marking fish with your electronics. Just watch local regulations. Use of minnows is illegal in many designated trout waters—but may be okay in

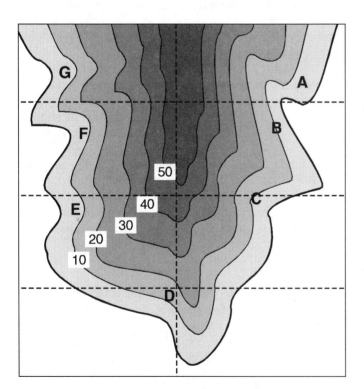

**To make locating productive holes a more efficient process on large Great Lakes bays, fish in large groups and assign individual anglers in your group to cover specific sections, then arrange a meeting place and time to review any established patterns.**

lakes featuring a mixture of trout and "warmwater" species, which usually aren't labeled designated trout waters.

Tip-up presentation for deep water Great Lakes trout is slightly different, and should include an effective combination of thoroughly covering channels and their respective banks narrowing into shallow flats and river mouths. To make locating productive holes a more efficient process, break bays into small sections, and after using sonar to pinpoint channel boundaries, migration routes and any structures on or within them, assign a section to each angler in your group so you can pinpoint the location of migration routes being used by active trout more quickly.

Cut numerous holes along the channel to cover water, and begin setting tip-ups, placing them strategically along the channel edges and covering a depth range from the base to the top of the break. Also stagger a couple of tip-ups over the middle of the channel, setting them about halfway down—this covers you in the event a suspended school tries slipping by. If you don't catch a fish within 30 minutes, try moving along the channel in 20 or 30 yard intervals, repeating the process until you contact fish. By sticking with this plan, you're likely to find an active school.

While tip-downs and ultralight umbrella-style tip-ups are better for light-striking stocked trout in smaller ponds, lakes or protected Great Lakes bays and harbors, because of the amount of wind and blowing snow often encountered in larger bays, underwater tip-ups set with thermal hole covers or thermal tip-ups are your best bets.

To rig your tip-ups, use premium Dacron such as Gudebrod, HT, or Mason's for backing, and tie the tag end to one side of a barrel swivel. To the opposite end, tie a long, light monofilament leader of 2 to 6 lb. test, or a nine-foot fly leader, then terminate the rig with a sharp #10 hook, using only as much weight as needed to sink your bait to the desired depth and hold it there, which varies with depth and current. With slight modification, this rig will cover most stocked trout winter fishing situations. Don't horse fish much; these light line rigs and tippets won't withstand much abuse. Of course, no matter what trout species you're seeking, set the tip-up as lightly as possible so fish won't feel resistance when the bait is taken.

Where legal, I prefer to use small, live emerald or golden shiners—although I've seen anglers using dead

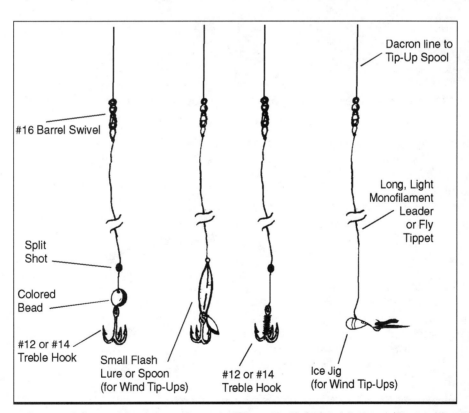

**A variety of tip-up rigs work for stocked trout, but you'll have to lighten things up. Dacron backing line should be light, 10-15 lb. test. Better yet, go with a 10-12 lb. monofilament backing. Use small #16 barrel swivels to attach light leaders or fly tippets rigged with small, number 12-14 treble hooks and ultralight fly fishing shot. Small flash lures and spoons or tiny jigs may work when fished beneath a wind tip-up or tip-down. Set your trips as lightly as possible; finicky trout often drop a bait if they feel even the slightest resistance.**

**When trout are finicky, you'll have to slow your presentation down and fish smaller ultralight lures and baits.**

baits come home with heavy pails, too. If minnows aren't legal, go with grubs, maggots or wigglers, and hook them so the bait remains alive, wiggles, and remains in a horizontal position. Also try periodically raising and "jiggling" your tip-ups slightly—this action often triggers additional hits.

## Jigging

While jigglesticks work fine for smaller stocked brook or rainbow trout, jig poles with ice reels offer some drag and are better applied to most winter stocked trout fishing situations. Be prepared to use slightly heavier lines of 4 to 6 lb. Test as jig poles are usually considerably stiffer than most light and ultralight style spinning rods, and you'll risk line breakage using lighter lines.

In areas where you're fishing deep, such as reclamated mine pits, Great Lakes bays or the deep alpine lakes or mountain reservoirs of the western United States—especially those offering opportunity for a true trophy—considerably heavier equipment may be neces-

sary. Some Great Lakes bay and Western trout anglers fish 24 to 48-inch stiff, "broom handled" action rods

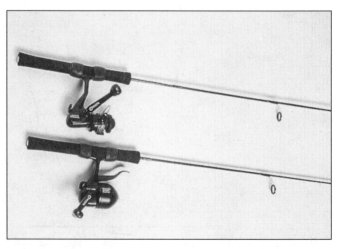

**When tackling down, good equipment begins with a sensitive, light-tipped ice rod and a smooth high-quality spinning or underspin reel featuring a smooth pickup and reliable drag. (Courtesy Zebco/Quantum)**

with large #16-20 ringed guides outfitted with large baitcast reels and heavier monofilaments or the so called "super lines." The heavier rods help set the hook in deep water, and the strong, thin diameter "superlines" reduce line stretch, providing better power for superior deep water hook-sets.

In these cases, a sturdy, three- to four-foot ice rod with some "give" toward the tip such as HT's Trout/Pike Systems, or, if you prefer, a five- to six-foot one-piece medium light action spinning or baitcasting summer graphite rod such as St. Croix's Premier Graphites or HT's Prominence Series should provide all the strength, give and power you need—qualities that are a must when fishing deep water or trophy trout through the ice. For best results, combine your rod with a large spinning or baitcasting reel and coat the gears with a lightweight oil that won't get stiff in cold weather.

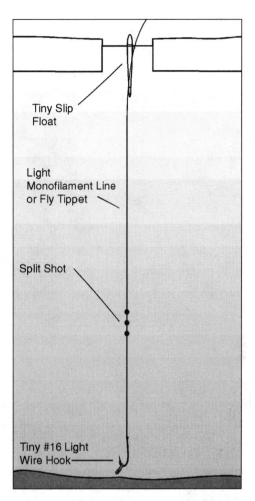

**When trout are really negative, naturally presented tiny waxworms, maggots or nymphs rigged ultralight on light monofilament leaders of 1-3 lb. test or light fly tippets can be excellent producers. They must be rigged carefully using tiny slip floats, ultralight split shot and tiny, baited ice flies or light-wire short-shanked hooks.**

Typically, relatively long, 36 to 48-inch medium-light action spinning rods such as HT's Polar Lite Elites, Jiggin' Sticks or four to five-foot Silver Lites or Micromaster ultralight rods are the choice of most trophy trout specialists. They offer greater presentation control, leverage and hook-setting power than standard length ice rods, and allow ample opportunity to fish lighter lines. Combined with a good spinning reel, these make excellent winter trout outfits.

Personally, I prefer a fairly stiff backboned, fast action 24 to 36-inch ice spinning rod with a limber, sensitive tip. The stiff backbone provides power for setting the hook and fighting fish, the soft tip helps add lure action, registers even the slightest of bites and as with other panfish, allows you to fish lighter lines. Balanced

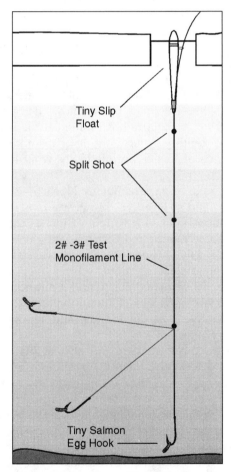

**For spooky trout, some ice anglers fish a tiny #4 salmon egg hook tipped with spawn sacs or chunks, waxworms, minnows or corn beneath a tiny slip float using just enough specially placed ultralight split shot to get the bait down. Then, barely jig the bait to attract fish.**

**By properly setting your drag, holding your rod tip high, taking your time as you retrieve and never attempting to ice a trout until it's fully played out, you'll lose very few fish, even those occasional trophies!**

with a good quality light or ultralight spinning reel, the systems work well.

On waters where trophies are rare, 24 to 32-inch light or ultralight ice rods are often sufficient and add to the fun. On clear lakes, some winter trout experts prefer short, 15 to 20-inch light action rods so they can jig close to the hole and watch the trout below react to their lure movements. These lighter rods also allow use of ultralight and "micro" lines or fly tippets. Again, an ultralight or micro size spinning reel rounds out the system.

However you fish, keep in mind stocked trout are powerful, and can really be tackle busters—be prepared. When fishing light, have the drag on your reel set accordingly, and check your line frequently for abrasion.

## Lures and Techniques

Since stocked trout can be quite active, swimming lures such as smaller-sized Normark Jigging Rapalas or Northland's Mini Airplane Jigs can be quite effective.

For best results, try tipping these baits with a minnow head or grub, various colored one- to two-inch plastic twist-style tails, tube jigs or twist-tail grubs. Plastics add extra color, bulk, action and taste—and also slow the fall of these baits just enough to trigger a few extra fish into swiping at your bait.

The biggest drawback to using swimming lures is most anglers tend to overfish them. For stocked trout, just periodic, short lift-drops interspersed with slight shimmying or shaking motions—barely enough to move the hook on the lure body—is enough. Overdo it and you'll spook trout instead of attract them.

Most winter trout anglers agree the best winter fishing baits include flash lures such as HT's 1/8-ounce Marmooska Spoons, Bay de Noc's #2 Swedish Pimples, Bay de Noc's smaller Vinglas, and lighter, slow falling spoons such as Bad Dog's Crippled Minnows, Bait Rig's Willospoons, Reef Runner's Slender Spoons and HT's #6 Walleye Spoons. My favorite colors include gold, orange, lime, watermelon and chartreuse, followed by silver and hammered copper.

To work these baits, periodically "pop" the lure upward to attract fish, lower your rod to allow the bait to swim or flutter downward, then pause for 15 or 20 seconds. The "lift" portion of this method attracts trout to the bait, while the drop/pause allows fish an opportunity to strike as the lure settles. Repeat the process at a variety of depths, experimenting with modifications and variations of this technique to see what best interests them.

For the sake of variety, Bay de Noc's Swedish Pimples, Northland's Fire-Eye Minnows or HT's Marmooska Spoons spliced a couple of inches up the line from a small ice lure tipped with a grub, waxworm or—where legal—a live minnow also work well. The weight of these spoons helps get tiny ice lures deep quickly—while their movements, flash and vibrations attract trout in for a closer look, and the baited stinger lure tipped with live bait encourages and tempts strikes almost every time.

If the trout are striking but shy, a tiny minnow, mealworm, waxworm, nymph or slice of spawn sac rigged on a small teardrop, ice jig or ice fly fished as a dropper on a long, light monofilament leader or fly tippet below a small flash bait such as a large, prism teardrop is another popular ultralight option. To rig one, simply remove the hook from the spoon and tie a short, light leader rigged with a tiny hook or ice jig tipped with your favorite live bait directly below it, jigging gently to trigger fish, interspersed with occasional "jumps" to attract distant fish.

Experiment with various lure sizes and colors to see if there are any preferences, and be sure to try different jigging actions and grubs. Trout can be fussy, and sometimes the smallest details such as changing lure size, bait type or method of rigging your grub can make a tremendous difference in catch rates.

If you still find the trout uncooperative, you'll have to slow things down and fish smaller ultralight rigs. Smaller horizontal baits such as Northland's Sink 'N' Jigs, Custom Jigs and Spins Rat Finkees or HT's Marmooska Jigs are good bets. Tip these tiny, lightweight lures with a single salmon egg, lightly hooked redworm, waxworm, mealworm, maggot or nymph, add a splitshot or two to get your bait down, fish slowly and, where applicable, let the bait dangle from the hook, allowing it to wriggle seductively to attract fish. Such practices often turn many slow days into special "limit" days you'll remember for many years to come.

Properly balance your gear when tackling down. I prefer to use smooth, high-quality spinning reels featuring smooth bail pickups and reliable drags. Combined on lighter-tipped rods, such features make fishing deep water practical, and use of light lines feasible. For best results, spool with premium, low-diameter memory resistant monofilaments in 2 to 3 lb. test, and to minimize break-offs regularly check your drag settings and examine your line and knots for signs of wear.

For spooky trout, some anglers simply tip a #4 salmon egg hook with spawn sacs or chunks, waxworms, mealworms, minnows or corn, then barely jig the bait—but if you try this approach it's a good idea to stagger some splitshot up the line to help keep your bait down, especially if there's current present. Using a spring bobber or tiny slip float to indicate strikes is necessary when using a stiffer rod. However, unless you're fishing in deep water beyond the reach of sunlight penetration, since the water in most winter trout environments is ultra-clear, sticking with lighter tackle and 2 to 3 lb. test monofilament is a bonus.

When trout are really negative, tiny waxworms, maggots, or nymphs rigged ultralight can be excellent producers—but they must be rigged carefully using light 1 to 3 lb. Test lines or light fly tippets, ultralight shot and tiny, #16-20 ice fly or light-wire, short-shanked hooks to appear natural. When ultralight rigging a small grub, just nick the skin and let it wiggle; with a nymph or other insect larvae, run the point of your hook through the middle of the insect's back, then slide it gently underneath the shell or skin until the barb comes out near the head. This causes the bait to be positioned naturally in a horizontal manner, and the compact design of this presentation combined with a subtle jigging approach is a tremendous attraction advantage during periods of slowed feeding activity.

Where live bait isn't legal, tiny hooks and soft, 1/2-inch plastic bodies in black, brown or green rigged on a jighead and dipped in fish attractant closely match the trout's preferred forage in profile, size, color and scent, and can be highly effective. I've even seen successful fishermen hide tiny hooks within Uncle Josh's pork rind Ice Flecks, Johnson's Ice Magic Baits and Berkley Power Baits. I know some trout anglers also use whole kernel corn, but I recommend avoiding this practice. Trout cannot digest the "shells" on whole kernel corn, and this can harm or even kill them if the the corn is ingested by the biting fish.

Once you've selected a bait, lowered it to the correct depth and a fish appears on your electronics, you'll have to convince them to bite. I've experienced most success fishing "tightline" on a sensitive ultralight ice rod like HT's Ice Blues, gently raising and lowering the bait with short, subtle twitches before dropping the bait to bottom—or when using stiffer action rods, sensing strikes with the help of a super-sensitive spring bobber or balsa slip-float such as Thill Tackle's Center Slider, and barely "quivering" the bait in place to tease fish into striking.

When you receive a strike on an ultralight rig, pause briefly, then set the hook with a firm, upward movement. Adjust your drag if necessary, and hold your rod high while fighting the fish. This allows more control and extra play should your trophy make a fast, hard run. Often trout are lost within just a few inches of the hole simply because overzealous anglers aren't able to react quickly enough when the fish makes a long, last-ditch head-shaking run for freedom. However, if you remember to properly set your drag, hold your rod tip high, take your time as you retrieve and never try

**High country stocked trout fishing: Quality scenery, quality fish, quality experience.**

landing a trout until it's fully played out, you'll lose very few fish.

Incidentally, for proponents of catch and release, winter-caught trout are releasable, provided they're handled gently, not deeply hooked or taken from excessively deep water. So fish responsibly. Pay attention to designated trout water regulations and bag limits, and keep only fish that are taken from very deep water, hooked badly, or you're sure you can eat—and practice catch and release with the rest.

## The High Country Trout Experience

Because a big part of the high country trout experience is the adventure and novelty, no discussion of winter stocked trout fishing would be complete without a couple of stories from the field.

Such ice fishing waters are unquestionably placed amid the most beautiful and rugged winter terrain. Mountain scenery is filled with breathtaking, panoramic winter scenes of majestic grandeur, including vertical, snow-covered rock ledges, sheer, ice coated craggy precipices, steep, icy mountain passes and rug-

ged expanses of pine covered hills and mountain meadows criss-crossed by rushing trout streams speckled with snow covered rocks.

Gorgeous.

While some of these waters are accessible by vehicle, most high country trout are often more for adventurous ice anglers ready to ski, snowshoe or snowmobile into backcountry lakes beyond plowed roads. Most of these high country waters support brookies, rainbows and browns, but some Western lakes yield cutthroat, cutbow, golden and Dolly Varden trout as well.

Once there, don't expect to find much classic fish-holding structure on these lakes, but if you search hard enough, you may locate points, shoals, bars or high banks featuring rock ledges and outcroppings, boulders, trailings and talus from rock slides. Once you've located these high-percentage locations, top this off with a suitable presentation incorporating the proper rods, reels, lines, lures, baits, rigging and jigging methods to best suit the situation at hand.

Trout on these high country lakes will bite virtually all day long. It's not uncommon to have a strong flurry

**Many high-country trout lakes offer little classic fish-holding cover, but productive points, shoals, bars or outcroppings, rock slides or rip-rap lining dam faces may be located if you search for them.**

of action during the middle of the day if you hit the right spots—although these waters are typically very clear, the most consistent catches seem to come during twilight periods, with the early morning hours between daylight and 10 a.m. generally producing the best results. A good secondary bite also occurs from about 3 p.m. until dark, often with a strong flurry right before the sun dips below the horizon.

Safety should always be a primary concern. Safe travel to and from these lakes should never be taken for granted—and neither should the ice, particularly early and late in the season. Be especially cautious of creek mouths and shore ice, and always be mindful of the weather. Access to mountain lakes is highly dependent on local weather, and conditions can change on the turn of a dime, so don't be frustrated by last minute plan changes.

## High Country Trout in South Dakota

If you're fortunate enough to live near South Dakota's Black Hills, you're in prime winter stocked trout country. I admit I wasn't exactly sure what to expect when I first shook hands with friend Larry L. Gimbel of Hill City, South Dakota, but I had a feeling I was in for a real treat.

Larry mentioned over the phone stocked trout were biting well in his area. After revealing several of his countless Black Hills ice fishing accomplishments, including a beautiful five pound splake, eighteen inch brook trout and limit catches of stocked rainbows on just about every trip in recent weeks, I have to admit he had me fired up. But before taking me to the lake, Larry wanted to visit.

"There's more than just exceptional trout fishing involved with the Black Hills high country ice fishing experience," he pointed out.

And he was right. As Larry's pick-up clambered up steep, winding Black Hills roads in second gear, breathtaking, panoramic scenes of majestic grandeur appeared around each corner. Vertical, snow-covered rock ledges, sheer, craggy precipices, steep mountain passes and rugged expanses of pine covered hills and mountain meadows coerced me to have Larry pull over

**The author with the last fish to round out he and his partner's South Dakota stocked trout limit. Since most Black Hills trout are stocked in waters designed as "put and take" style fisheries, catching a few fish for the frying pan is common practice.**

on several occasions as I fumbled with my camera to capture the landscape on film.

Larry just smiled and continued his narrated tour, noting the wide variety of scenic snowmobile and cross-country ski trails winding through the pristine mountainous terrain. Rushing trout streams speckled with snow-covered rocks provide fly anglers open water and a chance to test their skills throughout much of the winter. Best of all, the Black Hills lakes offer a year-round fishing season. Provided safe ice exists, trout are fair game on any of the lakes throughout the winter, and since many of these waters are found within state parks or are completely surrounded by undeveloped, state-owned lands, the scenery and atmosphere are fabulous. For adventurous anglers, snowmobiling or snowshoeing treks to backcountry lakes beyond plowed roads are also available. And for the budget-conscious, Black Hills room rates are lowest in the winter and many motels offer special winter recreation packages.

I soon learned the location patterns for catching Black Hills trout vary, because each mountain lake is slightly different. But general location patterns are fairly simple.

At first ice, which is usually formed and safe around Christmas, you can expect to find excellent fishing, with most trout located in easily accessible shallow water close to banks and shorelines. High-percentage features include long shoreline structures such as points, bars, drop-offs and ledges found in approximately 12 to 14 feet of water.

Fishing right off bottom at the base of drop-offs and breaks is most productive, probably because these fish are largely foraging on a variety of aquatic insects and crayfish on the bottom—so if you're simply relying on a small clip-on style depthfinder, fishing close to bottom is probably the most efficient first-ice approach.

Toward mid-season, there's a progressive movement into deeper water, and trout tend to scatter and move frequently, still feeding on invertebrates and other critters along the bottom—but often suspending to feed on drifting masses of plankton. While these roaming, suspended trout are often quite active and still very catchable, anglers must work a little longer and harder to catch them compared to first ice, when the fish tend to be more concentrated and easily accessible at the base of dropoffs.

If you're experienced using electronics on the ice, you'll likely increase your mid-season catch of mountain trout, because you'll periodically mark clouds of plankton and catchable fish swimming through suspended at a variety of levels. Of course, since suspended trout are apt to move through at a wide variety of depths, to be consistently successful, your best approach is to start fishing on or close to bottom as you

**Use of electronics is very helpful when winter trout suspend, a phenomenon common on many Western trout waters.**

would earlier in the season, and when you notice forage and fish coming through higher up, simply reel up to their level. This creates a different dimension that will add to the activity, excitement and fun of your Black Hills ice fishing experience.

As the season wears into the late ice period, fishing can be sporadic, but again, for best results, focus your efforts in deeper areas, and move often in search of fish. You may only catch a fish or two from any given hole, but by moving around you'll usually be able to work up a limit by day's end.

This basic pattern will continue producing until very late ice, when the meltdown begins and runoff from feeder creeks and melting snow draws fish back toward the shallows. This time of year, most trout tend to group up again in the vicinity of shoreline structure, cover and drop-offs near creek mouths—just be cautious in these areas, as the combination of current, warming temperatures and melting snow can cause ice conditions to deteriorate fast.

**A Black Hills guide hefts a stocked rainbow from a mountain reservoir. This 11-inch fish is a typical catch, as rainbows average 10 to 14 inches in size.**

Seasonally, the best bites generally occur at first ice, from mid-December until the first part of January, when trout are concentrated near shoreline breaks, and again at late-ice just prior to ice-out, usually throughout the latter part of March.

On a daily basis, trout on these lakes will bite virtually all day long—in fact, it's not uncommon to have a strong flurry of action during the middle of the day if you hit the right spots—although the most consistent catches seem to come during twilight periods, with the early morning hours between daylight and 10 a.m. generally producing the best results. A good secondary bite also occurs from about 3 p.m. until dark, often with a strong flurry right before the sun dips below the horizon. After that, things seem to slow down. For reasons unknown to me, night fishing generally isn't very productive.

As for equipment, you can leave your tip-ups behind in the Black Hills. These trout generally bite lightly and don't strike hard enough to trip most tip-up flags. Jigging seems to be the answer—and you don't

necessarily have to be elaborate in terms of equipment. A variety of light action ice rods will perform; rigs simple as a fiberglass jig stick rigged with a linewinder and bobber will catch fish, provided you're set up in the right location.

A light action fiberglass or graphite ice rod/ice reel combo such as HT's Little Jigger series spooled with braided tip-up line and a four to six-foot length of 4 lb. test leader and a slip float provides convenient line and depth control, very little line stretch when fishing deep water, easy visibility, and a helping hand when trying to bring fish from deep water to the surface.

For increased sport and fun—and some will argue, effectiveness—try an ultralight ice rod such as HT's Ice Blues, Polar Gold Micro or Micro Brim Rods, rigged with an ultralight spinning reel and 2 lb. test line. Again, Black Hills trout can bite light, and the sensitivity provided by these light action rods is helpful. Quality ultralight spinning reels with reliable drag systems also make the use of light lines more feasible, and makes raising and lowering baits more efficient when trying to catch suspended, deep water fish. Remember, the possibility of a double-digit splake is real, so set the drag light and be prepared. A 10 lb. splake struggling on a light rod and 2 lb. line will test your angling skill to its maximum.

As for lures, if the fish are active, #6 teardrops, ice ants, Daphnias, Rat Finkees or small spoons such as a #2 Swedish Pimple fished below a bobber, slip float, or simply tight line on a super-sensitive ultralight are productive. On days when the fish are fussy, drop down to a size 10 or 12 hook—bend the hook point slightly to widen the hook gap and increase your hooking percentages.

Try tipping your favorite jigs with a salmon egg, waxworm, mealworm, mousie, wiggler or maggot—and let the bait dangle from the hook, allowing it to wriggle seductively to attract fish.

Also note that where present, bonus catches of occasional brown trout, jumbo perch, slab crappies and other panfish species may add to the excitement—and at times, the action "explodes" for all the above species—and because Black Hills trout and other panfish species bite fairly well all winter long, with a little practice it's really not that difficult for most anglers to get good at catching them consistently.

## Regulations

South Dakota regulations for Black Hills trout are straightforward. Currently, the season is open year-round, and with the exception of a couple of specially managed lakes, the general limit on trout is relatively liberal—as I write, eight fish per person, in any combination. Please keep in mind that typical native brookie populations rely completely on natural reproduction, so catch and release of these precious beauties comes highly recommended. Remember, catch what you can—and keep the rainbows and splake for the frying pan.

As in most stocked trout areas, be advised that regulations often change. The use of live minnows is also limited, so be sure to check local regulations before drilling any holes.

## More on High Country Trout

High country trout fishing isn't limited to the Black Hills. Areas in Washington, Oregon, Colorado, Montana, Idaho, Wyoming, Utah—even Arizona, Nevada and New Mexico—offer high country, winter stocked trout fishing. In fact, I've been in the White Mountains of Arizona in June and still seen ice and snow at higher elevations! It's probably not a surprise that Colorado has numerous deep, clear trout lakes that freeze over or that Montana offers many world renowned winter trout fishing lakes of various sizes. But don't let states like New Mexico and Arizona fool you. Although these areas often conjure up visions of hot sun, dry sand, rattlesnakes and cacti, both states offer fabulous high country stocked trout ice fishing opportunities for rainbow, brook and brown trout—if you can get through the deep snow to the lakes.

Of course, ice fishing classic high country lakes such as those in Colorado or Montana offers greater opportunities. Small, glacial and alpine lakes offer limited access, but also memorable fishing experiences.

More common, however, are high country lakes located at lower, more easily accessible altitudes. One of my favorite Western stocked trout ice fishing experiences took place at Montana's Lake Hebgen, an impoundment on the famed Madison River near West Yellowstone, Montana. I was fishing with my good friend Mr. Paul Grahl, avid ice fishing partner and developer of the famous Polar tip-up. Determined to reach a remote area we felt held fish, Paul and I snowshoed down the side of a mountain, clambering over an estimated 40 feet of snow in -30° weather just to test our intuition and experience the thrill of snowshoeing in the high country. For us, the reward was more than worth the risks—the fishing and scenery were tremendous, and I'll treasure the memories of that special trip forever.

And why not? Out in these Western climes, uniquely marked and colored beautiful trout grow big, and are as challenging as any species you'll ever fish through the ice. Lake Hebgen, for example, is big water, and while a good portion never develops safe ice because of strong current flow, certain areas offer excellent fishing. In this case, our target was browns, a roaming species that pose one of the ultimate challenges in western "big water" ice fishing. However, we found an area where, during an earthquake a century ago, a chunk of mountainside had slid into the water along an otherwise steep, structureless wall. This formed

**The author's fishing partner prepares to drill a hole through the waters of a high-country lake. The tremendous scenery of a winter high country trout experience is considered unparalleled by many ice anglers.**

"point", covered with rock and trees, provided excellent structure and secondary cover, and on the map, it looked good.

Using electronics, we were able to find the rock point, its edges and primary cover laden areas, and we caught our share of moderately sized trout, along with several unidentified fish that snapped our light lines with the crack of a lightning bolt striking, providing a thrill beyond compare.

So regardless of the lake you're fishing, once you've made the commitment and chosen an area to fish high country stocked trout, researched stocking records, checked regulations for the waters you intend to fish, considered the species you're seeking, forms of available cover and forage, time of year, your target lake's classification, time of day and prevailing weather conditions, try using a combination of hydrographic maps, electronics and mobility to efficiently cover all major structural elements in search of active trout. Then top this off with a suitable presentation incorporating the proper rods,

reels, lines, lures, baits rigging and jigging methods to best suit the situation at hand.

No matter where you fish, by following these approaches you'll be well on your way to enjoying one of the most peaceful, pristine and pleasurable of all ice fishing outings.

**Most high-country stocked trout lakes are surrounded by breathtaking, panoramic scenery.**

# Chapter 9

# *Understanding Ciscoes During Winter*

*L*ate ice.

This isn't typical ice fishing. There's no wind, no drifting snow. The warming sun is shining brightly, the air temperature is hovering near 50°F, and our light jackets are open to allow body heat to escape the warming layers of clothing underneath. Yet I urge those around me to be careful. Exposed winter white skin and harsh, direct and reflecting sunlight are a dangerous combination and this time of year, even with sunscreen carefully applied, sunburn is a concern. We must be careful to keep our hands, arms, neck and face protected.

The fat tires of my four-wheeler spin, kicking up slush and water as we bounce off the muddy access onto the now-softening ice. Gradually we accelerate, hauling a trailer full of coolers, ice augers, electronics, jig rods and baits. Enthusiasm is the word to describe the day. After all, the conditions are perfect for an excellent cisco bite.

As we near an area that typically holds large schools of cisco, I notice two of my fishing partners hooking up the batteries on their electronics. I smile, knowing they're trying to get a jump on me. But not to worry. Once we find them, we'll likely all catch fish, because ciscoes are highly prolific, school tightly, and once located during late ice, generally aren't that difficult to catch.

Stopping, we scatter in different directions with our sonar, searching for an active school. Fifteen minutes of effort reveals nothing, so we hop back on the four-wheeler, move a few hundred yards away and repeat the process.

This time, things happen. I mark fish 18 feet down over 32 feet of water—big, suspended fish, and lots of

**Silvery, hard-fighting cisco sometimes fight and splash onto the ice with a strength and fury that reminds me of a thrashing steelhead.**

**Cisco are easily identified by their long, silvery iridescent bodies and prominently forked tails.**

them—probably cisco! I quickly drill a hole and lower my grub tipped jig, stopping my lure just above the huge school. Immediately, a fish rises to my bait and strikes, and I set the hook into a heavy fish. Moments later, a silvery, hard-fighting two-pound cisco splashes onto the ice with all the strength of a thrashing steelhead.

Again, I lower my bait and repeat the sequence to a tee. Realizing I'm on an active school, I drill a second hole and begin fishing two lines, and for several hours, stay in the same two holes, catching fish after fish almost constantly, seldom hooking into anything less than a pound. Best of all, my friends get into the action, too, and we all fish in a relaxed, social group, visiting, eating sandwiches and catching fish until we've iced all we care to clean and eat.

It's funny though. Relatively easy as ciscoes are to pattern, fun as they are to catch and good as they taste when fried or smoked, it seems many ice anglers have never even heard of ciscoes, much less considered fishing them. Late last winter I fished ciscoes three days straight during the midst of the day without seeing another angler approach me, although I did notice a few other people fishing ciscoes in other areas of the lake—discreetly, I might add.

However, while often passed up, my prediction is the cisco "secret" will soon be let out of the bag, and this silvery, muscular, hard-fighting, great-tasting fish will grow in popularity among ice anglers in future years, perhaps even becoming a primary-sought winter species.

Of course, like any other species, to catch ciscoes consistently, you must understand the fish, their primary locations and forage bases, and the best methods for hooking them.

Cisco are easily identified by their long, silvery iridescent bodies and prominently forked tails. Some ice anglers have called them tullibee or lake herring, although their proper name is cisco. Their preferred environment consists of cold, well-oxygenated water, so they are most often found in deeper, clear waters such as Great Lakes bays and large, deep natural lakes and reservoirs. Thanks largely to stocking they also may be found in limited numbers in smaller, relatively infertile lakes boasting moderate depths.

While some river spawning movements have been noted, spawning occurs mostly within the lake environment from early November to mid-December on shallow, clean bottoms, although some cisco have been known to spawn pelagically over deep water. Following the spawn, cisco move deep under the ice.

Since cisco are largely a pelagic species, their diet consists primarily of pelagic forage, especially plankton in the form of copepods and cladocerans, insects and insect larvae, fish eggs, and crustaceans like freshwater shrimp. The presence of clams and water mites in some stomach samples also provides evidence that limited bottom feeding occurs, although this is an exception to the rule.

One of the finest qualities of ciscoes is their willingness to bite during the middle of the day, so there's no need to be on the ice at sun-up or fumbling in the darkness of night. Rather, you can wake up at will, prepare your tackle, have a nice breakfast, hit the ice around mid-morning, leave by mid-afternoon and have a relaxing evening—and still catch plenty of fish. If you're a night owl, try night fishing suspended ciscoes actively feeding on crustaceans just under the ice. As with other panfishes, action can be fast and furious, although some mid-winter days getting a cisco to budge is harder than turning a well-rusted lug nut. I've also noticed ciscoes seem to feed aggressively before the advent of a major snowstorm, but cold fronts seem to slow feeding activity.

Average-sized ciscoes run about 10 to 16 inches in length and weigh one to two pounds, although in the right

While a roaming species, cisco also tend to hold in or near the same areas each winter. If you can obtain productive waypoints and travel directly to and from them checking each area out carefully with sonar, you'll likely have an easier time locating active schools and making consistent catches, year after year.

environment, they may grow to weigh several pounds. A 4 pound, 10 ounce cisco was taken from Big Green Lake, Wisconsin, in 1969; and really digging into the archives, an eight-pounder was taken from Lake Erie in 1949.

While somewhat oily, the cisco has excellent food qualities and is delicious—in my opinion featuring a taste and texture similar to trout. Either fillet or steak the meat, then deep fry the fillets in your favorite batter with lemon pepper, butter and onion. I've also discovered ciscoes are excellent when smoked, featuring a flavor similar to smoked salmon.

## Primary Winter Location Patterns

To begin with, ciscoes live mainly in deep, cold lakes, so choose waters with a fishable population. Larger, deeper inland waters and Great Lakes bays are your best bets, although some smaller, shallower cool water lakes, flowages and reservoirs may contain marginal populations. Keep in mind that winter fishing for cisco is not common so for more detailed information, you'll have to check with knowledgeable bait shops or your local fisheries agency to discover lakes in your area worth angling effort.

Be prepared to move in search of fish, and on many of the larger lakes cisco inhabit, traveling several miles

In the hunt for winter cisco, be prepared to move in search of fish, perhaps traveling distances of several miles from your launch site to find roaming schools.

from your launch site to find roaming schools is not unusual. Your best bet is to have a snowmobile, four wheeler or six wheeler to gain mobility, and a hand-held GPS to exchange productive waypoints with other knowledgeable anglers.

This might sound like consistently locating winter cisco is difficult. However, while cisco tend to suspend over deep water and roam, they also tend to hold in or near the same areas each winter. If you can obtain productive waypoints and travel directly to and from them checking each area out carefully with sonar, you'll have an easier time locating active schools and making consistent catches, year after year.

In terms of specific winter location, cool-water-loving ciscoes may be found almost anywhere, but are highly dependent on their primary forage bases—largely comprised of plankton and crustaceans—so the key is to find concentrations of such forage, and this can easily be accomplished using sonar. Remember, such forage bases typically suspend; consequently, so do the ciscoes and both register well and are easily recognizable on sonar.

Furthermore, while ciscoes are a restless fish constantly roaming in search of forage, they really aren't known to be long-distance movers even on large lakes, and often school heavily. So again, while cisco may be somewhat difficult to locate initially, once you find locations that typically support ciscoes for the time and conditions you're fishing, you'll usually find them following the same or similar winter patterns, year after year.

After finding a few productive winter locations, be sure to mark them on your GPS as waypoints and record the current water and weather conditions so given a similar situation, you can return to the same spots.

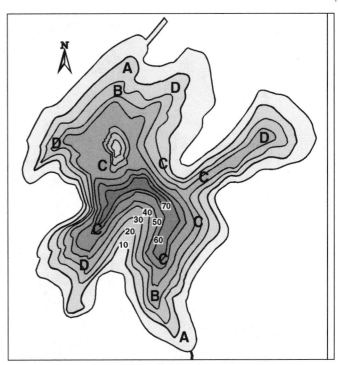

Early ice, ciscoes will be found holding over shallow and mid-depth rock and hard bottom areas (A). By mid-winter, there is a noticeable movement of cisco from inshore areas toward deeper water (B,C,D), where large schools gather and suspend at various depths. Late winter, ciscoes move into mid-depth, even shallow water regions and become quite active (A,B). Deep pockets and holes in mid-depth bays may also hold late ice cisco.

## Early Ice

Because ciscoes spawn in late fall over shallow to mid-depth rock and hard bottom areas, first ice typically finds post-spawn fish congregating in shallow, inshore areas consisting of depths up to 30 feet. Depending how early first ice sets in, fishing can be slow as they recuperate from the spawning ordeal, but generally by the time ice has formed solidly, active schools can be found along shallow and mid-depth shoals. Soon after, you'll find ciscoes moving down the drop-offs into deeper water, or suspending off steep breaks near these hard-bottom spawning flats and shoals. On smaller inland lakes, a similar pattern is noted, just on a smaller scale.

In some waters, cisco run up feeder streams to spawn, so river mouths and adjoining flats and drop-offs can be first-ice hot spots given early ice on these waters. In other environments, cisco have been known to spawn pelagically, meaning they simply dump their eggs while suspended over deep water. Be prepared to move while searching for active fish.

**Since plankton are the primary forage of ciscoes and typically suspend, so do ciscoes. Both register well and are easily recognizable on sonar.**

**In terms of timing, late ice is the best time to catch numbers of ciscoes.**

## Mid-Winter

By mid-winter, there is a noticeable movement of cisco from inshore spawning areas toward deeper water, where large schools gather and suspend at various depths. Often, they'll be found suspended between 20 and 70 feet down over water of equal or greater depths. Ciscoes are known to become finicky this time of year, and change depth frequently. In some waters, vertical, diurnal mid-winter movements may even bring cisco up at night to feed on minute crustaceans that move into the upper strata directly beneath the ice. The search for active, mid-winter cisco can be tough, but once found, good catches can be taken.

## Late Ice

Late ice is the best time to catch ciscoes. In late winter, ciscoes tend to move into mid-depth or even shallow water regions and become quite active. Action can be outstanding. Depending on the lake type, I usually begin looking for them at my waypoints for depths between 25 and 40 feet, where they'll often be suspended several feet off bottom.

Remember, ciscoes may change depths from day to day, depending on the conditions and whether or not their forage rises or drops. If you experiment while using sonar to establish daily depth patterns, you should be successful.

## Effective Winter Fishing Strategies

Ciscoes have notably small mouths, and therefore must be fished with small lures, hooks and baits. Tip-ups

Many cisco have been taken using simple jigglesticks and jig poles with ice reels. Provided you're not fishing unusually deep water, either is sufficient for containing the average cisco.

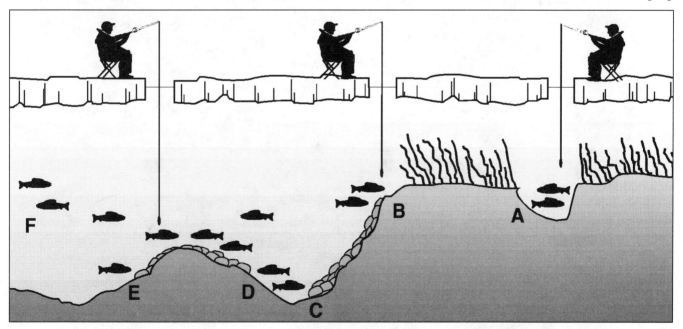

Early ice, you'll find cisco holding or suspended along the edge of shallow and mid-depth bays and shoals (B). Mid-winter, they'll hold along or suspend over the base of main lake drop-offs and structure features (C,D,E) or less often, suspend over deep, open water °F). Late ice, they'll move toward the edges of shallow and mid-depth bays and shoals (B) or deeper pockets and holes in shallow and mid-depth bays (A).

are rarely used to catch ciscoes simply because they're so willing to bite and fun to catch on light jigging equipment. However, I've found wind, ultralight and ultralight "umbrella"-style tip-ups rigged with light monofilament leaders and small, gold treble hooks affixed with yarn or paint, Bad Dog's jeweled treble hooks, or any variety of small, colorful jigs or spoons tipped with a tiny minnow or grub can be an effective means of catching cisco.

Many cisco have been taken using simple jigglesticks and jig poles with ice reels, and provided you're not fishing unusually deep water, either is sufficient for containing the average cisco. Be prepared for a strong battle—linewinder poles without reels and drags will require use of a little heavier line, and with jig poles, be sure you're ready to loosen the drag knob and "feather" the spool, just in case a larger, scrappy cisco makes a hard, line-breaking run.

I enjoy jigging ciscoes with a light action ice rod such as Berkley's light action Lighting Rods, HT's Blue Polar Lites or HT's Jiggin' Stick Systems. Ultralight rods also work, but since ciscoes feature average weighs between one and two pounds and may be larger, consistent catches of these size fish on ultralight tackle will often find you a little underpowered. A light action stick with a strong butt and sensitive tip is ideal.

Since ciscoes are larger than typical panfish, fight hard, and tend to hold fairly deep, a smooth, light action spinning reel with a quality drag is also helpful. Spool with 2 lb. test minimum; in my experience, 4 lb. is a better bet.

When it comes to lures, because the fish have such tiny mouths, most cisco enthusiasts use ultralight lures such as Custom Jigs and Spins Rat Finkees, HT's Marmooska's, Bad Dog's Water Fleas, Northland's Jig-A-Bits, K&E's Mid-Tear, or System Tackle's Copepods to catch them. Tipping the hook with a small grub and adding a squirt of fish attractant is also helpful. In deep water, attractors such as rattle chambers, glow beads or cyalume sticks can be an asset.

During mid-winter when ciscoes hold deep, lowering these smaller baits is difficult. To compromise, some anglers use small, thin, perch-style hanger rigs—or more commonly, ice spoons or flash lures rigged with light-line droppers down to tiny ice jigs or hooks to help get their tiny baits deep fast. These spoons also create the added attracting features of flash and vibration. For best results, these small lures should be tipped with small grubs, insect larvae or tiny minnows.

For intermediate depths, smaller, lightweight spoons such as Bay de Noc's smaller Swedish Pimples, Bait Rig's

**Since ciscoes have such small mouths, small lures tipped with a grub and squirt of fish attractant are helpful for increasing hooking percentages. Attractors such as rattle chambers, glow beads or cyalume sticks can also be an asset in deep water, as they help cisco find your bait.**

Willospoons, Reef Runner's Slender Spoons or HT's 1/8 ounce Marmooska Spoons or Custom Jigs and Spin's Stinger will also catch cisco. Replace the standard hooks on these lures with a smaller, well-sharpened single hook. Tipped with a grub; such a rig will often outfish any other presentation.

If the cisco are fussy, a slip-float rig consisting of a small slip float, split shot and tiny, #10-14 light wire hook or gold treble tipped with a grub or maggot can be the answer. For best results, lower your bait to a foot or two above the school, and jig the bait in one or two inch movements. When active, schooled ciscoes are highly competitive, and will usually rise for the bait. Lowering your presentation directly into the school will also catch fish, but may spook the school, breaking it up and making consistent catches more difficult as the day rolls on.

Finicky cisco can sometimes be tricked into striking. When fishing ciscoes with simple jigglesticks and heavier line in environments offering larger fish, for example, somewhat larger Bad de Noc Swedish Pimples and Vinglas, Jig-A-Whopper spoons, or HT's Marmooska Spoons and other larger flash spoons can be effective. Those with

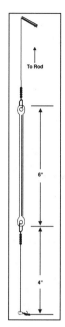

**When ciscos are holding deep, ice spoon/dropper line rigs or perch style hanger rigs help get small baits deep fast. For best results, the lure should be tipped with small grubs, insect larvae or tiny minnows for increased appeal.**

**When cisco become really finicky, simple jigglesticks, heavier line and larger, white or phosphorescent high-profile flash lures fished rapidly may arouse their curiousity and trigger a strike.**

a high profile and highly visible white or phosphorescent color seem to produce best. Fish them with rapid movement amid the school in an attempt to attract the fish's curiosity and tease one into striking or initiate an anger strike. For best results, replace the standard hooks with special, chemically sharpened treble hooks such as Mustad Triple Grips or Pradco's Excalibur. They'll increase your hooking percentages tremendously.

If you wish, try jigging with one of these lure presentations while watching a second "sitter" line rigged with a simple slip-float rig including a splitshot, hook and minnow or grub, or jig while another member of your group watches their "bobber" line. The flash of the lure often draws fish in, and the suspended bait draws the hit—an excellent way to get everyone involved in this fun-filled fishing. Use a slip-float or slip-bobber design on the sitter poles—these fish usually hold deep, and a clip-on style bobber won't be easy to work with.

Don't miss out on this unique opportunity. Cisco are a relatively untapped ice fishing species that doesn't require being on the ice early or late in the day, doesn't require specialized tackle, usually bites willingly, fights hard, tastes great—and provided you have a working knowledge of how to use electronics on the ice and are willing to be mobile, they aren't difficult to locate.

What more could an avid ice angler want?

# Chapter 10

# *Understanding White Perch During Winter*

$M$id-winter ice fishing, south central Maine. Using a lake map, I've located several mid-depth, hard-bottom bars and shoals likely to attract panfish, and using my sonar, I've finally pinpointed one holding fish.

In fact, the screen lights up, revealing a medium-sized school of suspended fish roaming the edge of the shoal. Given my Midwestern mentality, I immediately suspect they're crappies, so I tie on a small, silver #2 Swedish Pimple, tip it with a minnow and lower it just above the school. I lift the spoon six inches, and allow it to start fluttering down. The spoon never settles. A fish quickly rises for the falling lure, and hits with almost reckless abandon.

The little ice rod doubles, the drag sings. My immediate thought is this does not by any stretch of the imagination feel like a crappie, and my intuition proves correct when a scrappy, striped, white bass-looking fish pops from the hole. Two eastern seaboard friends come running over to drill holes, exclaiming something about a school of "humpies." I sit confused, trying to tell them the fish is a white perch, but they already know that. "Humpy" is simply the local term for this scrappy, warm water fish.

White perch are a somewhat confusing panfish species for a variety of reasons. First, they're not really a perch at all, but rather a member of the bass family that also includes white, yellow and striped bass. To further confuse the issue, the term "white perch" is also used throughout parts of the ice fishing belt as a nickname for freshwater drum and white crappie—somewhat understandable, considering white perch resemble the white crappie in appearance, closely follow many similar winter patterns, behave and fight much like them—but nonetheless, this is still a source of confusion. Further

**White perch not only provide good sport, but are often ranked as superior to even yellow perch in many taste tests—and that's good eating. (Bob Harris photo)**

**White perch are essentially a marine species, but have been successfully introduced to some New England ponds and lakes, creating additional sport for ice anglers. The fish show here, weighing 3 and 2-1/2 lbs, are true trophies. (Bob Harris photo)**

**White perch traditionally bite best in late afternoon and create excellent twilight bites, although night bites can be good where it's legal to fish them after dark. (Courtesy Maine Department of Fish and Wildlife)**

misunderstandings arise simply because white perch are also only available to ice anglers in a relatively small portion of the North American ice fishing belt, so many ice anglers aren't even familiar with them.

However, white perch are an undeniably different species. While essentially a marine species, some isolated, landlocked freshwater populations have been stocked in ponds and lakes throughout the New England states, where they've been made available to ice anglers.

Like crappies, their populations are highly cyclic in nature. One year white perch populations may be high and fishing can be very good, only to find the next season poor. Stunting can also be a problem with this highly prolific species.

In terms of species-specific tendencies, white perch are very much akin to their close cousin, the white bass. While more limited in distribution, where present, white perch often roam vast, open water areas in search of forage, then gather in large, actively feeding schools around forage-holding structure. They have strong schooling tendencies, and at times, feed aggressively in packs, often while suspended over mid-depth or deep water structure.

Primary forage consists of largely insects, freshwater shrimp, crustaceans and minnows. Given the right environment with suitable forage, white perch catches average a respectable 8 to 10 inches and weigh about three quarters of a pound, although they may attain lengths exceeding 16 inches and weights of more than two pounds.

Once you've made your catch, fillet them out and fry them up as you would crappies or yellow perch. Mixed in with just such fillets, you'll notice only a slight difference in taste and texture. Surprisingly, many folks often rate white perch superior to either the crappie or yellow perch—and that's mighty fine eating.

**In natural lakes and ponds, structures such as sunken islands, reefs, rock piles, contour turns and drop-offs extending from shallow feeding flats toward deep, main lake flats attract white perch. (Courtesy Maine Department of Fish and Wildlife)**

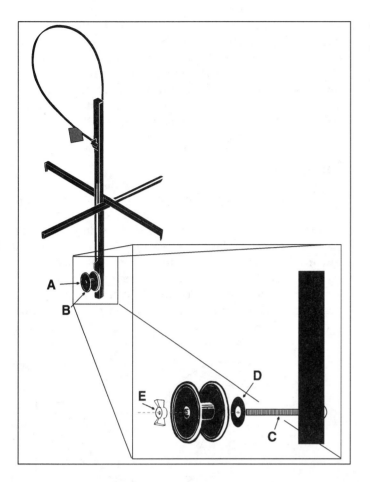

When using stick tip-ups for white perch, large capacity spooled models with drags are convenient. If your model doesn't have such features (A,B) spare large capacity spools can be purchased from companies such as HT Enterprises. The simple addition of a bolt (C), washer (D) and plastic wingnut (E) will allow you to build a customized drag system on basic tip-up systems.

Standard stick, underwater, thermal and ultralight balance tip-ups all provide effective means of hooking winter white perch, but wind tip-ups (shown at right) function even better because you can rig them with flashy jigging spoons and lures, which help attract active white perch.

## Primary Winter Location Patterns

White perch are roamers, and tend to suspend while following specific contours and structural edges in search of forage. Intercept them, and you'll do well.

In natural lakes and ponds, structures such as sunken islands, points, reefs, rock piles, contour turns and drop-offs extending from shallow feeding flats toward deep, main lake flats attract white perch. On reservoirs, main river channels and their edges, deep coves, flats or structures adjoining the mouths of feeder creeks or located near the deeper, impounded end of the lake and influenced by current are often good spots to check. If you find a particular structure holding a large concentration of preferred or available forage, white perch often hang around in large schools until the forage is scattered or eaten down and these bites may last several days. However, white perch are not necessarily structurally oriented, and may suspend over deep, open water areas provided adequate forage is available.

White perch traditionally bite best in late afternoon and create excellent twilight bites, although night bites can be good where it's legal to fish them after dark. However, in dark water environments, deeper water or during overcast days, white perch may start cracking best during mid-afternoon. If forage is readily available and conditions are right, they may also demonstrate productive early morning bites.

## Early Ice

Although winter white perch primarily use deep water where environmental conditions are more stable, shallow and mid-depth structures such as points, humps and shoals extending from shallow feeding shelves toward deep water and offering forage will draw active schools during the first ice period. Such areas influenced by current from an inlet or feeder creek are especially productive. Daily movements will occur based on the predominant weather, light intensity and water clarity.

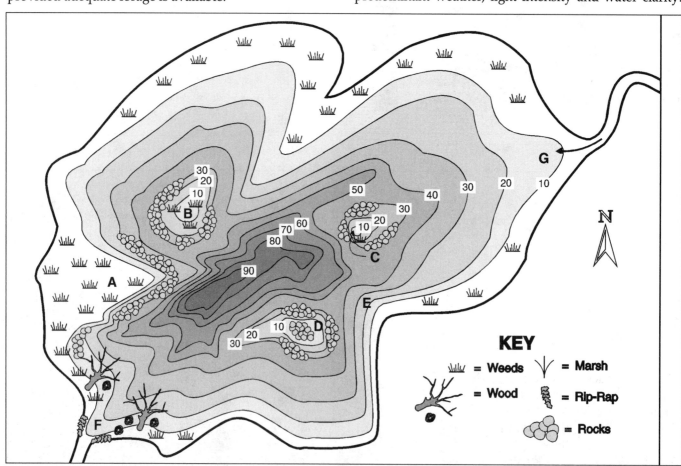

**Early ice, white perch relate to structures such as sunken islands, rock piles and reefs (B,D,C), points (A,E) and contour turns and drop-offs, especially those extending from shallow feeding flats toward deep, main lake flats. They use the same areas throughout mid-winter, although areas influenced by current are best. Late ice, white perch still hold deep, but tend to make movements toward gravel spawning shoals adjoining spawning tributary and inlet streams (G,F) especially those supporting sparse vegetation.**

Most activity seems focused around late afternoon as light levels diminish, although bites may occur earlier if the skies are overcast.

## Mid-Winter

White perch are known to make deep water movements during winter, and are prone to suspending over deep water structure. Because white perch don't particularly like cold water, good bites are not only dependent on finding a school, but finding an actively feeding one. Still, should you be fortunate enough to locate one of these schools as they're slashing into a deep water school of forage, the action can be phenomenal.

Also, if you do locate a larger, active school in deep water, especially during overcast conditions, late afternoon bites may begin earlier in the day, and extend later because light penetration isn't as great in deep water.

## Late Ice

Late ice, as the melt down begins and warm-water runoff enters the lake environment, white perch still hold deep, but will tend to make movements toward gravel spawning shoals adjoining spawning tributary and inlet streams, especially those supporting sparse vegetation. Fish the deep edges of these structures during the day, then work your way up the break and onto the flats during overcast days and twilight periods.

Standard ice poles with plastic reels, depth markers and live bait slip-bobber systems work fine for white perch, although I prefer to use short, medium action jig rod combos spooled with 6 to 8 lb. line and some type of flashy, attractive jig or spoon.

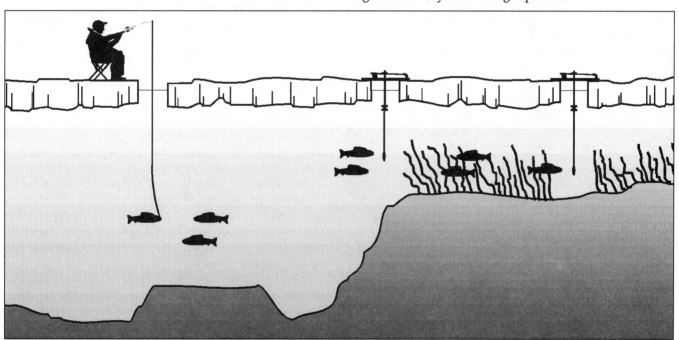

When planning a strategic approach for white perch, scatter your tip-ups across distinct structures, contours or migration routes likely to be used by wandering schools, setting some rigs on bottom, and others at various depths along migration routes. While waiting for a flag, search for suspended fish holding above or along the edges of deep water structures, using a jigging approach to reach them.

# Effective Winter Fishing Strategies

Once located, white perch generally bite quite readily on virtually anything, so a wide variety of presentations may be productive.

Standard, underwater, thermal and ultralight balance tip-ups all provide effective approaches for winter white perch. For best results, use tip-ups with large capacity spools and a drag. Spread them across a potential area, rigging them with light leaders, and small, one and a half to two-inch golden shiners or smelt hooked lightly on carefully sharpened hooks. Use just enough split shot to sink the bait to the desired depth and keep it properly positioned, then set your bait at the depth you've been marking active schools.

Often, wind tip-ups function even better because you can rig them with flashy jigging spoons and lures, which help attract active white perch. In fact, wind tip-ups so rigged will typically outfish other tip-ups by a 3:1 margin. Again, simply set them at the depth schools have been moving through. Monitor them carefully, making sure to adjust the angle to the wind, and carefully set your spring tension based on the predominant wind direction and strength.

Whether using standard or wind tip-ups, scatter them across distinct structures, contours or migration routes likely to be used by wandering white perch. This way, should a school move into the area, your tip-ups will let you know. Set some rigs right on bottom and some suspended at various depths surrounding the strata you've been marking fish; this will allow you to determine the primary strike zone. Once found, set all your lines accordingly. Again, since white perch are so aggressive and tend to school, if you get action on a tip-up, quickly set the rest of your units in the same area and set your baits at the same depth. You'll likely do well.

In the meantime as you wait for tip-up activity, try a mobile approach using a combination of sonar and jig-

**High-profile lures featuring at least some phosphorescence are especially good, primarily because winter perch often feed heavily in deep, dark water and during twilight—the size and the glow help fish find your bait. (Courtesy Maine Department of Fish and Wildlife)**

ging to continue searching for active fish. Standard ice poles with plastic ice reels, depth markers and a live bait slip-bobber system work fine for white perch, although I prefer to drop the bobber system and use a short, medium action ice spinning combo spooled with 6 to 8 lb. line and some type of flashy, attractive jig or spoon. You'll soon find when white perch are biting, such presentations allow a faster drop, hook and reel—plus better attraction qualities to draw white perch to your bait, enabling you to ultimately catch more fish.

For convenience in deeper water I prefer to use medium action ice rods like HT's Blue Polar Lites or Polar Gold Lights combined with good quality spinning reels spooled with 4 lb. test line. This allows me to change depth and work various depths and baits to pattern the fish more easily, plus with the better drag and faster retrieve ratio, provides the opportunity to fish lighter lines, and when in the midst of a hot bite, the ability to reel up and drop down more quickly, allowing me to better capitalize on the action. I also like to bring a couple of different ice rods rigged with various lure styles and sizes to make experimentation and pinpointing presentation patterns easier.

As for lures, small to mid-sized jigging minnows such as Normark's Jigging Rapalas, HT's Walleye Ice Jigs or System Tackle's Walleye Flyers, swimming jigs such as Northland's Mini Airplane Jigs, flashy, high-profile jigging spoons like Bay de Noc's Swedish Pimples, HT's Marmooska Spoons, Reef Runner Slender Spoons, Bait Rigs Deep Willospoons, or Custom Jigs and Spins Stinger, vibrating blade baits like Reef Runner's Cicada, large teardrops such as HT's Teardrops, Daphnias with

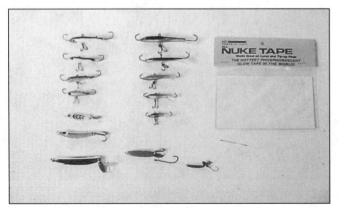

**Virtually any lure that gets down fast and wiggles, flashes or vibrates will attract and catch winter white perch.**

**Once located, white perch generally bite quite readily on virtually anything, so a wide variety of presentations can be productive. (Courtesy Maine Department of Fish and Wildlife)**

fins or Rockers—virtually anything that gets down fast and wiggles, flashes or vibrates—will attract and catch white perch. Tipping your lure with grubs or minnows will help sweeten your presentation by adding natural taste, smell and texture to the bait.

High profile lures featuring at least some phosphorescence are especially good, primarily because winter white perch often feed heavily in deep, dark water and during twilight periods, and the size and glow helps them find your bait. Rattle chambers such as Northland

Buckshot rattle rings add a slight attracting rattling noise that draws interest and may also be helpful.

However, as with any other panfish species, experiment with various lure sizes, colors and jigging motions to determine what's most productive for the time and place you're fishing. White perch can be phenomenally aggressive at times, but may be fussy and demand a lighter touch, so don't turn into a one-method Pete, or you'll miss out on some good bites—and perhaps the opportunity for some exceptionally delicious fish fries as well.

## *RIGGING BUCK-SHOT RATTLE RINGS:*

**1** Insert hook point into hole of silicone band.

**2** Thread rattle over hook shank.

**3** Push silicone band onto bait collar.

**When white perch are holding deep or in dark water, the addition of rattle chambers such as those available from Northland Tackle and called "buckshot rattle rings" add a slight attracting rattling noise that draws the white perch's interest.**

# Chapter 11

# *Understanding Smelt During Winter*

$I$ still remember my first iced smelt, taken from the deep, cold waters of Ontario's Lake Simcoe. Without being able to see the fish struggling on my sonar as I retrieved, I wouldn't have even believed I had a fish hooked. But when the small, thin-bodied, big-toothed silvery fish flopped from the hole, the entire picture became clear.

Despite the fact smelt will never win any awards for being large or hard fighting, they are willing winter biters, provide excellent winter action, and are certainly among the tastiest of fishes.

Smelt are essentially a marine species that have encroached into ice fishing realms through the St. Lawrence River and the Great Lakes. They've also been stocked in waters along the northeastern United States and deep, cold lakes throughout the ice fishing belt, primarily as a source of forage for other fish. On Lake Champlain on the New York/Vermont/Canadian border, the exceptional perch, walleye, salmon and lake trout fishing is, in part, because of the smelt forage base.

At the same time, smelt have gained a tremendous following as sportfish as well. In my home state of Wisconsin, smelt are usually fished by dipping with smelt nets in early spring as massive schools migrate into rivers and tributaries lining our Great Lakes to spawn—an event that draws shoulder-to-shoulder anglers lining the harbor mouths and riverbanks. As for ice fishing, most are taken incidentally by anglers fishing other panfish.

In other regions of the country, however, smelt have gained tremendous popularity among winter panfish anglers. Ice fishing for smelt is popular sport with a long history in the eastern part of the United States and parts of Canada. Ontario's Lake Simcoe, the New York Finger Lakes, Schroon Lake, the Saranac Chain, and Lake Champlain are especially popular areas for such pursuit.

In fact, smelt are likely the most sought after winter species by winter anglers in such regions. On Lake Champlain, for example, it's safe to say smelt are one of the more popular ice fishing species, if not the most important winter sportfish to the average ice angler. This is likely because of their willingness to bite and their food value, as smelt are considered a delicacy by many of these anglers.

As for the smelt's diet, they eat primarily freshwater shrimp, plankton including copepods, cladocerans and diatoms, along with insect larvae, fish eggs and some tiny minnows. Winter catches average four to seven inches in length.

## General Winter Location Patterns

Although essentially a deep water fish found in larger, deeper natural lakes, flowages and Great Lakes bays, smelt can be found in smaller, deep lakes sustaining cool water temperatures in the depths year-round, regardless of lake type. Because of their cool water pref-

**In parts of the North American ice fishing belt, smelt have gained tremendous popularity among winter panfish anglers.**

**Despite the fact smelt will never win any awards for being large or hard fighting, these thin, silvery fish are willing winter biters, provide excellent winter action, and are certainly among the tastiest of panfishes.**

erences, smelt often move more freely and become more aggressive and easily accessible in winter.

Though largely a pelagic species that tends to suspend over deep water in large, roaming schools, smelt may be found just about anywhere, sometimes relating to structure, relating to it loosely—or more often, suspended in deep, open water, relating to no structure at all. Depending on the lake type, finding these large schools suspended 20, 30, 40, 50, 60, even 70 feet down over deep water isn't unusual. However, smelt will often congregate in certain areas repeatedly winter after winter, so locating high-percentage locations is largely a matter of talking with experienced smelt anglers, then moving around in popular areas until you locate an active school.

A secret of modern winter smelt anglers is the knowledge that smelt can be taken by noting the characteristics

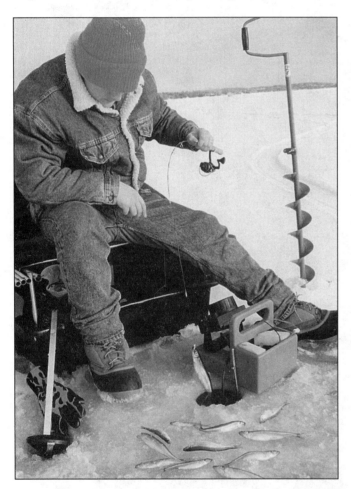

**Although mid-winter smelt are known to suspend and roam through open, deep water areas, deep mid-lake structures such as reefs and rock piles draw vast clouds of plankton, in turn drawing massive schools of smelt. Some smelt are also taken from shallow and mid-depth coastal estuaries, particularly in the northeastern United States.**

of traditional "hots spots," saving them as GPS waypoints, then, using lake maps and sonar, evaluating these traditionally good locations. This way, should traditional spots go dry, you can determine specific features and characteristics that might be drawing smelt to them, and by locating other such locations boasting similar characteristics throughout the lake, relocate active schools.

Consequently, by looking for similar productive areas using a mobile, versatile approach based on the conditions, situation and how far winter has progressed, more consistent winter smelt catches are possible.

## Early Ice

Early ice, smelt are relieved of their confinement to the deep, cold waters of summer, and gradually begin moving higher in the water column, often simply suspending in deep, open water areas. At times, they relate to mid-depth shoals, bars, points and main channels averaging between 20 and 40 feet deep. The best structures offer some form of plankton-attracting cover. I know one clear lake where a carpet of sandgrass covers a series of structural features extending from the shoreline down to 60 feet, providing fabulous migration routes from shallow to deep water. The sandgrass provides habitat for algae, which draws plankton, and hence smelt. Using sonar, I can determine holding areas along these features and migration routes attracting active schools of smelt and how deep, then focus my efforts there. The best bites generally occur during twilight and evening periods.

## Mid-Winter

Though mid-winter smelt are known to suspend and roam through open, deep water areas, often deep, mid-lake structures such as reefs and rock piles in close relation to deep water will draw vast clouds of plankton, in turn, drawing large schools of smelt—and if you're able to recognize and identify such features, it's possible to happen onto huge concentrations of fish on which nobody else is capitalizing.

Of course, like other times of the year, under-ice factors such as current, turbidity, ice, snow cover and wind all influence primary mid-winter smelt locations. One 1950 fisheries study verified that ice anglers fishing the main smelting area off Port Henry, New York, on Lake Champlain were doing poorly, whereas in a lightly fished area to the north, individual catches of 20 to 30 pounds were being recorded. At the same time, anglers fishing the so called "reef" in Vermont waters were doing well.

Furthermore, even people fishing in close-knit groups may note certain shanties doing well, while others are catching little or nothing. Because of such variations, mobility is often the key to modern approaches and consistent smelting, so don't get hung up on traditional spots. If you're not catching fish, don't be afraid to move. It pays.

As for timing, the best mid-season bites typically occur during twilight and evening periods.

## Late Ice

Like the rest of the winter, locating late ice smelt can be a challenge because of their inherent roaming nature. If you locate a school of late-ice smelt and stay with them, you're likely to do well, because scattered schools begin assembling in large, active schools as they begin making large migrations from mid-winter, open water holding areas toward spawning streams. These smaller schools eventually gather along drop-offs and breaklines adjoining these stream mouths, forming massive schools and often feeding actively. In fact, these large, late ice

schools tend to be quite voracious. Find them, and you'll measure your overall catches in pounds, not number.

As for the best timing on a daily basis, smelt can be caught throughout the day, but since they don't like direct, bright light, the most productive fishing often occurs under the glow of a lantern during twilight and evening periods. Lesser bites may occur in deeper or darker water throughout the day.

## Effective Winter Fishing Strategies

Because smelt are so small, hold so deep and bite so lightly, traditional tip-ups and tip-downs aren't used to catch them, although "umbrella" balance tip-downs placed inside a fish house protected from the wind and rigged without heavy counterweights would no doubt work.

Better, however, is a modified unit of sorts. The winter smelt tradition dictates use of a large diameter spool

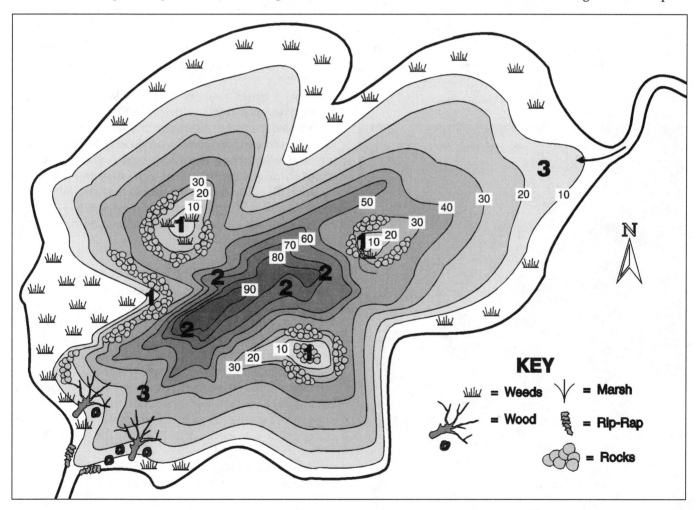

First-ice smelt gradually begin moving higher in the water column, often suspending over deep, open water areas (H), but also relating to mid-depth shoals and bars (A,B) and points (E,F) leading from deep to shallow water. Mid-winter, smelt typically suspend and roam through open, deep water areas, often on deep, mid-lake structures such as reefs and rock piles (D). Late ice, they'll hold in similar areas, but often demonstrate a noticeable shift as they move toward inlets and outlet areas (I) where they stage prior to the spawning run.

nailed to the wall of an ice shack, spooled with line and tipped with a small hook and bobber rig. When a smelt bites, the spool turns. Anglers simply grab the line and set the hook by pulling the line, then spin the reel to bring smelt up from the depths.

Many anglers fishing this way have constructed two spool units, one wrapped with line, the other with a cord. The rig is set so the spools are both on the same axle, and when the spool holding the line is unwound and lowered into the hole, the cord opposite the line wraps up. Thus, smelt can be brought up quickly by simply pulling and unwinding the cord, which then turns the spool holding line and retrieves it, winding fish up in one quick motion. Use sonar to locate the depth schools are holding, and set your presentation accordingly.

Jigging is another popular means of catching smelt. No fancy equipment is necessary, but since the smelt's diet is close to that of the yellow perch you can use similar jigging presentations. Traditionally, most smelt anglers fish simple wood hand lines wound with heavy monofilament to minimize tangles, and tip them with a heavy sinker-flasher and a light dropper line attached to a hook tipped with strips of smelt belly meat measuring about 1-1/4 inch long by 1/4 inch wide. The heavy

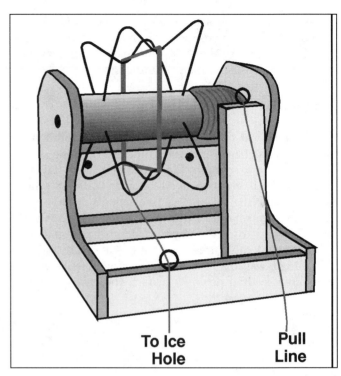

To Ice Hole          Pull Line

**The smelt speed-reel. Two spools are placed on the same axle, one filled with monofilament, the other with heavier cord wrapped in the opposite direction. Thus, smelt can be brought up quickly by simply pulling and unwinding the cord, which then turns the spool holding line and retrieves it, allowing the angler to wind fish up with one quick motion. When the monofilament is again lowered and set, the cord re-wraps itself in the opposite direction, so you're ready to pull up another fish.**

flasher allows quick drops, and the small, dangling bait attracts fish and is easy for smelt to strike.

After catching a fish, anglers repeatedly reposition their lines a foot or two above the preceding catch depth in an effort to bring the school up, guided by the philosophy it's more efficient to catch them from shallower depths—a trick that often works. I know some anglers who have brought schools up 10 or 20 feet using this technique, and increased their catches substantially by simply being able to lower their baits, hook fish and bring them up more quickly from the lesser depths before the school had passed.

Many New England anglers also use standard 20 to 25-inch jigstick with linewinders or ice reels. Light spring bobbers work well for helping sense strikes, although one inventive Vermont bait shop owner explained many of his customers suspend their rods from coffee mug holders over holes. When precisely balanced, this set-up allows them to jig by simply tapping the rod handle periodically and letting the rod swing. Even the softest

**Late ice, scattered schools of smelt begin gathering along drop-offs and breaklines adjoining the mouths of spawning streams, forming massive schools and often feeding actively.**

strikes are easily noted when the rod tip moves or tips. This system also works well if you're not using sonar, because when a fish is hooked anglers can note how many wraps of line are spun around the linewinder, or in the case of ice reels, you can employ depth-marker pins.

I prefer to use sonar to locate the primary depth fish are moving through, then use short 24 to 30-inch ultralight action jig rods featuring fast, sensitive tips. I combine these with small, ultralight or micro spinning reels to make sensing faint strikes easier, to allow the use of lighter lines, and to make lowering and reeling lines from deep water more efficient. If you plan to use lighter lines—I prefer 1 to 2 lb. test and small plankton imitating lures featuring hooks of size 12 and smaller—you have an excellent opportunity to try a perch hanger rig. For additional challenge and sport, when smelt move into more reasonable depths during late ice, micro ice rods, lines and tackle can also be employed.

**I like to use sonar to locate the primary depth smelt are moving through, then use short, 24 to 30-inch ultralight action jig rods combined with small, ultralight or micro spinning reels. Note the use of the hanger rig to drop my tiny, ultralight ice lure deep into the smelt's domain.**

Tiny "pinhead" minnows or small grubs work well as live bait tippers; pinhead minnows seem to work better for larger fish. And with any winter smelt presentation, adding a phosphorescent bead, small piece of colored yarn, plastic, pork rind fleck or "power bait" style fish attractant to the hook or line can have very positive results. This is especially true in deep, dark water, because they help passing smelt notice your bait, arouse their curiosity, and often, cause competitive strikes between fish within the school.

New England anglers often use splitshot and tiny #8-12 jig hooks called "bibbets," or fly hooks wrapped with silver and gold mylar and a small tuft of purple, black, dark brown or green bucktail. Phosphorescent beads threaded just up the line from these baits are also helpful for attracting smelt. To get more bang for their buck, some ice anglers use a small three-way swivel to attach a second lure or fly a foot and a half above the lower bait; this can increase catches by bringing up two fish at a time. For added attraction, brightly colored spinners, yarn, small cyalume light sticks or rattle chambers are sometimes incorporated into the rig as attractors. Fish attractants and scents are also helpful additions to these highly successful smelt presentations.

With any of these presentations—if you're not using electronics—start by fishing near bottom and periodically work your way up in one-foot intervals, preferably while fishing with other anglers and staggering your depth placement so you can identify the correct strike zone more efficiently.

Better practice, however, is to watch for suspended fish on your sonar, then adjust your presentation depth as necessary. Large schools of smelt will suspend at various depths throughout the winter, and predicting precisely where can be difficult. By watching for large, tightly concentrated schools on your electronics, you can quickly adjust your presentation depth to that of the fish, and by experimenting with different sizes, colors, live bait tippers and attractors, subtly jig your presentations and monitor their responses. You will note patterns.

Once caught, you can fry these little delicacies for the table, or where legal, store them for use as live or dead baits beneath tip-ups for larger predators.

# Chapter 12

# *Understanding Kokanee Salmon During Winter*

*T*he scene opens on a still, below-zero early January morning in Montana. Long, dark shadows darken steep, mountainside slopes as the bright, golden-orange sun rises behind an eastern precipice.

I stand amid this beautiful, frigid scene atop an ice-capped gorge, jigging. Eyes focused intently on my sonar screen, I watch as a fish approaches my bait, then turning my attention aside, note the faint strike of a biting fish on my spring bobber. I pull up, but don't react quick enough and miss the hook set. Now holding my breath, I wait, ready to spring, hoping for a second chance. This time when the bobber dips, I'm ready and instantly set the hook.

My rod suddenly comes alive. The lightly set drag on my spinning reel feeds out line as a seemingly crazed fish battles in the depths below, and the struggle becomes even more intense as the resistant fish nears the surface, where my line angles in one direction, then cuts to the other. Soon, however, a fish appears at the hole, and I'm amazed when a 10-inch fish flops onto the ice. Estimating by its sheer power, I would have guessed the fish to be three times its actual size. My fishing partner laughs when I suggest these mountain waters must be laced with steroids.

While fun to catch and undoubtedly one of the strongest of all panfishes, the kokanee salmon isn't a widely distributed species. Although found mostly in the far western portions of the United States in high country lakes and reservoirs, some stocking has been attempted within limited areas throughout other parts of the North American ice fishing belt. Success in these secondary attempts has been marginal, however, and most have been considered failed plantings.

Where available, kokanees, more often known as "kokes," are actually a dwarfed, landlocked form of the sockeye salmon. Unlike other salmon, they rarely grow large. An average catch through the ice is 10-12 inches, although they may grow larger—the world record is a tremendous six pound specimen taken in Idaho during the 1970s. Yet like other salmon, kokanee put up a strong, almost crazed battle when hooked—many anglers have

seen these fish run so hard and fast they literally jump right through their holes and onto the ice. Consequently they're a highly regarded winter sportfish.

Kokanee are pelagic fishes, and while they occasionally feed on small crustaceans and bottom organisms, they're largely plankton eaters, so they often suspend and roam open water while searching for clouds of plankton throughout most of the winter.

## Primary Winter Location Patterns

Being a nomadic, pelagic species, the main winter location pattern involved with kokanees is locating what region they're holding, and the specific depth active fish are feed-

**Kokanee salmon are among the strongest and most aggressive of all winter panfish species, so aggressive in fact, they're known for literally jumping right out of the hole when hooked! (Tom Brown photo)**

**For many high-country anglers, few species can compare with the satisfaction of icing a hard-fighting kokanee. (Courtesy Fishing & Hunting News)**

**Once located, kokanee salmon provide quality action for anglers of all ages. (Tom Brown photo)**

ing. It's not uncommon to find feeding kokanee suspended 25 feet down over 40 feet of water one day, then find them regrouped 35 feet down the next, sometimes in an entirely different region of the lake. For these reasons, sonar is imperative to consistent success. Just keep moving periodically until you locate a suspended school, note the depth, and present your lure at the depth the fish are holding. By doing so, you'll eliminate unproductive water and inactive schools efficiently, and be able to spend more time fishing high percentage locations and active fish.

## First Ice

Because kokanee spawn in outlet streams during the fall, first ice usually finds schools of kokanee scattered along the sharp breaks, drop-offs, walls and deep flats near the mouths of outlet streams, or suspended over deep water nearby—although preferred locations and specific movements may vary day to day. Remember, the effects of fall turnover may still be lingering, and forage may still be widely scattered due to the stratification breakdown—thus, most schools of kokanee are often scattered as well.

Since kokanee may suspend over deep, open water, or just off sharp, deep banks and "walls," especially those featuring rock ledges, overhangs or outcroppings near the mouths of spawning streams, you'll have to be mobile. The first trick to catching first ice kokanee is simply fishing the right area—at the right depth.

Use those electronics! When it comes to kokanee, sonar is your best friend. Speak with local, knowledgeable

**First ice, schools of kokanee often scatter along sharp breaks, dropoffs, walls and deep flats near the mouths of outlet streams, or suspend over deep water nearby.**

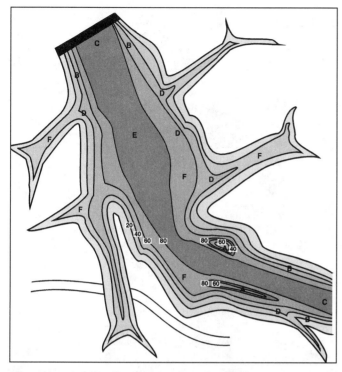

**First ice usually finds schools of kokanee suspended and scattered along mid-depth reefs, bars and shoals (A), sharp breaks, drop-offs and walls (B), deep flats near the mouths of outlet streams or current (C) or suspended over deep water nearby (E). Mid-winter, they suspend over deep open water or slots just off sharp, deep banks and walls, rock ledges, overhangs or outcroppings (D). Late ice, they suspend mostly over deep water holes (E) but may move toward mid-depth flats (F), depending where the most forage—namely plankton—can be found.**

contacts to determine where first-ice kokanee are likely to suspend on your target waters, then use your sonar to pinpoint them. Once located, you'll have to determine if they're active by trying a variety of depths to decipher the strike zone, or depth the kokanee are best taking lures and baits. Fish the wrong depth, and you'll miss a lot of fish.

Early morning bites are typically best, although in some stained waters or during overcast days, kokanees may turn on periodically throughout the day.

## Mid-Winter

Because kokanee aren't effected much by depleting oxygen levels or competing species in the deep, infertile reservoirs holding them, mid-winter patterns don't vary much from those of first-ice. The exception is that with winter stratification now intact, plankton and other forage are more likely to congregate at specific depths, and kokanee will relate to these suspended foods. Conse-

quently, you will often find mid-season kokanee suspended over deep, open water, or just off the same sharp, deep banks, walls and shoreline outcroppings that held them early ice—however, they're likely to be more tightly schooled.

The best mid-season action seems to heat up during early to mid-morning, especially in somewhat stained waters. As deep as kokanee often hold beneath all that water, ice and snow, this time of day offers better light penetration so they can feed more easily. In darker waters, the bite may occur anytime throughout the mid-day period.

## Late Ice

Late ice, kokanee will still be relating to forage, but are likely to be suspended over deep, open water, where plankton find adequate light penetration for survival. The best action seems to take place during early to mid-morning periods. Good sunrise and sunset or evening bites may occur on clear-water lakes and reservoirs, especially as the snow and ice subside, increasing light penetration.

## Effective Winter Fishing Strategies

While unbelievably strong, scrappy and hard fighting for their size, kokanees are well-known for their uncanny ability to strike light—if you're not right there to see the hit with a super-sensitive strike indicator and react quickly, you'll probably miss the fish. Consequently, tip-ups are seldom employed, although underwater, wind or balance tip-ups featuring larger line capacity spools with drag are occasionally used. For best

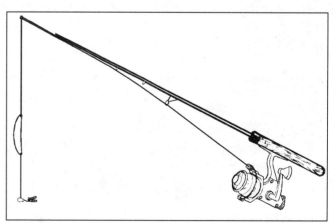

**Flash lure dropper lines are the most commonly used rigs for fishing kokanee salmon. The weight of the spoon allows you to fish heavier rods as required to set the hook and fight powerful kokanee up from deep water, and the dropper allows you to use the lighter line and lures needed to hook them. Note the spring bobber for improved sensitivity and strike detection with the heavier rod.**

results, set your tip-ups lightly at the desired depth, using light line rigs incorporating an attractor such as a spinner or flicker blade of some sort and small glow baits or hooks. Set your trip lightly; the faintest amount of resistance will cause kokanees to drop your bait.

Most kokanee anglers will agree jigging presents a more efficient means of catching fish, yet when it comes to jigging, kokanee offer a unique challenge full of contradictions. First, since kokanee are often found in deep water and have the ability to fight hard, a medium-length, medium-heavy action ice rod is needed to compensate for line stretch to set the hook properly, and power is needed to fight fish to the ice. However, because their mouths are relatively small, tiny lures are needed to catch them consistently—and because they have soft, tender skin surrounding the mouth, hook-sets cannot be overpowered or you'll tear the hooks free.

This poses significant problems, because smaller lures and baits aren't easily balanced on heavier rods and lines, yet sensitivity and light hook sets aren't typically associated with a medium or medium heavy action ice rod. On the other hand, if you try to balance your tiny lures to light or ultralight rods to sense strikes, you won't have enough power to set the hook properly and control these hard-fighting, deep water fish.

The best compromise involves using a medium action spinning rod and reel spooled with 8 lb. test line and outfitted with a sturdy, flat wire spring bobber. Run the line through the guides and spring tip, then tie a small to medium size, mid-weight spoon to the eight pound test, and run a 6 to 8-inch dropper line consisting of 2, 3 or 4 lb. monofilament down to a painstakingly small, well-sharpened ice fly, teardrop jig, #12 single hook, #14 gold treble, tiny painted hook or salmon egg hook tipped with a couple small salmon eggs, grubs or maggots.

Small, well-sharpened micro ice jigs, ice ants and ice flies allow kokanee the opportunity to get your bait into their tiny mouths—and offer better hooking percentages for you.

One of the most popular means of catching winter kokanee is a gliow-in-the-dark lure or hook suspended below a flash lure in dropper rig fashion. Use a snap swivel above your flash lure to eliminate line tangling. (Courtesy Fishing & Hunting News)

This is the best presentation compromise, because you'll be able to use the medium or medium-heavy action rod for presentation control, hook setting power and fish-fighting control, the heavier line you need to balance the rod to line connection, plus with the heavier spoon, the ability to feel your presentation and drop your small lure deep quickly. At the same time, you'll still have the sensitivity of the spring bobber to feel strikes, and the light line/small lure combination required to allow kokanee the opportunity to get the hooks into their tiny mouths.

Now the only remaining problem to solve is the hook-set, and the secret is to not set the hook overly hard, but rather just give the rod a firm lift to set the hook.

Some kokanee anglers also use keeled bead chains and diamond spinners with silver or gold finishes in place of the spoons, or perch style hanger rigs to get their smaller lures down. Still, spoons seem to work best because the added flash and vibration seems to help attract fish, and when fish move in and see the small bait, they strike. Some anglers, myself included, believe the flash of the spoon leads kokanee to think another fish in their school is feeding, and when they approach the area to capitalize on the

**The tremendous scenery surrounding most kokanee waters is enough to make a successful ice fishing trip in itself.**

available food and see the small grub slowing falling nearby, they strike out of a natural, competitive instinct to steal the bait from another fish. Works well.

As for jigging dropper rigs, use a slight "popping" motion to allow the spoon to flash and attract kokanee, then pause, allowing time for the smaller ice fly or hook and bait to drop down. Fish attracted by the flash will then suck in the smaller bait as it drops. Some anglers also use slight shaking or jiggling motions to help trigger hits on the dropper bait.

Several experienced kokanee anglers I know also vary their presentations to increase their catch when kokanee are finicky, and do so by using small jigs in 1/32, 1/64 and 1/80 ounce weights and in various colors, but featuring at least some phosphorescent color. Split shot are used to make the presentation heavy enough to work in deep water. These jigs are then tipped with small, 1-inch twister tails or maggots, and most anglers are careful to conceal their hooks. The addition of phosphorescent beads, rattle chambers or small cyalume-style light sticks just up the line from the hook is also helpful practice, especially when fishing deep. Remember, your goal is to do whatever it takes to help kokanee find your bait.

To work these smaller jigs and lures, start by jigging with periodic, 3 to 6-inch aggressive motions, then gradually reduce your jigging motion to smaller movements until you reach a fraction of an inch. Some experienced kokanee anglers do little more than spin their line slightly with their fingertips, while trying to swing the jig with a pendulum-like motion to attract fussy fish. Just remember: with any of the above presentations, establish regular jigging motions. This will allow kokanee to target your presentation more easily in the deep, dark depths, while at the same time, allowing you to detect faint strikes by simply watching for any interruption or unusual movement interrupting your established jigging cadence.

For best results, experiment at various depths above and below the marked school, and using your sonar, watch how the fish are responding to various presentations, lure types and jigging actions at each level. Kokanee will tell you what they prefer.

Most importantly, take the time to look up from your sonar to soak in the landscape. The tremendous scenery surrounding most kokanee waters is enough to make a successful ice fishing trip in itself.

**While fun to catch and undoubtedly on of the strongest of all panfishes, the kokanee salmon isn't a widely distributed species. Most are found in the mountain lakes and reservoirs throughout the western United States. (Courtesy Fishing & Hunting News)**

# Chapter 13

# *Understanding Miscellaneous Other Species in Winter*

*T*he preceding chapters cover basic winter patterns for the most commonly sought winter panfish species. But there are other panfish occasionally taken through the ice: Fish usually, but not always, taken incidentally by ice anglers seeking more commonly caught winter panfish species. These include rock bass, golden shiners, green sunfish and bullheads. Another species, grayling, can be taken through the ice, but because they're limited to a very narrow geographical range within the North American ice fishing belt and not as readily available or as active as many winter panfishes, they don't quite fulfill all the requirements of our original definition of panfish, so I've included them here.

Finally, although a marine species taken only from saltwater environments and available to ice anglers in only one unique location, sea bass, often called "ocean perch" by locals, constitute a panfish by our definition, so we'll cover them here, too.

## Rock Bass

Like many of the panfishes, rock bass are a highly adaptive, prolific species. While present in many kinds of environments, rock bass thrive in clear, cool to warm well-oxygenated waters featuring hard bottoms. They are a diverse feeder, with a diet consisting largely of crayfish, minnows, cladocerans, freshwater shrimp, insect larvae, mites and plant materials. Although they don't bite readily through the ice, when caught from well-oxygenated, cold water, they make a fine fish fry.

First ice, rock bass bite quite readily in shallow, vegetated, hard-bottom river backwaters, coves, bays and flats, and catches are usually made incidentally by sunfish, bluegill and crappie anglers. By mid-winter, rock bass relate primarily to mid-depth, hard-bottom vegetated flats and drop-offs, where they remain in a condition of semi-dormancy. Here, they are occasionally taken as incidental catches by anglers seeking other panfish. During mid-winter periods of low-oxygen they rarely feed, but by late ice as oxygen concen-

trations are replenished, vegetated, hard-bottom shallows and their associated breaks can provide good action. Most activity generally occurs during early morning and late afternoon, although night bites are prominent in some waters.

**Most winter rock bass catches are made incidentally by anglers fishing for other panfish.**

Although ultralight rigging of grubs or small minnows on most any tip-up can result in some fine rock bass catches, most are taken by anglers jigging with jigglesticks, jig pole combinations, micro or ultralight tackle. Rock bass especially seem to like a variety of small, flashy flutter spoons and ultralight blade baits, although rocker-style ice jigs, ice ants and horizontal ultralight and micro ice jigs can be productive, too, especially when tipped with a juicy grub or small minnow.

While rock bass typically strike with an almost reckless abandon and fight hard momentarily, they tire quickly. Their short, fat, football shaped bodies simply roll and twist as they're brought to the ice, so fighting quality is considered poor by most ice anglers.

## Golden Shiners

Golden shiners inhabit moderately to heavily vegetated, clear water river systems, ponds, lakes and reser-

Golden shiners are often caught incidentally by anglers fishing micro tackle for panfish in vegetated, relatively clear waters; on such light gear, they provide some sport.

To catch golden shiners consistently—as I occasionally do to collect them as baitfish for tip-up fishing—the best bet is to contact a local biologist to determine lakes offering a strong population, then search out shallow, moderately to densely vegetated hard-bottom flats during first and late ice.

voirs featuring moderate nutrient levels. While certainly not a commonly sought-after winter sportfish, they are caught incidentally with some regularity by anglers fishing micro tackle in vegetated, relatively clear waters, and on such light gear, provide some sport.

This highly prolific species grows rapidly in warm-water environments, more slowly in cooler water, and winter catches vary greatly in size—most average 4 to 5 inches, but fish exceeding 8 inches in length have been caught through the ice. Diet consists mostly of zooplankton such as cladocerans and copepods. Secondarily they also feed on insects, mites and plant materials.

If an ice angler wanted to specifically fish golden shiners, as I occasionally do to collect them as baitfish for tip-up fishing, the best bet is to contact a local biologist to determine lakes offering a strong population. Then, search out shallow, moderately to densely vegetated hard-bottom flats during first and late ice. Mid-winter, try slightly deeper, mid-depth, moderately to densely vegetated shoals and bars.

Because golden shiners have small eyes and small, upturned mouths, the best catches occur on micro and ultralight jig rod spinning combos, preferably spooled with light, 1/2 to 1 lb. test lines or fly tippets rigged with small, dark colored #12 or smaller ice jigs and ice flies tipped with tiny grubs and heavily soaked in fish attractant. Small, lightweight ultralight and micro jigs featuring thin, light-wire hooks tipped with mayfly nymphs, spikes, poppers or small waxworms also work well.

As for timing, twilight and evening periods are generally best, but on overcast days they can be taken throughout the day.

## Green Sunfish

Green sunfish are a hardy, aggressive member of the sunfish clan that prefer heavy cover such as dense weeds, large rocks, fallen timber or brush piles in small, fertile natural ponds and lakes. They seldom grow large, with the average catch measuring only 4 to 5 inches. Compared to other sunfishes, green sunfish have a large, almost bass-like mouth, which enables them to feed on larger prey than most sunfishes, including crayfish and minnows. They feed most heavily during twilight periods. Like other sunfishes, table fare is good, with a consistency and taste much like bluegill.

Because green sunfish prefer heavy cover and can tolerate low oxygen levels and cold water, they are typically found in shallow, heavy cover throughout the winter, although serious oxygen deficits may send them scurrying into deeper cover or suspending deeper with other sunfishes. They bite readily, are easy to catch and fight sportingly, but because they're small, aren't often fished specifically, but rather taken incidentally by winter panfish anglers fishing shallow, dense cover.

Since they typically hold in such shallow water, virtually any type of small jigglestick, jig pole or ice rod outfitted with light line will provide all the gear necessary to tackle even the largest green sunfish. As for baits, they will bite aggressively on a variety of tiny, colorful spoons, ice flies, jigs or lures tipped with grubs and fished tightly along the edges of pockets or openings in dense, shallow cover.

## Bullheads

Bullheads are inhabitants of small, shallow, nutrient rich, low-oxygen, dark or turbid water environments. Populations typically flourish in quiet backwaters, ponds and small lakes. They are largely bottom feeders and scavengers, feeding on basically whatever is available, including insects, insect larvae, algae, small crayfish and snails, leeches, silt and bottom debris.

Their meat is firm and well-flavored when taken from the cold, clear waters beneath the ice. However, while bullheads are commonly taken in open water, they're rarely taken through the ice consistently, largely because they enter an almost hibernation-like state on or within bottom sediments. In fact, the respiratory movements of brown bullheads have been known to become

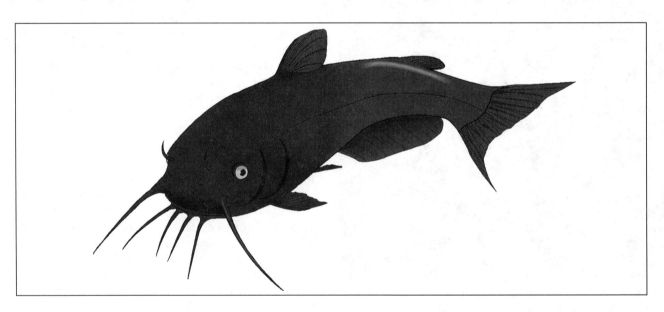

**Most species of bullheads become dormant during winter, but incidental catches are sometimes made by ice anglers fishing live bait tipped lures and rigs near bottom during first and late ice, or in areas influenced by warm water discharges, inlets or springs.**

so weak at temperatures below 37°F, they appear dead. Obviously, feeding all but ceases during such periods.

However, incidental catches are sometimes made during first ice, or throughout winter in areas influenced by warm-water discharges, inlets or springs. During mid-winter "thaws" and late ice warming trends in current-influenced areas, bullheads may resume feeding, although in a fairly lethargic manner. Most bullheads are caught by ice anglers jigging live bait tipped lures and rigs in a rather lazy manner near or directly on the bottom just prior to ice-out, or by tip-up anglers inadvertently placing tip-ups set with panfish rigs directly on bottom.

## Grayling

Only one species of grayling, the Arctic grayling, is found within the North American ice fishing belt. Although they have been stocked in some northwestern parts of the United States, the grayling's distribution is largely limited to remote areas of northern Canada and parts of Alaska. Their large, sail-like dorsal fin make grayling easy to differentiate from other panfish species. This feature also makes them hefty fighters, especially in current. While readily caught during open-water periods, ice fishing for grayling presents its share of challenges, and demands use of very specific finesse-style techniques.

Grayling, which are members of the salmon and trout family, prefer cold, clear, unpolluted hard-bottom lakes, and feed mostly on insects and salmon eggs, occasionally small fish. Like other panfish, grayling will relate to bottom configurations and structure, particularly vegetation harboring forage such as insect larvae or small minnows. They school, and can often be found in large aggregations under the ice.

Throughout the winter, the edges of shallow and mid-depth structural features, drop-offs and weed lines are productive winter holding locations, and although they relate mostly to shallow and mid-depth features, will move slightly deeper during mid-winter and the aftermath of severe cold fronts. A particularly good time to catch them is when they concentrate near small spawning streams and tributaries right before ice-out.

Although grayling are known to be willing biters during the open-water season, they often become quite finicky beneath the ice. Jigging presentations are the rule, and must be exact. Light to medium-light action spinning rods with a fast tip or outfitted with a sensitive spring bobber is recommended to create the best combination of sensitivity, strength and hook-setting power. Combine this with a spinning reel featuring a smooth drag and spooled with a supple, low-memory 3 to 4 lb. test monofilament, and you're all set. As with most panfish, tackling down an effective way to fish grayling, and is more fun as well.

When it comes to lures, experiment with a variety of small, lightweight ice jigs and flies. Smaller, chartreuse Blue Fox Foxee jigs are stand-bys, although 1/64 to 1/32 ounce chartreuse-green crappie jigs and tiny, light jigs and ice flies of various two-toned color combinations can be effective. Live bait isn't legal in many areas supporting grayling, but where you can, tip these small lures and flies with grubs, maggots, small salmon eggs, or tiny shrimp.

Jig subtly with simple, periodic flicks of your wrist and fraction of an inch jigging movements—anything radical tends to spook grayling. Work your jigs approximately 12 to 18 inches off bottom, adjusting your bait to the level of the fish when necessary. Winter grayling can be a real challenge, so experimentation and versatility are crucial. Once you find fish, exercise patience and try different combinations of lures, sizes, colors jigging actions and depths until you find the right combination.

Although ice anglers may catch graying measuring 20 inches or more in length, they average 12 to 14 inches.

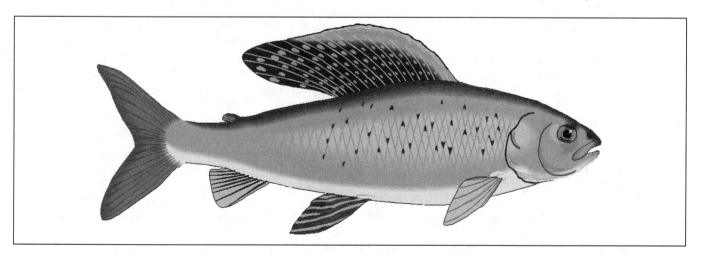

**Only one species of grayling, the arctic grayling, is available within the North American ice fishing belt. While very active and a good biter during the open water months, light, finesse style jigging presentations are required to catch these finicky fish through the ice.**

Ocean perch are a unique, colorful, goggle-eyed fish averaging 8 to 15 inches long—although they may attain lengths exceeding 30 inches.

Fighting quality is highly respected, and table fare is excellent, with a light, flaky, and less oily consistency than most salmon and trout.

## Sea Bass or "Ocean Perch"

Ocean perch are a unique, colorful, goggle-eyed fish averaging 8 to 15 inches long—although they may attain lengths exceeding 30 inches. Diet consists of a variety of marine worms, crustaceans and fishes. From an angler standpoint, table fare is excellent—and when it comes to ice fishing unique panfish, it doesn't get any more exotic than ocean perch, which can be caught through the ice in only one global location: Quebec's Saguenay River.

Located just inland from the Gulf of the St. Lawrence, tidal action has caused the Saguenay to become a deep, brackish water environment. The Saguenay averages between 300 and 800 feet deep throughout much of its length. And with temperature and salinity gradients between the outflowing freshwater from Lac St. Jean and influx of frigid saline water from St. Lawrence tidal fluctuations, a thermal layer of

freshwater stratifies atop the saltwater rather than mixing, forming a complex ecosystem. Here, the fertile saltwater in these tremendous depths never warms beyond 2°C, and with a continuous, replenishing supply of oxygen from tidal movements, the Saguenay's depths maintain temperature, oxygen and salinity levels similar to those found in the Arctic Ocean, enabling this environment to support a viable marine fishery. Best of all, with the upper layer of freshwater allowing ice formation, anglers can enjoy ice fishing for saltwater species.

However, this long, winding, deep "fjord" does bring intimidation when considering where to fish. The greatest challenge is locating fish in such mind-boggling depths. To make matters worse, the effects of currents and tidal actions influence location patterns, and most ocean perch suspend along the Saguenay's steep banks in depths ranging from 55 to 300 feet.

To pinpoint them, you'll need to use sonar and equipment allowing you to drop your bait into the immense depths, then bring them back to the surface efficiently. Accordingly, sensitive, strong backboned medium-heavy action rods 30 to 48 inches long featuring large guides and good tip action for sensitivity should be combined with quality spinning reels spooled with 150 yards of 8 to 10 lb. monofilament.

As for lures, heavy, flashy, fast-dropping jigging minnows, jigs and jigging spoons work best, because their weight gets them deep fast, and their vibration, large size and high profile make them easier for ocean perch to locate in the dim depths. Tip your favorite with colorful plastic action tails as additional attractors, or pieces of smelt to provide natural texture and scent. When considering color, phosphorescent is unquestionably the color of choice for helping ocean perch find your baits in the dark, immense depths. I usually splice in HT's Hanger Rigs to drop my lures deeper, faster, and add Berkley Cold Water Formula Power Baits that act as additional attractant and seem to increase my catches. Rattle chambers and small cyalume sticks incorporated into the rig just above the lure can also help attract fish.

When jigging, use standard lift-drop tactics, experimenting with different jigging motions, but always maintaining continuity in your rhythm. If working a spoon, for example, always lift it to about the same height, and lower it back to roughly the same initial depth after the fall. Remember, the depths of the Saguenay are dark, and by maintaining established jigging motions, ocean perch seem to have an easier time finding and striking baits. Because the fish can't see well and strikes aren't always directly on target, however, be sure your hooks are carefully sharpened to reduce missed strikes.

In this unique environment, keep a close watch on tidal movements. When you notice the ice creaking along shore or the depth changing on your sonar, be prepared to reset your lines. Shifting underwater currents stir changes in preferred fish location, causing increased activity—and often, improved catch rates. Depending on where you're fishing and how far winter has progressed, the action may improve as the tide comes in or as it retreats.

Learn to coincide your fishing with these periods using tide-tables, and you'll soon note patterns.

**Most ocean perch suspend along the Saguenay's steep banks in depths ranging from 55 to 300 feet.**

# Chapter 14

# *Winter Panfish Tips from the Pros*

*O*ver the years, I've spent countless hours fishing and talking with numerous ice tackle manufacturers, ice fishing writers, guides and experts from all over the world. Often, these trips and discussions include comparisons of observations and notes, discussion of various ice fishing secrets, tricks and techniques used for advancing and enhancing established location and presentation patterns. I've enjoyed each of these special round-table occasions with everyone I've ever spoken with, and learned from each and every conversation, interview and outing.

Some of my favorite learning experiences, however, have come sharing notes and experiences with several innovative individuals from prominent ice tackle manufacturing firms, and with five of my favorite fishing partners: Jim Lindsey, Larry Smith and Tim Duffy of Wisconsin, Steve Heem of Minnesota, and Wil Wegman of Ontario, Canada. So now, after taking an in-depth look at total winter panfish patterns in the preceding chapters, I thought you—now being a fellow knowledgeable winter panfish angler—might find it interesting to have them share a few of their most learned, "short and sweet" winter tips, tricks and secrets. Here's what they had to say.

### Scott Stecher, Reef Runner Lures

Scott is unquestionably one of the industry's leading innovators, and as a result, his Cicada bladebait and Slender Spoon flash lure have become staple items in my ice tackle box. I asked Scott for tips on how to fish these two unique baits.

- "When fishing the Cicada, try cutting the body off a tiny plastic twist tail grub, and threading the thin curly tail onto the rear hook. Not only does this slow the lure's fluttering action and result in more subtle vibration, but also adds color and natural texture to the lure."

He also suggests "loading" the hooks.

- "Loading simply means placing a small minnow on each hook, which seems to draw the interest of bigger panfish."
- "With Slender Spoons, try replacing the standard hooks with VMC reverse-barb trebles, or jeweled treble hooks.

Reverse barbs improve hooking percentages, and jeweled hooks add color and attraction that cause fish to strike more readily."

### Paul Grahl, HT Enterprises

Paul operates not only one of the foremost ice tackle manufacturing facilities in the world and manufactures the world famous Polar Tip-ups, but is also a close friend. We've spent many hours on the ice together, refining products and techniques.

- "When it comes to winter panfish, keep it simple. Stick with ultralight presentations. With tip-ups, use well-machined, smooth operating units like those in the Polar family, and rig lighter. Go with long leaders of light monofilament and smaller, light-wire hooks, use just enough split shot to drop and hold your bait at the desired level, and always set your trips on the lightest possible settings. Also, to avoid tangles when transporting or storing a rigged tip-up, stretch a rubber band across the upper portion of the frame, wrap some line around the spool handle, then extend the leader and clip the hook around the rubber band. You'll never experience another tangle or twisted leader."
- "With ice rods, use only models featuring fast action tips for sensitivity, use light lines of 1 to 2 lb. test, and round out your system with a lightweight ultralight jig."

### Barry Day, Berkley

When it comes to fishing lines, Berkley has unquestionably been among the industry leaders in quality, and the same could be said regarding this company's research in fish scents and attractants. I recently asked Barry for some tips regarding use of his products on the ice.

- "Probably the most recent innovation is the use of our 6 lb. Fireline, a superline with the diameter of standard 2 lb. monofilament. Aside from fishing extremely finicky, clear water panfish like bluegills, Fireline works tremendously well, particularly for deep water jigging, because line stretch is reduced from approximately 25 percent to 2 percent. When it comes to strike detection, this difference in stretch makes a noticeable difference in sensitivity and increased hooking percentages.

**Paul Grahl, president of HT Enterprises, a company offering more than 1,000 ice fishing products. Paul is also the inventor of the famous Polar Tip-Up.**

**Full time pro angler and guide Larry Smith.**

- "Also, Berkley Power Bait attractant works well when you're marking panfish on your electronics, but they're inactive and won't strike. By coating your lures and baits with Power Bait, as the attractant disperses, these fish will often become more active."

### Larry Smith

Larry, of Berlin, Wisconsin, is a fishing pro is the truest sense of the word, making his living by fishing tournaments, guiding and writing. He's one of the few ice anglers I know who will sit in the open on a five-gallon bucket, moving from hole to hole and staring at his electronics searching for winter panfish, regardless of the temperature, wind chill or fish activity levels. The guy's a die hard, the type I most enjoy fishing with.

His tips?

- "First, use electronics. This takes the guesswork out of fishing—and catching—winter panfish. Use those electronics to find pockets within heavy to moderate cover offering adequate oxygen, and always use light tackle. Tip your lures with one grub threaded up the hook and squished to disperse fish-attracting juices, then nip a second with the hookpoint, allowing it to wiggle.

- "Plastic strips also work well as additional attractors, especially when fishing fussy winter panfish, and this is a presentation option many ice anglers miss. Finally, be sure to watch your electronics to see how the fish react, and adjust your presentation until you find what works best."

### John Peterson, Northland Fishing Tackle

When you consider selection in fishing jigs, you won't find many companies offering the variety of Northland Tackle.

- "One of my favorite ice jigs for active panfish such as perch, crappies or white bass is the mini airplane jig. For best results, these should be attached directly to your line, but to prevent line twists and tangles, a crane swivel should be placed approximately 12 to 24 inches ahead of the jig. When jigging, work the entire water column, but concentrate on the 'twilight zone'...the area just below the light penetration point. It's the primary strike zone.

- "When fishing deep or dark water, I like to place a buckshot rattle ring onto the hook, too. These versatile rattles can be jigged aggressively, thumped or shook to create the extra attraction necessary to draw fish in, especially in deep or dark water."

### Steve Baumann, Vexilar Electronics

Vexilar is unquestionably the pioneer company promoting use of electronics for ice fishing, a concept that has helped thousands of winter anglers improve their catches. So when Steve offered his tips, I listened closely.

- "Probably the best tip I can offer is to keep your sensitivity set low as you possibly can and still read your bait. Also, lower your bait until the line goes slack, then raise it until the bait appears on the screen, and measure this distance on your line. This is important, because the 'bottom' as read on your screen could be the top of a breakline, or an object such as a rock located directly within the cone of sound. If the break is steep or the rock tall, this measured distance could be considerable, meaning even when you think you're fishing just off bottom, you may actually be several inches off.

- "Finally, never charge your battery when it's cold. A cold battery features diminished charging capacity, so even when it reads fully charged, it's actually only charged up to the diminished charging point. In other words, if the diminished charging point is half the actual capacity, when you check the charge on the cold battery, it may appear to be fully charged. But checked again at room temperature, you'll find the same battery is really only half-charged."

### Dan Redman, Jiffy Ice Augers

Jiffy was one of the first companies to offer power ice augers to the market, and continues to be a leader in ice auger technology.

- "With power augers, add a fuel stabilizer with the pre-mix. This will preventing gumming of the carburetor and maintain the octane level of unleaded gasoline, which otherwise breaks down over time. Also, never fill your tank more than half full. You'll still get an hour's worth of continuous operation, and when your drill with the black gas tank sits inside your vehicle in the warming sun, the gas has room to expand without being forced into the carburetor and spilling inside your vehicle.

- "When using hand augers, be careful not to drop or bang your drill on the ice. This bends the blade holder, and once damaged, the drill will never work as well, no matter how often you sharpen the blades."

### Mark Gostisha, Frabill Ice Shelters

Mark and I discussed features incorporated into high quality portable shelters.

- "The features many ice anglers should look for are the ones you might not think of until after you're on the ice. Things like arched doors for easy entry and exit while wearing heavy clothes, high ceilings enabling you to stand up straight while inside, two-way self-repairing coil zippers and draped windows are several such considerations. Also be sure the floor plan fits your intended style of fishing. This may sound funny, but having two holes in a four man shelter is a problem—and I've seen models constructed this way."

- Mark also emphasized the importance of a lightweight model with removable canvas or nylon material that can be easily removed for drying or repair.

### Paul Thorne, Zercom Marine

Paul is one of the people promoting the newest innovation in flasher technology, the LCD flasher.

- "To improve your efficiency looking for key spots, use your electronics as your underwater eyes. Pour a small

**Walt Matan of Custom Jigs and Spins, manufacturers of a full-line of premium quality ice fishing lures. (Courtesy Custom Jigs and Spins)**

amount of water on the ice, then place your transducer flat within the water. You'll get a depth reading—perhaps even be able to see cover such as weeds and fish. This can make the difference between catching fish or just drilling holes.

- "You can also use your depthfinder to make the difference between a successful day on the ice or just plain boredom. Once you've located fish and drilled your hole, lower your ice fly and watch it drop on your screen. When you've identified your fish target, raise or lower your jig to bring the two targets in line. If the fish doesn't hit right away, raise the bait up slowly, watching to see if the fish target moves with it. More often than not, the fish will rise with the bait and strike within the first two or three feet of upward movement. This video game of teasing is not only fun, it's deadly!"

## Walt Matan, Custom Jigs and Spins

When it comes to producing high quality ice lures, Walt at Custom Jigs and Spins is certainly among the top manufacturers. Among their highly effective creations are the ever-popular 2-Spot and legendary Rat Finkee.

- "When fishing shallow water panfish, I like to use the smallest and lightest poles I can find. In water less than six feet deep you really shouldn't use a spinning reel, but rather just a small plastic ice reel. I also usually go with a highly visible 4 lb. line like Stren because it's easier to detect strikes—I simply twist my line into a slight crinkle, then watch for it to straighten out when a fish hits. From here, I'll go with a 2 lb. test leader and a little Fastsnap type eyelet instead of tying direct."

- "My favorite lures include size twelve 2-Spots or Rat Finkees. The best ways to fish these tiny lures include letting them slowly fall—or when the fish are lethargic, a jiggle and pause motion—then watching the line for slack indicating a strike. Waxworms work best for the slow fall presentation, while maggots work better with the jiggle."

## Ray Peterson, Strikemaster Augers

Strikemaster has made great strides in ice auger innovation in the last decade, including the "Lazer" hand and power auger technology.

- "For smoother engine performance with power augers, always mix your gas and oil at the correct ratio, and be sure to drain gas from your tank and carburetor before storing them away for the season. To prolong blade life, it's also a good idea to spray both power and hand auger blades with lubricant before storing them, as this helps prevent rusting. Also, for both longer blade life and safety, always store your unit with the blade guard intact."

## Mike Carney, Lowrance Electronics

Lowrance Electronics was one of the original pioneers of sonar use for sportfishing applications, and in many respects, has remained a pioneer introducing new electronics technology to the sportfishing market. Recently, most of this innovation has been in liquid crystal graphs and global positioning systems.

- "For ice fishing, my tips would include using a liquid crystal you're familiar with—namely the same one you use for your open water fishing. Since you're more likely to know this unit inside and out, understand the features and how to properly set, adjust, configure and fine-tune its settings, you'll likely be able to put it to better use on the ice as well. With Lowrance LCGs, this is accomplished by simply removing the unit from your boat, adding a second transducer and the porta-pack to accommodate your gel-cell battery, and placing all the gear in a transport box. Now your unit will serve double-duty, both summer and winter."

- "As for GPS on ice, the advantages are clear: Entering the electronic address for your hot spots takes you directly where you want to go, precisely, quickly and accurately. And saving your launch site as a waypoint is extremely helpful in the event of a sudden "whiteout" and loss of direction, making GPS as much a safety device as a handy convenience."

## Jim Lindsey

Jim isn't with a major manufacturer of ice tackle, doesn't guide, doesn't do much outdoor writing, but his warm-weather outdoor career leaves him free throughout the winter—leaving him a lot of time to ice fish. And of all the people I've spent time with on the ice, he's unquestionably one of the best—a silver medal in the 1992 World Icefishing Championships will attest to that. His philosophy for catching panfish is simple.

- "For panfish, I follow three rules: One, be prepared to be mobile looking for hot fish. Two, keep your presentations small and light. And three, keep it simple. I can't tell you specifically how to catch winter panfish in every instance, but I can say every ice angler I've ever witnessed not doing well operated on a philosophy directly opposite these three rules. They tend to sit still in one hole, fish gear that is too heavy, and make things too complex. Follow these three rules, however, and you'll improve your odds."

## Steve Heem

Steve operates Iceman Guide Service in northern Minnesota. Having ice fished as a hard-core his entire life, he knows the formula for success. He knows how to research the best waters, understands how to pinpoint location and presentation patterns given a wide variety of conditions, and has a vast knowledge of the best gear and equipment to accomplish his goal: to ice winter panfish consistently. Best of all, he openly shares his knowledge by showing people what he's doing to locate and catch fish—the mark of a truly expert guide.

His advice?

- "First, have all your equipment ready and organized before setting out on the ice—batteries charged, reels spooled, lures ready—then move strategically from location to location searching for fish. Don't die in one spot. Move and keep moving until you locate fish, then be pre-

**Jim Lindsey, ice fisherman extraordinare and world champion ice angler, shows a nice winter yellow perch catch taken by himself and the author.**

**Steve Heem of Iceman Guide Service, a premier winter guide service from northern Minnesota.**

pared to work them with a variety of lures and presentations until you come across the one producing best. Mobility and versatility are the name of the game."

## Wil Wegman

Like the other anglers listed here, Wil is a die-hard ice angler. Countless hours of on-the-ice experience and experimentation have led him straight down the path of pinpointing winter panfish patterns, to the point he's been authorized to offer college-accredited courses in ice fishing at Ontario's Seneca College for the last 10 years.

Wil strongly emphasizes mobility and versatility.

- "Mobility is one of the real keys to success. Don't wait for the fish to come to you. Instead, search them out, and when you find them, adapt your presentation to their activity level. If they're aggressive, use larger baits, when they're less cooperative, use lighter lines and smaller baits, and fish slowly with long, frequent pauses to allow your bait to settle. In fact, I've often found setting my rod down completely for a couple minutes and just watching the rod tip and line for unusual movement is one of my top-producing methods for detecting the subtle bites of light-striking panfish."

## Tim Duffy

Tim is a full-time, licensed Wisconsin guide from the famous Hayward, Wisconsin, area. I've seen Tim repeatedly spend countless hours searching for active fish, whittling and fine-tuning winter panfish patterns down to the sharpest nubbin through every conceivable condition, simply to help his clients enjoy a satisfactory ice fishing outing. His determination has made him a top-of-the-line winter guide.

Tim emphasizes the importance of the total ice fishing pattern.

- "First, you must use sonar—these units usually are the difference between catching and not catching. Often, panfish relate to specific home areas. For example, these may consist of a hole amid or a pocket along the edge of a weed line. If you're hole is drilled three feet away from this spot, you might be dropping your jig into thick weeds or over an open mud flat—and you won't catch nearly as many panfish as you will when you're located on that sweet spot. You need to search for these 'best of the best areas,' and the only way to do it efficiently is with sonar. Remember, whether or not you're catching fish, there's almost always a better spot to be found.

- "Once a sweet spot is found, I'm always surprised how frequently I mark concentrations of panfish, but find them shut off or unaggressive. Without using sonar, I'd have to assume no fish were present when I wasn't catching any, and eliminate such areas. With sonar, however, I can work these fish, and refining my technique using sonar and light rods, lighter lines and small-

er lures, can watch how the fish respond and determine how to catch them—or if necessary, return later, often to find them more cooperative. To me, this process is truly the fun of winter fishing."

**Tim Duffy, a prominent winter guide from the famous Hayward, Wisconsin, area.**

# Chapter 15

## *Putting It All Together*

**Y**ou now have gained an awareness, if not a good understanding, of the tremendous array of variables and conditions governing total winter panfish patterns. You know how to: Prepare for ice fishing trips by researching your waters; determine lake types and water characteristics; review lake maps; use sophisticated electronics to quickly identify and efficiently locate "high-percentage" fishing locations for a variety of panfish species throughout the winter; then strategically establish working location and presentation patterns using mobile, versatile approaches specially modified to a wide variety of potential winter situations and conditions.

Yet we've just scratched the surface. Unique combinations of various factors will always make ice fishing a challenge. But whether you consider yourself a beginner, experienced veteran or advanced winter panfish angler, the solid, skeletal winter panfish patterns and awareness of detail we've outlined here should help you successfully tackle virtually any water, under a variety of conditions, anytime throughout the winter. And by using and

applying this foundation of elementary secrets and tricks you will be able to confidently develop, elaborate and fine-tune your winter panfish approaches even further, regardless of the conditions.

Along the way, the road to success can be enhanced by watching educational ice fishing videos, reading outdoor magazines and books and clicking through internet pages offering helpful ice fishing tips. All of these build on the basics and will help you stay on top of the newest tactics, techniques and equipment. Interacting with other knowledgeable ice anglers, bait shop owners, guides and ice tackle manufacturers is also helpful. Like you, they're constantly experimenting; trying new twists and wrinkles in their foundations of success to stay ahead of the crowd. They also realize the value and benefits of comparing notes and ideas. So should you.

One of the best ways to share observations and ideas is to compare your findings at sport shows, networking with manufacturers, sales reps, resort owners, guides and fellow anglers. Ice fishing presentations and semi-

**By using a systematic, mobile, versatile approach incorporating use of lake maps and electronics, you'll find there are plenty of panfish available to catch through the ice. To help increase your odds, try networking with other knowledgeable anglers at sport shows, seminars, fishing clubs, fisheries meetings and ice fishing tournaments.**

**There is no substitute for experience. The more time you spend on the ice, the better you'll get.**

nars by experienced ice anglers are also becoming increasingly common at these sport shows, and can be a great way to learn. But to really comprehend this information and turn it into working patterns, I encourage you to sort out the "good" information from the poor, take this information onto the ice, and apply what you've learned to the fundamental system outlined here.

Participating in the "on the ice programs" many of the more confident educators and ice guides provide is a great way for beginners who haven't yet invested in gear and tackle to learn more about what equipment will best suit their needs. Here, in an interactive environment, you not only have the opportunity to witness and take part in the process of researching, reviewing maps, using electronics, moving, setting-up and breaking down in search of active panfish and catching them on the various types of gear and equipment best adapted for each situation—but also play an active role in the entire process—right on the ice. This is not only educational in the purest sense, but provides background information on what types of gear and tackle you may want to invest in.

**Asking for up-to-date information on ice conditions and fishing at a local bait shop while picking up last-minute essentials can be extremely helpful in providing leads for a productive ice fishing outing.**

Let me emphasize there is no better teacher than experience, and to gain that experience while fishing with a seasoned veteran offers no compare. Skilled winter guides willing to share their knowledge are well worth the investment of a day's fishing. Whether you're new to the sport and desire a basic introduction to methods and techniques; would like to take your kids or a beginning angler fishing and have them experience the thrill of knowledgeably assembling winter panfish patterns; plan to fish a new area; want to learn more about the local waters and patterns; or simply want to spend time fishing and comparing notes with a fellow expert, a knowledgeable guide is well worth the money spent.

Fishing clubs are another good means of advancement. Find an active club with knowledgeable members willing to share and network, and you'll make great strides learning where and how to fish a variety of waters and panfish species in your area. Club interaction also allows the opportunity to fish with anglers of different backgrounds, expanding your wealth of knowledge. Many of these clubs also draw good speakers, allowing you to confer, perhaps even fish with, some highly skilled anglers. Many clubs also have regular club outings, where again, notes can be compared between knowledgeable ice anglers.

Another excellent, yet often overlooked source of information includes fisheries journals, fish management meetings, conferences and symposiums open to the public. Scientific studies seldom provide actual fishing information, but offer related technical information about various fisheries, such as the characteristics of specific waters, including clarity, bottom content and cover availability and breakdowns, forage species available and their densities throughout the winter, fish movement studies, interactive competition and relationships between various fish species and their forage bases, population cycle data and creel census surveys—all of which can be critically important to piecing total patterns together. If you can obtain such information, then call or meet with the scientists and biologists involved with these studies; they can be worth a tremendous amount of accurate, valuable data.

A final means of gaining information that's becoming more and more popular is ice fishing tournaments. Not the fund-raising derbies and fisheries, mind you—but actual ice fishing tournaments. By organizing friendly, yet competitive contests between skilled anglers, numerous knowledgeable people are facing similar conditions on the same water during the same time—and by comparing notes between the successful and unsuccessful means of patterning and catching fish, much can be learned.

Again, there is no substitute for experience. The more time you spend on the ice, the better you'll get.

**Not every day on the ice will result in outstanding winter catches, but follow the system, tactics and techniques presented in this book, and by day's end, you should often feel a sense of satisfaction with your day's fishing.**

And as you fish strategically by yourself, or preferably along with other skilled ice anglers, applying and modifying the basic principles presented here on various waters and under a variety of conditions, the more you'll learn to better pattern winter panfish. In fact, you'll learn strategic, fine-tuned approaches often brought out by attention to details—details that often make the difference between a great catch and a mediocre one; perhaps even the difference between a good catch and none.

Believe me, by putting the basic, modern system outlined here together with your new-found knowledge, building on it through an interaction with other knowledgeable ice anglers, maintaining an open mind and utilizing a mobile, versatile approach on the ice, you will experience increased winter panfish success, thereby constructing the building blocks of a foundation for catching more and larger winter panfish...and gamefish, too, but that's another topic in itself, and likely the subject of a future *Hooked On Ice Fishing* series book.

For now, however, while I sit hunched at my kitchen table alongside a sink of soiled dishes, elbow on the table and chin in hand, facing a window revealing a drive that needs shoveling and staring at a checkbook that requires reconciliation, my young daughter stands beside me with hopeful eyes, tugging at my shirt with one hand, holding her little pink boots with the other, begging me to take her ice fishing.

I turn and smile. Faced with such a predicament, the choice is clear.

# Index

## A

access, 25, 32, 55–56, 93, 120–121, 147, 180, 185, 198, 200
accessibility, 121
aggressive, 38, 75, 78, 116, 118, 134, 153, 159–160, 163, 167, 171, 175–176, 214–215, 218, 227, 230, 242
airplane jig, 237
alcohol, 26–27, 69
alpine lakes, 182, 187, 190, 198
attractor, 135, 162, 171, 226

## B

backwater, 42, 45, 52, 60, 86, 117, 166–167
bail roller, 102, 110–111, 156
bait, 29, 58, 60, 62–64, 72–73, 75, 79–80, 102–106, 108, 114, 116, 118, 134–138, 154–156, 159–160, 162–163, 172–175, 182, 188–190, 192–193, 197, 201–202, 207, 214–215, 220–222, 226–227, 231–232, 234, 237, 239, 242, 244
baitfish, 37, 39, 59, 71, 89, 100, 120, 147–150, 156, 159, 161–162, 164, 167–168, 182, 186–187, 229
balance, 17, 100, 102–103, 110–111, 113, 133, 170, 193, 214, 226
balsa float, 157
banks, 127, 185, 189, 194, 196, 224–225, 232
barb, 136–137, 159, 163, 193, 234
barometer, 18
barometric pressure, 18
bars, 16, 37, 49, 71, 101, 164
basin, 49, 127, 150, 168
battery
    alkaline, 67
    gel-cel, 67
    lithium, 67
    nickel-metal hydrate, 67
bays, 11, 13, 21, 30, 32, 51, 56, 82, 86, 89–90, 93, 100, 120–122, 126, 129, 131, 138, 145, 146–149, 167, 180–182, 186–187, 189–190, 202, 216
beads, 105, 221, 226
behavior, 18, 49, 81, 92–93, 118, 129, 148, 152, 164
bibbets, 221

Black Hills, 195–198
blade baits, 78, 140, 172, 175, 214, 229
blanks, 102, 110, 113–114
bloodworms, 126, 128
bluegill, 11, 30, 60, 74, 82, 84, 86, 88, 92, 93, 99-101, 104, 106, 108, 114, 116, 117, 230
bobber, 81, 102, 113, 131, 142, 156, 171, 174, 193, 197, 207, 214, 220, 222, 226, 231
bottom content, 15–17, 19, 34, 37–39, 47, 49, 52, 55, 58, 63, 70–71, 73, 76, 90, 93, 95–96, 99, 101, 124, 127, 130, 178, 246
breaklines, 17, 38, 46, 49, 97, 99, 237
brush pile, 145, 230
buckshot rattle ring, 237
bullheads, 228, 230–231

## C

cabbage weeds, 76
carbon monoxide detector, 29
center slider, 157
channels, 38–39, 45, 65, 86, 93, 121, 123, 127, 145, 166–168, 184, 189
cisco, 11, 13, 73, 166, 200–203, 205–207
cladocerans, 201, 216, 228
clarity, 16–17, 19, 30, 32, 34, 39, 52, 55, 78, 102, 152, 212, 246
clothing, 21–27, 29, 88, 200
club, 246
cold front, 13, 15, 17–18, 30, 36–38, 42–43, 47, 49, 52, 86, 201, 231
color, 49, 54, 62, 75, 78–79, 103, 105, 108, 112–114, 116, 131, 137, 156, 159, 162, 192–193, 207, 227, 231, 233–234
compass, 55–56
competition
    interspecies, 16, 181, 186
    intraspecies, 17, 181, 186
conducted heat loss, 22
cone angle, 65, 69–70, 127
cone, 62–65, 69–74, 127–128, 174
contours, 49, 212
copepods, 201, 216
corn, 193

# M

magazines, 10, 244

maggots, 61, 105, 112, 114, 137, 140, 193, 197, 207, 226, 231

Marmooska
    jig, 105, 112, 136–137, 193
    spoon, 164, 192, 207, 214

mayfly nymphs, 230

mealworm, 192–193, 197

memory, 56, 67, 111, 156, 193, 231

micro, 19, 61, 63, 99, 102, 108, 110–114, 116, 156, 159–161, 192, 221, 229–230

microstructure, 34, 39, 76

mid-winter, 167

migration routes, 15, 38, 44–47, 50, 52, 54, 86, 91, 95–96, 99, 105, 129, 131, 149–150, 154, 168, 170, 189, 214, 218

minnows, 19, 79, 81, 84, 90, 92, 131, 134–135, 138, 140, 156, 159, 161–164, 170–172, 174, 176, 185, 188, 192–193, 206–208, 210, 214, 216, 221, 228–231, 233–234

mites, 201, 228–229

mobility, 27–29, 101, 129, 131, 141, 170, 176, 199, 203, 218, 242

modern system, 247

monofilament, 103, 113, 131, 133, 135, 154, 156, 170, 188–189, 192–193, 206, 220, 226, 231, 233–234

mountain, 178, 182, 190, 194–196, 198, 222

mousies, 114, 136, 197

movement, 16, 18, 21, 24–26, 32, 34, 37–38, 42, 44, 47, 49, 55, 61, 76, 86, 91, 93, 96, 103, 114, 121, 134, 148, 154, 167, 185, 193, 196, 205, 207, 227, 239, 242, 246

# N

niche, 123, 176, 178

nutrients, 16, 118, 129

nymph, 162, 192–193

# O

ocean perch, 228, 232–233

open water, 18, 21, 52, 81, 84, 88, 96–97, 110, 112, 144, 147–148, 161, 164, 166–168, 176, 178, 188, 196, 210, 212, 218–219, 222, 224–225, 230, 239

outlet, 224

oxygen, 13, 16–19, 21, 32, 34, 37, 44–47, 50–52, 76, 86, 89, 92–93, 95, 97, 121–122, 126, 128, 131, 145, 148–149, 167, 176, 182, 186–187, 225, 228, 230, 232, 237

# P

panfish, 10–20, 30, 32, 34, 36–38, 43–47, 49–52, 54–56, 58, 60–61, 71, 73–76, 78–81, 84, 88, 92, 100, 108, 110, 112–113, 116, 131, 142, 148, 152, 161, 164, 166, 176, 181, 191, 197, 206, 208, 215–216, 228, 230–232, 234, 237, 239, 242, 244, 246–247

patterns, 15, 18, 32, 73, 75–76, 78, 81, 97, 99, 101, 124, 138, 140, 153, 187, 196, 201, 203, 214, 222, 237, 247

pelagic, 144, 150, 161, 178, 188, 201, 218, 222

pencil reeds, 91

perch
    white, 208, 210, 212–215
    yellow, 52, 118, 122, 124, 126–127, 164, 166–167, 210, 220

personal floatation device (PFD), 21, 26

phosphorescence, 160, 215

photosynthesis, 16, 18, 50, 92

pinhead minnows, 221

pits, 180, 188, 190

pixel, 59–60, 64

plankton, 15, 17, 19, 37, 39, 51, 59, 79, 84, 89, 93, 95, 97, 99–101, 106, 112, 116, 118, 147–150, 154, 159–162, 186–187, 196, 201, 203, 216, 218, 222, 225

plastics, 32, 69, 102, 112, 114, 135, 137, 154, 159, 162, 170, 172, 188, 192–193, 214, 221, 233–234, 239

pocket, 39, 93, 114, 237

points, 13, 23, 34, 36–39, 42, 45, 55, 60–61, 65, 71, 73, 76, 91–92, 105, 112, 114, 118, 126, 128, 136, 149, 159, 161, 167, 193, 199, 237, 242

Polar Therm, 131

polypropylene, 23, 25–26

ponds, 11, 13, 34, 42, 108, 117, 229

poppers, 114, 230

population cycle, 12–13, 15, 17, 19, 34, 144, 246

pork rind, 114, 171, 193, 221

portable heater, 29

portable shelter, 27–28, 188, 239

positioning, 15–17, 44, 46, 52, 239

power bait, 221

Precise Positioning Service (PPS), 56

predator, 17, 46, 75

predator/prey relationships, 17, 46, 75

presentation, 18–20, 49–50, 58, 64, 74–75, 78–82, 103, 105, 108, 110–112, 114, 116, 133–138, 141, 148, 154, 156, 159–162, 170, 174, 189, 191, 193–194, 199, 207, 214–215, 220–221, 226–227, 234, 237, 239, 242, 244

prism, 104, 162, 192

# R

radiant heat loss, 22

rattle chamber, 172, 206, 221, 227

# T

tactics, 135, 160–161, 173
taper, 102
target, 11–13, 15, 17, 30, 32, 34, 36, 38, 44, 46, 52, 54–55, 60, 63–65, 76, 78, 145, 180, 182, 198–199, 225, 227, 239
taste, 79, 131, 160, 162, 192, 201–202, 215
techniques, 56, 104, 192, 220, 237
temperature, 23, 25, 27–29, 34, 44, 47, 50–52, 88, 90, 96, 176, 200, 232, 237
texture, 79, 131, 160, 162, 202, 215, 233
thermal hole covers, 131, 189
Thermax, 25
thread, sewing, 111, 113
tidal movements, 232–233
tightline, 193
tiny tears, 103
tippets, 103, 192
tips, 25, 29, 72, 79, 91, 102, 108, 110, 112, 114, 131, 136, 154–156, 159, 162, 164, 170, 188, 191, 193, 197, 206, 220–221, 226, 229–231, 233–234, 237, 242
tip-up
    Polar Therm, 189
    Polar, 234
    tip-down, 102, 188, 219
    ultralight balance, 102, 188, 214, 225
    umbrella, 19, 131, 154–155, 189, 206, 219
    wind, 171, 214, 225
tools, 101
tournament, 81
trailer, 26–27, 200
transducer, 59–60, 62–64, 69–74, 160, 163, 174, 239
transition, 32, 93, 96, 126, 149
trout
    brook, 30, 176, 178, 181–182, 186, 194–195, 198
    brown, 176, 178, 181–182, 194, 197–198
    cutbow, 176, 179, 182, 185, 194
    cutthroat, 176, 178–179, 182, 185, 194
    Dolly Varden, 176, 179, 182, 194
    golden, 176, 179, 182
    rainbow, 30, 176, 178–179, 181–182, 185, 194–195, 198
    splake, 176, 178, 181, 185, 195, 197–198
    stocked, 11, 73, 176, 178, 181–182, 185–189, 192, 194–195, 198–199
tullibee, 201
turbid, 144, 230
turbidity, 144, 218
turnover, 89, 224
twilight zone, 237
twilight, 13, 17, 32, 84, 97, 102, 116, 142, 144–145, 149, 152, 154, 159–160, 162, 195, 197, 212–213, 215, 218–219, 230, 237
two-story lakes, 180, 186

# U

ultralight balance tip-up, 188, 214
ultralight, 19, 80, 102–105, 108, 110–114, 116, 133, 135–137, 140, 154, 156, 159–162, 170–171, 188, 190–193, 197, 206, 214, 221, 226, 229–230, 234

# V

versatility, 101, 112, 117, 140–141, 150, 154, 172, 231, 242
videos, 10, 239, 244

# W

walls, 29, 224–225
water mites, 201
waxworms, 63, 114, 136, 162, 192-193, 197, 230, 239
waypoint, 56, 80, 118, 239
weather, 13–15, 18–20, 22–27, 32, 34, 36–39, 42–43, 45–47, 49–50, 52, 54, 62–63, 67, 75–76, 78, 81, 90–92, 97, 111, 116–117, 122, 130, 145, 153, 156, 179, 188, 191, 195, 198–199, 203, 212, 242
weed line, 13–14, 16, 145, 147, 149, 161–162, 167, 231, 237
weeds, 15, 32, 34, 37–38, 42, 49, 63, 71, 76, 84, 89–91, 97, 101, 120, 147–149, 178, 230, 237, 239
Wegman, Wil, 234, 242
white bass, 164, 166–168, 170–176, 208, 210, 237
white perch, 208, 210, 212–215
wicking, 24–26
wiggler, 114
wigglers, 135, 138, 197
wind chill, 24, 237

# Y

yarn, 135, 170, 206, 221
year class, 12

# Z

zooplankton, 89–90, 93, 101, 116, 120, 144, 176, 229

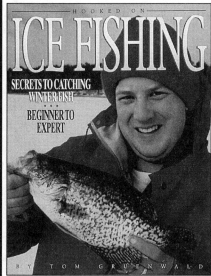

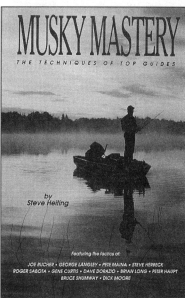